THE TRUTH BEHIND THE NEW ATHEISM

DAVID MARSHALL

HARVEST HOUSE PUBLISHERS

EUGENE, OREGON

Cover by Dugan Design Group, Bloomington, Minnesota

Cover photo © Paul Souders / Photodisc Red / Getty Images

THE TRUTH BEHIND THE NEW ATHEISM
Copyright © 2007 by David Marshall
Published by Harvest House Publishers
Eugene, Oregon 97402
www.harvesthousepublishers.com

Library of Congress Cataloging-in-Publication Data
Marshall, David, 1961-
  The truth behind the new atheism / David Marshall.
    p. cm.
  ISBN:13-978-0-7369-2212-8
  ISBN:10-0-7369-2212-1
  1. Apologetics. 2. Atheism. I. Title.
  BT1103.M37 2007
  239'.7—dc22   2007021425

Printed in the United States of America

07 08 09 10 11 12 13 14 15 /VP-KB / 10 9 8 7 6 5 4 3 2 1

I dedicate this book to our boys, John and James.
I've always told you the truth, as best I could see.
I thank God for you. May you always know him, and
may he always guide you not only to, but in, the Truth.

Acknowledgments

The beginnings of this book came in a flurry of bullet points while I was studying at the Commonwealth House of St Aldates. Thanks to Michael and Celia Mowat for their gracious hospitality to all us scholastic nomads—and the juice, the cheeses, the music and discussions, and making us feel at home. Thanks to fellow scholars and friends at the Oxford Centre for Missions Studies, and apologies for too many untimely remarks about Richard Dawkins—now you know what I had in mind.

Thanks to Drs. Ben McFarland and Dave McCorkle for kindly reviewing the scientific portions of the book and offering extremely helpful criticism. Thanks also to Dr. Ard Louis for the many helpful conversations about Christians in science, and to Todd Chapman. Thanks to Dr. Hiawatha for arguing for so many untenable positions with persistent grace and unflagging good humor.

My wife and parents also deserve thanks as usual, and then some, for support in too many ways to count.

Contents

Introduction

I arrived by bus from Heathrow Airport to begin a research program at the Oxford Centre for Missions Studies. I began walking up High Street jet-lagged, dragging a suitcase and carrying a backpack, but curious for my first look at the famous little town. After about 100 paces, I noticed a plaque on the stone wall to my left, and set down my luggage to read:

> In a house on this site between 1655 and 1688 lived ROBERT BOYLE. Here he discovered BOYLE'S LAW and made experiments with an AIR PUMP designed by his assistant ROBERT HOOKE, Inventor, Scientist and Architect who made a MICROSCOPE and thereby identified the first living cell.

Boyle and Hooke were founding members of the Royal Society, which put Francis Bacon's famous call to apply science for the good of humanity into action. Hooke, an inventor and experimental scientist of many talents, published breathtakingly beautiful still life drawings of microscopic herb spores, woven silk, mold, and even fleas that are still admired today. Boyle, one of the leading scientists of his day and a devout Christian, established a lecture series in his will for "proving the Christian religion against notorious Infidels, to wit, Atheists, Theists (Deists), Pagans, Jews and Mahometans; not descending lower to any controversies that are among Christians themselves."[1]

Religious controversy, one might say, has come to a new "Boyle" today. The most notorious infidel of our time works in New College across the street and down an alley. Richard Dawkins, Oxford Professor of the Public Understanding of Science, is—like Boyle and Hooke— passionate about science. And like Hooke, he is meticulous and artistic in the pictures he draws (verbal rather than engraved) of the living world. But besides his artistry with words (he won the 1987 Royal Society of Literature Award), Dawkins is known for a concept of evolution that focuses on the "selfish gene," for a controversial branch of knowledge called *memetics*, and most of all for his impassioned public attacks on religion, Christianity in particular.

With his friend the American philosopher Daniel Dennett and a young protégé named Sam Harris, who, like Dennett, studies human consciousness, Dawkins has attempted to parlay the prestige science has accumulated since the time of Boyle and Hooke into overthrowing *The God Delusion*, as the title of his bestselling 2006 volume put it. Dennett's book, *Breaking the Spell: Religion as a Natural Phenomena*, also released in 2006, attempts to show that evolution can explain religion away without change. Harris also hopes to make an *End of Faith*, as his first book advocated. Harris's bestseller *Letter to a Christian Nation* added to the chorus.

These books are aptly titled. They argue not only that religion is wrong and there is no God, but that faith is a curse upon the human race. Harris's books were written in the context of 9/11 and are passionate about the dangers of religion. He describes the Bible as inarticulate, morally repugnant, and false. Dawkins enlists a company of adjectives to battle the Old Testament Yahweh:

> Arguably the most unpleasant character in all fiction: jealous and proud of it, a petty, unjust, unforgiving control freak; a vindictive, bloodthirsty ethnic cleanser; a misogynist, homophobic, racist, infanticidal, genocidal, filicidal, pestilential, megalomaniacal, sadomasochistic, capriciously malevolent bully.[2]

Dennett finds a bit more good in religion, but in a way, his criticism is even more radical. He offers a theory as to how the human race fell into this trap. By backwards muttering, he hopes to "break the spell" of faith.

These attacks don't come in a vacuum. In recent years various schools of skepticism have argued that religion can be explained naturally, the Gospels are unhistorical, Gnostic "Gospels" are just as good or better than the ones in the Bible, the Vatican was led by "Hitler's Pope" during World War II, and the "religious right" brings the threat of "Christian fascism" to the United States. One is reminded of the passengers in the airline disaster spoof *Airplane* who line up with boxing gloves, a whip, a baseball bat, and a gun to take their anxiety out on one of their fellow passengers.

Dawkins, Harris, and Dennett form the core of what I call the New Atheism. They agree much, and quote one another often and warmly. They borrow what they like from many schools of skepticism and from rationalist arguments going back to Voltaire, Tom Paine, and Bertrand Russell (to whom Dawkins is often compared). Between them, they advance seven arguments: (1) Faith is irrational. Faith means "believing not only without evidence, but in the teeth of the evidence," as Dawkins famously put it.[3] (2) Evolution undercuts any reason there may have once been to believe in God (which is why few eminent scientists are religious). (3) Biological and social evolution can explain the origin of religion. (4) The Bible is, at best, a jumbled aggregate of theological cullings that do little to enrich humanity and much to harm us. (5) The Jesus of history was (at best) mortal. (6) Christians in the United States (the "American Taliban," Dawkins calls them) constitute a profound threat to democracy. (7) All in all, the world would be better off without the gospel of Jesus Christ, or any religion.

The trio harmonizes in tone almost as much as in substance. None mourns the death of God: They are eager to heap dirt on his coffin, and volunteer to dig his grave deeper. Dawkins is called an "evangelist" or "Darwinian fundamentalist" even by some secular colleagues, like his *bête noire* Steven Jay Gould (who, with the likes of biologist E.O. Wilson and Michael Shermer, offers skepticism in a mellower tone). Dennett compares himself to a "revivalist preacher,"[4] while Harris's passionate jibes at theistic religion ("an average Christian, in an average church, listening to an average Sunday sermon has achieved a level of arrogance simply unimaginable in scientific discourse") seem designed to rankle as much as subvert.[5]

The talented polemicist Christopher Hitchens chimed in a year later with his subtly titled *god Is Not Great: How Religion Poisons Everything*, violating all the rules of grammar, never mind courteous discourse, to express contempt for his Creator.

How should a Christian respond?

An answer to such "notorious infidels" needs, I think, to find a middle path between two errors. On the one hand, a mocking or sarcastic response would feed the Us vs. Them mimesis, giving readers something to cheer or jeer, depending on who you're rooting for, but not persuade anyone. Such a tone is also unworthy of the gospel. On the other hand, the New Atheists are often contempuous of moderates (and for Gould's well-intentioned suggestion that religion and science be assigned separate spheres of influence—"Non-Overlapping Magisteria," or "NOMA"). The New Atheists have set the cathedral on fire. I plan to put it out, not roast marshmallows while it burns. The skeptics, I will argue, are flatly and often spectacularly wrong.

But I also think these and other critics do believers, and those who want to know whether or not to believe, a favor. The Christian tradition has always taught that faith needs to be tested by reason. Dawkins consolidates the most common modern objections to Christianity. Harris asks a few key questions with "burning anxiety" (to borrow a phrase from one of those issues, the debate over the role of Christianity in the Holocaust). Dennett popularizes new anti-God theories, giving us a chance to look more closely at this strange phenomena called *man* and consider why he tends to believe in God, even at gawdforsaken times and places.

Some of Jesus' greatest sayings came in response to criticism. In the second century, a skeptic wrote an attack on Christianity known today from the philosopher Origen's response, *Against Celsus*. If the blood of martyrs is the seedbed of the church, intellectual criticism can be the showers that make those seeds grow.

Of course I won't cover all the issues that these or other new atheists (Christopher Hitchens, Carl Sagan, Steven Weinberg) bring up. I won't venture too deeply into philosophical "proofs" for or against God. Dawkins disputes Thomas Aquinas's arguments and offers what he sees as a telling blow against theism: "Who designed the designer?"[6] Any Creator must be more complex than what he creates, so doesn't belief in God just complicate matters? Better philosophers than Dawkins or I, including Alvin Plantinga and Richard Swinburne, have answered these questions. Dawkins also assumes the cosmological argument for God ("the universe had a beginning, therefore a Beginner") has fallen into disuse. In fact, William Lane Craig jousts with leading unbelieving philosophers on this very issue in debates that can easily be found online, and the big bang theory has moved quite a few physicists and astronomers to discuss it openly. I leave readers to judge for themselves how moribund that argument is.

Evolutionary biologist Alan Orr doubts the question of God should center on abstract reasoning too much, however:

> Since when is a scientific hypothesis confirmed by philosophical gymnastics, not data? The fact that we as scientists find a hypothesis question-begging—as when Dawkins asks "who designed the designer?"— cannot, in itself, settle its truth value. It could, after all, be a brute fact of the universe that it derives from some transcendent mind, however question-begging this may seem.[7]

What we've learned about the origin and nature of the universe has given these old debates new life in recent years. But I, too, prefer brute facts. I'll concentrate my response on earthbound evidence for the rationality and value of the Christian faith.

The challenge of the New Atheists can be summarized in three sets of questions, and High Street in Oxford, standing across from St. Mary's Cathedral (where C.S. Lewis preached his famous "Weight of Glory" sermon), outside the home where Boyle and Hooke worked, a block from the garden where penicillin was discovered, and the college where Schrodinger's cat first met her fate, is a good place to ask them. First, we ask about God and science. Is faith irrational? Does evolution make belief untenable? If not, why do so few modern heirs of Boyle and Hooke believe? Did God create man, or did man create God?

Second, Dawkin's friend and colleague Sir John Krebs is the principal of "Jesus College." The richest college here—where John Wesley, Lewis Carroll, and John Locke taught, and 16 future prime ministers studied—is Christ College. Who is Jesus Christ? How does he help solve the riddle of God and the meaning of life? The answer, of course, lies in the Bible, which the New Atheists see as a dubious document. Are they reading it right?

Third, look around this town, founded in the early eighth century as a monastery by the semilegendary shy princess St. Frideswide (whose unwanted suitor, following a tradition already half a millennia old, was struck blind in a forest, then healed by the virgin saint). Does faith blind or heal? Is an incipient "American Taliban" on the verge of dragging the United States back into the Dark Ages? Does morality evolve? What did the Enlightenment have to do with Adolf Hitler and Joseph Stalin? Is religion mainly a horror story of witch-hunting, inquisitions, and caste oppression? (Such as the burning of three famous Anglican bishops for heresy a five-minute walk from this spot?) Or has the gospel molded the very stones upon which the New Atheists walk, the key foundational principles of Western, and now world, civilization?

The value of any viewpoint lies in what it allows us to see. The makers of the modern world—Rousseau, Voltaire, Freud, Marx, Darwin, Kinsey, Mead—often tangled their facts. But they inspired people to see life from new perspectives. They opened doors to what followers perceived as a wider world.

Dawkins, Dennett, and Harris are talented storytellers too. The power of their arguments lie primarily, I think, in the map of reality they draw as apprentices to the aforementioned and other Enlightenment cartographers.

After describing the flaws in their map of reality, therefore, I will briefly sketch a map of my own. If Dennett aims to break the spell of faith, you might accuse me (in this final chapter) of casting a new one. But enchantments are set to liberate as well as to bind, to help people see as well as to blind them.

PART ONE

GOD AND SCIENCE

Have Christians Lost Their Minds?

If the modern world is confused about anything, it is the idea that Christianity demands "blind faith."

That Christians have a soft spot (their heads) for faith unsupported by reason is a core tenet of the New Atheism. One of Daniel Dennett's chapters is called "Belief in Belief." "People of all faiths," he explains, consider it "demeaning" to ask God tough questions. "The meme for blind faith secures its own perpetuation by the simple unconscious expedient of discouraging rational inquiry." Christianity in particular, he asserts, is addicted to blind faith.[2] He says this, ironically, without offering any evidence it is true—quoting no Christian philosopher, scientist, or theologian who thinks so.

In *Letter to a Christian Nation*, Sam Harris calls faith "nothing more than the license religious people give one another to keep believing when reasons fail."[3] The title of Harris's previous book, *The End of Faith*, set the point clearly in the wood. The first two chapters, "Reason in Exile" and "The Nature of Belief," pounded it home. Harris wrote, "It should go without saying that these rival belief systems are all equally uncontaminated by evidence."[4]

One blinks at this. Why should the claim that there is no evidence for religion "go without saying"—in other words, be accepted with no evidence? Harris continues:

> Tell a devout Christian that his wife is cheating on him, or that frozen yogurt can make a man invisible, and he is likely to require as much evidence as anyone else, and to be persuaded only to the extent that you give it. Tell him that the book he keeps by his bed was written by an invisible deity who will punish him with fire for eternity if he fails to accept every incredible claim about the universe, and he seems to require no evidence whatsoever.[5]

If opinions need to be supported by evidence, let's begin with this one. How does Harris know Christians don't support their beliefs with evidence? Dennett cites Pascal, Dawkins cites Harris, and everyone takes this alleged Christian doctrine for granted, but no one cites any Christians!

Richard Dawkins set the tone. In his seminal 1976 work *The Selfish Gene*, he defined faith as "a kind of mental illness," and, more specifically, "a state of mind that leads people to believe something—it doesn't matter what—in the total absence of supporting evidence."[6] Christians make a virtue of believing "not only in the absence of evidence, but in the teeth of evidence."[7]

But what if *this claim itself* is held "not only in the absence of evidence, but in the teeth of evidence"? What if the real "blind faith meme" is the unsupported and false theory that Christians believe for irresponsible reasons?

Much is at stake here for non-Christians as well. I will argue that in its idea of "faith," the gospel defends us against simplistic and dehumanizing models of truth. Christianity, I will argue, stands on the side of ordinary people against the intellectual imperialism of those who imprison the human spirit in credulous, tunnel-visioned scientism.

We've been bamboozled into accepting (in the name of science, though not always from scientists) a lie about truth and how to find it, an untruth that narrows life and hands truth to tunnel-visioned specialists. "There is no way a tunnel can feel like home," says Huston Smith.[8] The Christian concept of truth, rightly understood, sets us free from some of the deepest intellectual errors of our time.

Let's begin with the allegation that the Bible recommends "blind faith."

What Does the Bible Say About Faith?

Information scientist Hubert Yockey doubts that life can come from nonlife by chance mixing of chemicals. He wants his readers to understand, however, that his doubts are scientific, not religious. Socrates said go to cobblers to learn cobbling. So go to theologians, he suggested, and see how they look for truth:

> The views of the theologians are discussed in the Letter to the Hebrews: "Now faith is the substance of things hoped for, the *evidence* of things *unseen*"...The same theme appears in the Gospel of John 20:24-28 where Thomas "The Doubter" demanded positive and specific evidence before he would believe. But he got chewed out by his Boss who gave him the evidence but reproved him: "Have you believed because you have seen me? Blessed are those who have not seen and yet believed." So much for the point of view from religion.[9]

Yockey finds this "theological" attitude suspiciously similar to the Marxist mentality. True believers of every creed ignore experience and believe blindly based on holy writ.

But look more closely at the holy writ quote mined here.

The story of doubting Thomas is often cited to prove Christianity demands blind faith. When the other disciples reported they had met the risen Jesus, Thomas (true to character as developed in the Gospel of John) found the story hard to swallow. "Unless I see in His hands the imprint of the nails...and put my hand into his side, I will not believe," Thomas famously retorted. When he met Jesus he was told, "Reach here with your finger, and see My hands; and reach here your hand and put it into My side; and do not be unbelieving, but believing." By contrast, Jesus blessed those who do not see, and yet believe (John 20:25,27-29). Dawkins cited the same text in *The Selfish Gene*: "Thomas demanded evidence...The other apostles, whose faith was so strong that they did not need evidence, are held up to us as worthy of imitation."[10]

There are several problems with taking this passage as a general repudiation of critical thought. First, Jesus did give Thomas—and the other disciples—enough firsthand evidence of his resurrection that they were willing to die for him (Thomas, reportedly in India.) Second, Jesus often did miracles, calling them "signs," which (even skeptical historians often admit) show strong evidence of historicity. In the very next sentence (usually omitted by those making the case for blind faith), John explains that the signs Jesus did were recorded "so that you may believe that Jesus is the Christ" (John 20:31).

Is it rational to believe things on the basis of human testimony? It'd be a pity if it weren't, because, as Samuel Johnson put it, most of our knowledge is based on "implied faith" in other people. Almost everything we know—not just about first-century Palestine, but about dwarf stars, neutrinos, state capitals, vitamins, and sports scores—we believe because we find the person telling us the information is credible. If trusting human testimony were irrational, we wouldn't be able to know much.

The other popular proof text used to support the contention of blind faith is Hebrews 11. In that chapter, the author describes faith as the "substance of things hoped for, the evidence of things not seen" (verse 1 NKJV). He adds that through faith we know that the universe was created "by the word of God, so that what is seen was not made out of things which are visible" (verse 3).

To read this as an intellectual copout is a grave error. What does the author mean when he says faith "is" evidence? There's nothing mystical about this. It's clear and sensible. Evidence is a reason to believe something. Hearing about it from a credible source is the most common such reason. By faith we know not only that the physical world is made of "things unseen"—physicists now take a different path to the same conclusion—we know pretty much everything we do know. We'll talk more later about the role of human testimony in knowledge.

So even passages cited to defend the "blind faith meme" can easily be read to mean the opposite: that Christian belief demands evidence, though it is a broader and more social evidence than the scientific method in the strict sense allows.

The Bible also frequently appeals to reason, empirical facts, and experiment ("Taste and see that the Lord is good!" "Come let us reason together!"). Take a slow walk through the book of Proverbs. "Simpleminded" ones and "fools" who "hate knowledge" are rebuked (1:22). The Lord "gives wisdom," and "from His mouth come knowledge and understanding" (2:6). He used wisdom to create the heavens and the earth, and knowledge to form the oceans, the atmosphere, and its canopy of water vapor (3:19-20). Wisdom enters the heart of the good son, and knowledge is "pleasant to your soul" (2:10).

What about later Christian tradition? Dawkins builds his case for blind faith not even on a selective reading of that tradition, but on ill-informed cheap shots at the expense of a few thinkers (Harris and Dennett offer even less). Looking at some of those shots, and why they are unfair, carries the triple benefit of refuting common misconceptions, rehabilitating his victims, and tracing the Christian view of faith more deeply.

Richard Swinburne: Can There Be Too Much Evidence?

To defend his claim that the Christian faith doesn't demand evidence, Dawkins quotes a "typical piece of theological reasoning" from Richard Swinburne, a colleague and one of the world's leading Christian philosophers. Swinburne explained why, in his view, we aren't surrounded by such an overwhelming number of miracles that we would have to believe. "There is quite a lot of evidence anyway of God's existence, and too much might not be good for us." Dawkins responds indignantly:

> Too much might not be good for us! Read it again. Too much evidence might not be good for us…If it's a theologian you want, they don't come much more distinguished. Perhaps you don't want a theologian.[11]

It's hard not to admire the pizzazz of these lines. This is the sort of touché moment that those who enjoy debate live for.

But in the interest of a good repartee, Dawkins misses Swinburne's point. Dawkins had just said Christian theologians don't have any evidence. Here Swinburne says, "There's quite a lot of it." Dawkins doesn't stop to look at Swinburne's evidence (he's written tons of books). He doesn't even pump his brakes in the rush to broadside the man.

In fact, Dawkins is brutal. When both men appeared on a TV show, Swinburne attempted, Dawkins says, to "justify the Holocaust." This is an ambivalent phrase. It could mean showing why Hitler was right to kill Jews. It could also mean, (as Swinburne meant), the far different and difficult task of asking why God may have allowed the Holocaust. Dawkins leaves the two potential meanings tangled, then ends with the borrowed quip, "May you rot in hell!"[12]

On his Web site, Swinburne replies with remarkable generosity. "I am grateful to Richard Dawkins for having looked at some of my writings." He suggests, however, that Dawkins join the philosophical debate over God and suffering "and not try to win by shouting."[13]

As for "too much evidence," one should earn the right to mock by thinking first. Can there be such a thing as too much evidence? From the point of view of a relationship, there can be. An honest husband may feel dejected if his wife insists on 24-hour streaming webcasts from his hotel room when he's on business trips. Swinburne meekly admitted he should have cited his explanations, and referred his assailant to them. I hope Dawkins does not mistake courtesy for weakness.

What you shouldn't want is a biologist who insists on belittling philosophical ideas that he hasn't shown the patience to read and understand.

Alister McGrath: Is Faith Supposed to Be Blind?

Dawkins writes, "Ask a religious person to justify their faith and you 'infringe on religious liberty.' "[14] One can, of course, find Christians too tongue-tied or unreflective to offer a clear explanation of their faith. But most thoughtful Christians are only too eager to explain themselves— church library shelves are full of books written by such individuals, including those by Swinburne. Dawkins has every right to ask Christians to justify their faith; his protest that no one does so would be more convincing if he paid closer attention to informed responses.

Another of Dawkins's Oxford colleagues, Alister McGrath, took Dawkins's claim that Christianity demands blind faith to task in his book *Dawkins's God: Genes, Memes, and the Meaning of Life*.[15] As to Dawkins's definition of faith as "blind trust, in the absence of evidence, even in the teeth of evidence," McGrath responded: "This may be what Dawkins thinks; it is not what Christians think." On the contrary, McGrath explained, quoting Anglican theologian Griffith Thomas, faith begins "with the conviction of the mind based on adequate evidence." McGrath added that he had never even met a Christian theologian who agreed with Dawkins's "skewed and nonsensical" definition, adding, "I see no point in wearying readers with other quotations from Christian writers down through the centuries."[16]

Dawkins read that book. In *The God Delusion* he describes how he pored over it, making notes in the margins. He claims the "only point" McGrath offers in response to his own arguments was "the undeniable but ignominiously weak point that you cannot disprove the existence of God."[17]

McGrath is one of the world's leading experts on the history of Christian thought. If he says, "This is what Christians believe," he may be wrong. But it would be unwise in the extreme to simply dismiss his opinion without first doing careful research on how Christians actually see faith.

I've done that research, and McGrath is right. Great Christian thinkers across the centuries, and up to the present, no more agree with Dawkins's absurd definition of faith than do McGrath's theological friends. Justin Martyr wrote, "Reason directs those who are truly pious and philosophical to honor and love only what is true, declining to follow traditional opinions." Origen pointed out that not everyone can drop everything and go on a research sabbatical: most people can and must believe on the testimony of others (the "implicit faith" Samuel Johnson referred to). But he argued that there was good evidence (in archaeology, history, miracles, and prophecy) that the Christian faith was, in fact, reasonable. Augustine argued that rationality was a prerequisite of belief. Therefore, "heaven forbid that we should believe in such a way as not to accept or seek reasons." Much of what we know, he added, is based on facts not visible to the senses. "But they are much deceived, who think that we believe in Christ without any proofs concerning Christ." Thomas Aquinas said Christianity was uncertain not because the evidence is poor, but because of "the weakness of the human intellect." William Law said that "unreasonable and absurd ways of life...are truly an offense to God."[18] Johannes Kepler added that religion "cannot be but rational," since God is "supremely rational, and the human being is also rational, being created in the image and likeness of God."

McGrath is right—one could go on like this for many pages (as I do, in "Faith and Reason" at christthetao.com).

Rather than refuting McGrath's claim, which is irrefutable, or changing his mind, which seems unchangeable, Dawkins ignores McGrath's challenge and repeats his original claim:

Faith (belief without evidence) is a virtue...Virtuoso believers who can manage to believe something really weird, unsupported and insupportable, in the teeth of evidence and reason, are especially highly rewarded."[19]

Dawkins can only be writing about himself. For 2000 years Christians have defined faith as inseparable from reason and evidence. One of the world's leading experts on Christian theology wrote a book specifically to educate Dawkins. Having read it, Dawkins continues to define Christian faith as "belief without evidence," without deigning to respond to contrary evidence. Clearly it is Dawkins whose faith in blind faith is held not only without evidence, but "in the teeth of the evidence."

Nicholas Wolterstorff and the Sin of Blind Faith

In a series of lectures, and in the book that grew out of them, Yale philosopher Nicholas Wolterstorff meditated on the claim that God speaks. In the process he offered, in the algebraic terms philosophers favor, the following view of what justifies a belief (pardon the initial obscurity):

A person S is entitled to his belief that p just in case S believes p, and there's no doxastic [ie, "ethically warranted belief"—DM] practice D pertaining to p such that S ought to have implemented D and S did not, or S ought to have implemented D better than S did. (Notice that a person may be entitled at one time to believe p without having implemented D, and at a later time no longer be entitled to believe p without have implemented D.)[20]

What does this mean? Wolterstorff is saying that a person has a right to believe something if he does believe it and there's no course of investigation open to him by which he could test its truth, or if he has studied contrary evidence and is still convinced.

How does this apply to the omnipresent claim that Christians rely on blind faith? (Aside from the fact that Wolterstorff, as an eminent Christian philosopher in the Reformed tradition, is another person who thinks faith "in the teeth of the evidence" is wrong?) Let's key names and ideas into the formula:

> *Richard Dawkins* is entitled to his belief that *Christians rely on blind faith* just in case *Dawkins* (really) believes *this*, and there's *no course of study in Christian history or theology* that *Dawkins* ought to have *undertaken* and did not, or that *he* ought to have *studied* better than *he* did, or else he has done the study and still honestly thinks so.

It seems clear that before writing a book on an important subject that may affect what hundreds of thousands of readers believe, one is responsible to do one's best to see if those ideas are true. Clearly, Dawkins did no such research. It is even more clear that, having read McGrath's rebuke, Dawkins was obliged to see if McGrath was right, admit his error, or at least put the subject on hold until he had time to look into it. Instead, Dawkins admitted he read McGrath carefully, praised his kindly tone, but said nothing at all in response to McGrath's argument about faith. In fact, Dawkins not only ignored the rebuttal, he repeated his prior false claims.

So we paraphrase Wolterstorff's formula and apply it as warranted:

> Dawkins might have been entitled at one time to believe that Christians believe in blind faith without having studied Christian theology, without reading McGrath, Wolterstorff, or any of dozens of other key thinkers. But having read McGrath's rebuttal, he ought to have gotten his act together and begun to question his dogma. Having failed to do so, and written a new bestseller (to paraphrase Flannery O'Connor, "many a best-seller might have been prevented by a good theologian") in which he appears to have learned nothing, Dawkins therefore condemns himself by believing not only without evidence, but in the teeth of the evidence.

Do Ordinary Christians Believe for No Good Reason?

But all this is irrelevant, some may say. Whatever dead white theologians or ivory tower intellectuals think, "real" Christians believe for no good reason, as everyone knows.

In 1998, Frank Sulloway and Michael Shermer asked 10,000 Americans, "Why do you believe in God?" and "Why do you think other people believe in God?" The two most popular answers to the first question had to do with "good design," the "natural beauty," "perfection," or "complexity" of the universe, and "experience of God in everyday life."[21] Together, these two answers constituted just under 50 percent of the responses (and about two-thirds of the answers Shermer enumerated in his book).

Both answers, Shermer (a leading skeptic) recognized, are essentially rational. By contrast, when asked why *other* people believed, most people said because faith was comforting, gave meaning to life, or those other people had been raised to believe. So they saw their own beliefs as *rational,* but assumed (not surprising, considering the spread of the "blind faith meme") that others believed for *irrational* reasons.

In a more limited but focused study, I found that evangelical Christians are even more likely to offer rational reasons for their faith. I asked 76 Christians at two conservative churches (Presbyterian and Assembly of God), "Why do you believe in God?" The least popular responses had nothing to do with reason: "You have to believe in something" (six circled this answer), and "I enjoy the fellowship in church, and that makes it easier to believe" (20 chose this answer). Apart from "I feel the presence of God in worship and prayer," which 58 people circled, the most popular responses had at least some intellectual component: "Faith in God helps make sense of life" (60 agreed); "The evidence seems good" (47 circled this item, 62 percent of those who took the survey); and "I have had supernatural experience that taught me the reality of the spiritual world" (42 agreed, or 55 percent of those who took the survey!).

When asked, "What does *faith* mean to you?" only one person, in either group, circled Dawkin's nonsensical definition "Believing what you know isn't true." One person also circled "Believing even when evidence is against it, just because you want to." By contrast, 63 agree that faith means "Sticking to what you have good reason to think is true, in the light of difficulties."

Apparently unaware, like Dawkins, that theology has always linked faith and reason, Shermer suggested that Christianity had been contaminated by the Enlightenment. He even seemed to think Pope John Paul II, who agreed that faith should be based on evidence, was confused about Christian orthodoxy. I can hardly blame Shermer: Few views are drilled into our heads more deeply than the "blind faith meme." One must at least give him credit for asking modern Christians and listening to their replies, however.

But what about Blaise Pascal's famous wager? Didn't the great scientist tell us to bet on God even if the odds are bad because the potential payoff is higher than the alternative? It's good that Dawkins brings up this popular question, because Pascal's wager points to something important about faith and how it helps us live more reasonably.

Pascal's Wager

Blaise Pascal, the great French mathematician, scientist, and philosopher, compared life to a game of blackjack or poker:

> You must wager. It is not optional. You are embarked. Which will you choose then?...If you gain, you gain all; if you lose, you lose nothing...
>
> "But, still, is there no means of seeing the faces of the cards?" Yes, Scripture and the rest, etc. "Yes, but I have my hands tied and my mouth closed; I am forced to wager, and am not free. I am not released, and am so made that I cannot believe. What, then, would you have me do?"
>
> Endeavor, then, to convince yourself, not by increase of proofs of God, but by the abatement of your passions...Learn of those who have been bound like you, and who now stake all their possessions. These are people who know the way which you would follow, and who are cured of an ill of which you would be cured...[22]

Dawkins says Pascal "wasn't claiming that his wager enjoyed anything but very long odds." Maybe Pascal was even joking. In any case, one can't believe just because one wants to. Even if you go to church, mouth Christian creeds, and swear on a stack of Bibles that you believe it all, if you're not convinced, that won't make you believe. Dawkins concludes, "Pascal's wager could only ever be an argument for *feigning* belief in God."[23]

This is like Archie Bunker explaining the errors of Zen Buddhism.

Pascal is writing to thoughtful people who are wondering whether to follow the Christian path but find the evidence ambiguous. Even though they can "see the faces of the cards," the evidence Pascal talks about in the rest of the book, "Scripture and the rest," some people find themselves constitutionally inclined to doubt. He points out that faith often follows action. As Jesus said, "If anyone is willing to do His will, he will know of the teaching" (John 7:17 NASB). Begin obeying God, and he may show you his reality. Often our minds are clouded by sin or lust, and training in righteousness will make them more clear. These are practical principles that I and many others have found helpful.

Dawkins reads this as the "odd assumption that the one thing God really wants of us is belief."[24] I don't think Pascal saw it that way. What he tells us is that if we orient ourselves correctly to the true nature of things, evidence that we are, in fact, so oriented will appear. Locate yourself rightly on a map, and you begin to find your way. As we will see, Dawkins asks for a similar step of faith when he upbraids biologist Michael Behe for giving up too early on naturalistic explanations of biological complexity.

And why do people write as if the wager were the only thing Pascal wrote? (Aside from the obvious reason that some apologists of all kinds confuse *research* with *Web search*?) Read Pascal's *Pensées* as a whole. While he was only making notes for a planned apologetic, and hadn't brought them into final form, clearly he had positive reasons for belief! Among them are traditional arguments for Christianity that the New Atheists overlook, some of which will come up later. Pascal didn't concede that the odds against God's existence were long. Rather, "There is enough light for those who desire only to see, and enough darkness for those of a contrary disposition."[25]

Pascal showed that while faith requires evidence, it takes nerve as well. Life is a gamble: "You must wager." We are not detached sifters of data, nor is the choice other than deciding what we will become. We are deeply involved in our choices because they are part of who we are.

What Is Faith, and Why Is It Useful?

Faith is not blind. If it helps us see further, what does it help us see? Why is it impossible to please God—or get up in the morning, drink coffee, or drive down the road—without reasoned trust? How does rational faith enrich our lives and widen a world that naïve empiricism tends to narrow?

In the Christian sense, *faith* means courageous trust in an object one has good reason to see as credible. As Pascal said, we must choose. But choice is risky and requires courage. And faith must not be lightly given, for "reason is a thing of God," as Tertullian put it.

Faith involves a continuum of four kinds of trust. First, we trust our own minds. There's no way to prove our minds work—this is often forgotten by people who uncritically praise the scientific method. Even to do math or logic, which are more basic than science, we have to take our brains more or less for granted. How could we prove them? Any proof for mind would depend on what it assumes: the validity of that endless electrical storm in the skull.

Brain surgery is tricky. Some atheists seem to think a simple evolutionary "bash" to the head will shake the religious nonsense out of our skulls, without stopping to think what harm the blow may do their own theories. Dawkins writes:

> Just as the primitive brain rule of sexual lust passes through the filter of civilization to emerge in the love scenes of Romeo and Juliet, so primitive brain rules of us-versus-them vendetta emerge in the form of the running battles between Capulets and Montagues; while primitive brain rules of altruism and empathy end up in the misfiring that cheers us in the chastened reconciliation of Shakespeare's final scene.[26]

But if there is a "misfiring," there must also be a proper firing, a normative working of the mind. Is this an error on Dawkins's part, or can the function of our brains be described in terms of purpose?

If it can't, we're all in trouble. If we reduce art and morality to Darwinian mechanisms, why not science and math as well? Presumably our ability to count has Darwinian roots. Is calculus a misfiring of mental faculties? It'd be hard to argue the brain of man evolved on the plains of the Serengeti to do differential equations. The problem is not that skeptics have teleology, it is that they are arbitrary and authoritarian in applying it. Even to say, "The mind cannot be trusted," one must trust the mind.

The second level of faith is trust in our senses. How do you know you're reading a book? Why do you think it's hot or cold, that starlings are looking for seeds on the ground, or the washing machine is running? Again, there's no way to prove your eyes, ears, nose, mouth, and skin are giving you the real scoop about the outside world. At an extreme, you could be stuck in some "virtual reality" world with false impulses feeding untrue data to your brain through wires. Matter may be less real than it looks—ephemeral, like a cloud—but most of us find it reasonable to assume the cloud is really there.

Third, to learn anything, we accept "testimonial evidence" from parents, teachers, books, street signs, Wikipedia, and "familiar" voices transmitted as electronic pulses over miles of wire and electromagnetic signals, then decoded into waves in the air. Almost everything we know comes from other people in one way or another.

This is as true in science as anywhere. That's why terms such as *peer review, footnotes, mentors,* and *review of the literature* are not words of reproach, except when neglected. In her book about the scientific revolution, Lisa Jardine speaks of the "crowded, motley lives" of seventeenth-century scientists "in which conversation in the coffeehouse and vigorous correspondence with like-minded individuals in other countries figured as importantly as strenuous private study and laboratory experiment."[27] Science is and always has been a social enterprise. In theory, everything can be tested with one's own hands, but in practice, no one has time, funds, and equipment to do it all. Every general story of evolution (by Darwin, Mayr, or Dawkins) is built on facts borrowed in trust from other researchers.

Dawkins says with assurance, "What I, as a scientist, believe (for example, evolution) I believe not because of reading a holy book but because I have studied the evidence."[28] Is that so? Certainly Dawkins has pointed to a great deal of evidence that he thinks supports his view of evolution. But did he originally "come to faith" by studying the evidence? Or by seeing pictures of fossils taken by people he'd never met, in books printed he couldn't say where, explained by strangers? There's nothing wrong with that. Reason almost always relies on a complex web of faith. But it should be aware of its debts.

The problem is that hubris about the "scientific method" often masks an almost childish naivete about what constitutes a good argument in nonscientific fields. The skeptic's historical views may not derive from careful and honest study—even at second or third hand—of the evidence. Too many "facts" on which key arguments are based may be gleaned off the Internet or from an elite corps of fellow skeptics operating outside their specialties, and accepted too quickly.

Dawkins responds to the argument that scientists also have faith:

> If I am accused of murder, and prosecuting counsel sternly asks me whether it is true that I was in Chicago on the night of the crime, I cannot get away with a philosophical evasion: "It depends on what you mean by 'true.'" Nor with an anthropological, relativist plea: "It is only in your Western scientific sense of 'in' that I was in Chicago. The Bongolese have a completely different concept of 'in,' according to which you are only truly 'in' a place if you are an anointed elder entitled to take snuff from the dried scrotum of a goat."[29]

This is fun, but obscures the real issue. In fact, scientific evidence *is* based on faith—exactly the same sort of faith as informed Christians have in God. Science is always based on at least three kinds of reasonable but fallible faith: trust in the mind, in the senses, and in other people. None of these can be proven—to use mind to prove mind is to argue in a circle. And the senses might be wrong. And there is no scientific test to prove our colleagues honest, reliable, and competent—only social tests. Yet without reliance on all three, good science can't be done. Maybe it could in the age of Galileo, Boyle, and Hooke, when scientists could make their own instruments, but nowadays most scientific work is simply too complex. And even then, as we have seen, science was as much a product of coffeehouses as home laboratories.

Of course there are hoaxes. One can fall for a mirage, trap door, traitor, or archaeologist who plants specimens in the ground at night and "uncovers" them during the day. This is why reason is vital. We were given minds, said Augustine, and heaven forbid we don't use them. And heaven forbid we lean too heavily on friendly Web sites, he might have added—as we will see, that's one thing that gets Dawkins into trouble.

The idea that science is the only valid way of finding out things is called *positivism*. Among those paid to think carefully, this view has fallen out of favor, partly because it disproves itself. Why believe that only truths grounded in scientific evidence are worth believing? That idea itself can't be proven scientifically! Another problem is that one extreme often pushes us to its opposite, like a swing or pendulum. Those who make wild claims about the scientific method often base their arguments not on good human evidence (which they discount), but rumor, wild guesses, and extrapolations that would embarrass a shaman.

Dawkins tells us that "atheists do not have faith."[30] But most atheists in modern times have been Marxists. If the Marxist-Leninist enterprise didn't involve canyon-spanning leaps of unwarranted belief, what did? The past two centuries have seen an unending succession of pseudoscientific cults, of popular hoaxes and swindles, of wild guesses that have struck the cognosphere like the 24-hour bug: Freud, Kinsey, Mead, Ayn Rand, Haeckel, Galton, Skinner, a quack in every pot. It seems that the alternative to reasonable faith is not science, but unreasonable faith.

Faith means, then, not believing poorly evidenced claims, but "sticking to what you have good reason to think is true, in the light of difficulties." In that sense, if their lives are reasonably happy, almost all atheists have faith—in memory, senses, wives, children, colleagues, and peer-reviewed literature.

The fourth level of faith is religious. Faith in God is "higher" in some ways. God can (if he exists) tell us that which "lower" levels of faith cannot. We "go out on a limb" further in trusting him than in trusting people, just as trusting a person involves both more risk and reward than believing only what I see for myself. In this sense, as Gregory of Nazianzus put it, faith "gives fullness to our reasoning." Faith must "precede" reason, Augustine said, because there are some truths that "we cannot yet grasp by reason—though one day we shall be able to do so."

Why are Christians stubborn about faith? Science, Dawkins tells us, is different. "We believe in evolution because the evidence supports it, and we would abandon it overnight if new evidence arose to dispute it."[31] But as Karl Popper pointed out, scientific paradigms are not in fact so easily dislodged, even when evidence against them grows.[32]

If Christianity accepts the need for evidence, what sort of evidence does it offer? It would be as unreasonable to demand that all the evidence conform to the scientific method as that your wife prove she is faithful mathematically, or that you give a purely philosophical proof that you weren't inebriated in church last Christmas. God could choose to remain hidden. After all, the "Prime Directive" in an ancient science fiction TV program was that advanced races not interfere with the development of other worlds, generally by keeping secret. If God wanted to hide, he could do so better than Captain Kirk, one assumes.

But Christianity says God hasn't remained hidden. He reveals himself in creation, our hearts, and in history. Jesus said, "Love the Lord your God with all your heart, and with all your soul, and with all your mind" (Matthew 22:37). If faith involves a commitment of the whole person, and of different kinds of people, one might expect it to appeal to different facets of our humanity. And that, I will argue, is what we find.

You can add numbers in your head without getting out of bed. To study rocks, you may need to go outside. Rabbits are a bit smarter, and gain some initiative. They won't come to you, but they might run away. If you want to get to know a person, the initiative is shared more or less equally, depending on status, nerve, and wit.

It follows from this progression that in any relationship with God, he will retain the initiative. God may be the "hound of heaven," but he's not a lap dog who comes when called.

Dawkins thinks that theological ideas such as the Trinity and the incarnation are fragile and will be destroyed by the attempt to understand them. We're asked to "gain fulfillment in calling it a mystery."[33]

Dawkins is hard to please. Elsewhere he complains that if God were real, he would be "more incomprehensible" than religion represents him as (though showing that he doesn't really grasp what religion says). But when he meets with a difficult doctrine, he reverses himself and complains it's too obscure! That can't be helped. If religion is about any more than shadows in our minds, difficulty and mystery are inevitable.

In every discipline, complex ideas require patience to understand.

John Polkinghorne (who has worked with both) compares Christian formuli to scientific theories. A theory often encapsulates ideas that are not concretely imaginable—the indeterminacy of photons, the efficacy of magnetic fields—and can only be "grasped" by formulas. You can shape styrofoam balls into model atoms and molecules, but don't think real atoms bob like floats in a bathtub and make a squeaky sound when you rub them. The Trinity is mysterious because it's hard to picture, and also because we lack complete access to the mind of God—as to quarks, or to extraterrestrial planets.

The Virtue of Openness

So faith isn't an intellectual aberration or disgrace. It is the normal functioning of a healthy mind, probing its environment in concentric circles, taking the wild world to its lips, learning to love and fear in reasonable balance, open to truth but wary of error. Thought is the "greatness of man," said Pascal.

We're warned that fundamentalists are "hell-bent" on ruining the science education of the young. "Sensible" religion may not do that, Dawkins concedes, but it "is making the world safe for fundamentalism by teaching children, from their earliest years, that unquestioning faith is a virtue."[34]

I missed that Sunday school lesson. I do remember my old pastor drawing me aside one day and explaining that, as I continued my studies, I'd probably find reason to doubt my faith. But, he went on, "Don't give up too quickly! Keep searching!" I'm grateful for his advice, much like what Francis Bacon said at the beginning of the scientific enterprise: "A little or superficial knowledge of philosophy may incline the mind of man to atheism, but a farther proceeding therein doth bring the mind back again to religion..."[35] The pastor's words came true. Nor do I think Dawkins's faith in evolution is so different. Were he to find evidence that seemed to contradict it tomorrow, I don't believe for a moment he would quickly drop his theory. He would assume, as we'll see, that the overall evidence is strong, so with more study anomalous facts will fit in. That I take to have been the essence of my pastor's advice.

It's easy to confuse an opponent's unwillingness to change his mind for mere stubbornness:

> Fundamentalists know they are right because they have read the truth in a holy book and they know, in advance, that nothing will budge them from their belief. The truth of the holy book is an axiom, not the end product of reasoning. The book is true, and if evidence seems to contradict it, it is the evidence that must be thrown out, not the book.[36]

How does Dawkins know that "fundamentalists" never come to believe through reasoning? Many *say* they did. Has Dawkins read their books, considered their arguments, then concluded (as the "end product of reasoning") that they are, in fact, mistaken? Since he doesn't give any evidence for his generalization (and his bibliography is barren of contrary thinkers), I can only assume he finds it *axiomatic*. One can point to many books by believers in which they describe how reasoning and evidence brought them to faith,[37] but it appears that Dawkins has found a quicker solution than throwing evidence out—never reading it.

Dawkins tells the story of a "respected elder statesman" in the zoology department at Oxford before whom a scientific theory he had long believed was disproved by an American biologist. He strode up to the biologist and thanked him profusely: "My dear fellow, I wish to thank you. I have been wrong these fifteen years." The audience "clapped our hands red." Dawkins remarks, "No fundamentalist would ever say that."[38]

No doubt there are many believers who are closed to having sacred beliefs falsified. A cynic may add that Dawkins is one. But it's unfair to overgeneralize either about believers or unbelievers. Some people Dawkins would probably call fundamentalist are, I think, open to being proven wrong. I was one. As a teenager, I believed the earth was young. But the evidence persuaded me otherwise (beginning with a brief but helpfully confusing stint at the L'Abri Fellowship in Switzerland), and I moved on—along with a lot of other people.

Dawkins is right about one thing. Being open to learning new things is, indeed, a priceless quality. Is the kind of openness Dawkins depicts in his senior colleague why so many scientists disbelieve in God? Why were so many early scientists zealous Christians? Did Bacon have things backwards? Does greater familiarity with science cause researchers to lose their faith? What, in general, is the relationship between science and a reasonable Christian faith? Let's consider that question before we plunge into the frothy primodial waves of evolutionary debate.

Are Scientists Too "Bright" to Believe in God?

"A little or superficial knowledge of philosophy may incline the mind of man to atheism, but a farther procceding therein doth bring the mind back again to religion..."

—FRANCIS BACON

Richard Dawkins and Sam Harris are scientists, and Daniel Dennett is a philosopher who writes about science. Like some other famous atheists—Steven Weinberg, Carl Sagan, Bertrand Russell, Edward Wilson—they see science as a way of understanding the world that supersedes faith. These men are all good writers—Russell won the 1950 Nobel Peace Prize for literature—and each has much of interest to say. Each also tends to write well outside the bounds of the specialty in which his claim to scientific expertise rests.

Why should we care what these or other scientists think about God? (More than, say, union plumbers or minor league catchers?) Scientists are masters of the knowledge that has made the modern world—quarks, plate tectonics, genetics, radio waves, medicine. Few, Dawkins tells us, believe in God. Daniel Dennett has a word to describe this precocious, unbelieving elite: "brights"[1] (modeled on the use of *gay* to improve the image of homosexuals). A *bright* is a "person with a naturalist as opposed to a supernaturalist world view," and who possesses an "inquisitive world view."[2]

Dawkins holds the Charles Simonyi Chair for the Public Understanding of Science at Oxford, and claims a broad commission to speak on behalf of science. Since Charles Darwin undermined the argument from design with his publication of The Origin of Species in 1859, most eminent scientists have come to disbelieve in God, he argues.

Since the Enlightenment, progress has served as the central Western myth. Beginning with the first tentative touch of amino acids in a warm primeval bath, life has advanced. Darwin made human history part of the same saga. Humanity once made sense of nature by telling tales about divine beings and scribbling dragons or Terra Incognito at the edges of maps. Primitive man bled the sick, burned witches, cut into flesh with unsanitized knives, and feared sailing off the edge of a flat earth, we are told.

Science is a "candle in the dark," said astronomer Carl Sagan, while "superstition and pseudoscience keep getting in the way."[3] Christianity discourages attempts to understand the natural world, Dawkins claims, adding that theology is the only branch of thought that "has not moved on in eighteen centuries."[4]

Scientists, the high priests of progress, do want to move on. Only about 40 percent of American scientists are believers, in a country where atheists are rare. Top scientists are almost all atheists. A search for distinguished Christian scientists yields the "unmistakably hollow sound of bottoms of barrels being scraped."[5] Christian scientists are so rare in England that three names come up "with the likeable familiarity of senior partners in a firm of Dickensian lawyers": John Polkinghorne, Arthur Peacocke, and Russell Stannard. "The higher one's intelligence or education level," Dawkins adduces, "the less one is likely to be religious or hold 'beliefs' of any kind."[6]

Are scientists really too bright to believe in God? For that matter, does tipping test tubes, spinning particle accelerators, chipping fossils, or thinking systematically about the fruits of such activities really convey some special insight into the nature of reality?

Many think so. This is the logic implicit in Dennett's use of the term bright. It is also assumed in the reverential discussion of science and the scientific method one often hears from skeptics. Scientists such as Dawkins are the rock stars of the movement, and they show little timidity in expressing their views on all kinds of issues.

All this begs four questions. First, is it true that Christianity discourages the attempt to understand the natural world? Second, are modern scientists really so unlikely to believe in God? Third, if so, why? And fourth, if many scientists are atheists, does that make atheism more likely to be true?

In his history of Chinese science, Joseph Needham and his successors differentiate between the effect various Chinese religions had on science. Confucianists cared about "human society, and human society alone," and were unwilling to sully themselves with manual work.[7] They showed no interest in nature, neither aiding nor (much) hindering her study. Taoists, alone among mystics, reveled in the empirical nitty-gritty of experiment. Apart from esoteric Buddhists such as Yi Xing, who tinkered with clocks and studied stars, and may have been half Taoist himself, Buddhists were generally too busy with other worlds to do much with this one.

Does religion help or hurt science? The example of China shows how crude a question this can be, asking for comic-book clarity in the relations between two immensely complex phenomena. But no serious person doubts that in the West there has been deep influence. The question is, What sort?

Christianity and Science

In the last chapter, we saw that Christians seldom if ever see it as a "virtue not to understand." What a mystery the history of science would be if they did!

Early scientists were mostly zealous Christians. If the Bible teaches us to close our eyes to natural wonder, why did modern science arise among a church-educated elite steeped in such anti-intellectualism? How did they reconcile this stick-in-mud theology with their unabashed passion for understanding? Robert Boyle paid to help translate the Bible into Turkish and Lithuanian. Was he trying to undermine the science programs of outlying cultures? Like Newton and Pascal, his passion was defending the Bible. Next time Dawkins strolls down High Street, he should stop at Boyle's plaque and ponder this mystery.

According to sociologist Rodney Stark, of the 52 greatest scientists between 1543 and 1680, Edmund Halley was one of just two skeptics.

Most were "devout" believers.[8] It's not that piety was so common at the time. "Virgins are few, martyrs are few, preachers are few," Fra Giordano complained, and empirical research seems to back him up.[9] Elite, pious Christians steeped in the theology Dawkins scorns saw the attempt to measure and understand the universe as a natural outgrowth of their faith. Evolutionary philosopher Michael Ruse points out that even Darwin drew "heavily" on Anglican natural theology, concluding ironically, "Without Christianity, I doubt we would have Darwinism."[10]

The Royal Society was partly inspired by the ideas of Francis Bacon who, between 1597 and 1625, laid out a program for science. Bacon quoted Proverbs as calling it the "glory of God" to hide mysteries, and the glory of kings to research them (Proverbs 25:2). The natural world was packed with such mysteries: a "labyrinth" of "knotted and entangled" enigmas, wonders, and puzzles given us to explore.[11] By understanding nature, we could also (he believed) improve the lot of humanity. Atheism might result from "superficial" study, but "a farther proceeding therein" would bring one back.

Many skeptics seem to think science emerged from the so-called Enlightenment. Wilson, for example, marks Voltaire as a central figure in France.[12] But Voltaire wasn't a scientist, and did little to help science. Perhaps he lacked the faith. G.K. Chesterton points out that Voltaire "laughed openly" at the claim that a fossil fish had been found at the top of a mountain, ascribing the report to "monkish fraud."[13]

The rise of science marked no sudden break in history. Like other accomplishments of Christian Europe, it grew slowly like a tree from roots deeply entangled in the humus of the so-called Dark Ages.

Christian faith was not the only parent to the civilization that sprouted on the wooded fringes of the old Roman Empire. The baptized savages—Frank and Saxon, Viking, Visigoth, and Hun—who built clocks, Gothic cathedrals, and Atlantic sailing vessels were heirs to Greece, Rome, Arabia, and half the kingdoms of the earth. But it was the church that taught them to read and write. And what the newly literate read was mostly Christian theology. Every great European thinker from John of Paris to John Locke was steeped in the Bible (even Voltaire was educated by Jesuits). If theology makes it a virtue not to understand, as Dawkins claimed, then Western civilization can only be a massive artifact of reverse psychology.

By 1200, slavery had almost vanished in northern Europe. A hundred years later, Western Europe was the most technologically and socially advanced civilization the world had ever known. The use of waterwheels, armor, and other labor and lifesaving devices allowed Europeans to grow more food, defend their land against invasion, and create a rich, varied, artistically inventive society. Women had a far higher status than in competing civilizations. European ships began to explore the world, bringing new wealth, along with temptations (which may explain Bacon's worries).

But Dawkins claims modern scientists, at any rate, are inclined to atheism. Do scientists disbelieve in God? If so, should the rest of us embrace their doubts as well?

Scientists and God

The stats seem clear enough. Among American scientists eminent enough to have been elected as fellows of the National Academy of Science, only 7 percent believe in a personal God, compared to over 90 percent of Americans in general. Among biologists, only about 5 percent believe. According to Dawkins, a parallel survey in Great Britain shows (though only 23 percent of those surveyed responded) that just 3.3 percent of eminent scientists strongly believe in a personal God, while 78.8 percent disbelieve.

I find these stats a little hard to jibe with experience. I speak in churches on other topics, and the first people who come up to talk with me after I speak are often enthusiastic Christians who work in one or another area of science. It seems harder to find Christians working in the social sciences than the hard sciences such as mathematics, or in engineering (an engineering friend explained, "We engineers like things that work!").

I also notice some discrepancy in Dawkins's account of British colleagues who are Christian. He writes of "my trio of British religious scientists":[14] Arthur Peacocke, who helped determine the shape and soluble nature of DNA, John Polkinghorne, who studied elementary particles at Cambridge, and Russell Stannard, who researched the structure of matter and, like Dawkins, helps popularize science. The point of the jibe is that scientists who believe are so few that people point to the same rare examples. But one of the theologians Dawkins discusses, Alister McGrath, did research in molecular biophysics at Oxford. Richard Swinburne, the eminent philosopher and neighbor whom Dawkins mocks mercilessly—and whose arguments he neglects—has a strong scientific education. In other contexts, Dawkins mentions physicist and futurist Freeman Dyson and a distinguished Cambridge geologist who are believers. So Dawkins's Dickensian law firm, while a colorful construct, is a bit of a bluff, even by his own account.

I questioned Dr. Ard Louis, who studies the physics of protein folding at Oxford, about Dawkins's claim. A devout Christian, and the son of Dutch missionaries who are also scientists, Louis told me he knows at least ten of about 100 or so in the physics faculty to be evangelical Christians (by contrast, a girl who worked in an office of 60 or 70 in London said not one of her English coworkers were believers!). Furthermore, Louis added, the largest Christian fellowships in Britain are at the most prestigious (but not largest) colleges, Oxford and Cambridge. So anecdotally, Dawkins's stats merit scrutiny at least as regards the United Kingdom.

Still, with due caution over possible bias or miscounting, it seems that scientists in America at least are less likely to believe in God than "civilians." If Stark is right, the demographics may have even flipped from the time of Kepler, Newton, and Pascal. Why is that? And what, if any, conclusions about the existence of God might we draw?

Why Do Scientists Doubt?

Some of the best evangelists I met in East Asia were gangsters. Or rather, they had been gangsters. They had made a predatory living off heroin, girls, and rigged games of chance. After becoming Christians, they dedicated their lives to spreading the faith that freed them. They seemed especially effective among blue-collar workers. I often visited a large church in an industrial suburb of Taipei whose pastor once sold drugs and ran brothels. A Christian girl wrote to him daily while he was in prison. When he got out, he married her, went to Bible school, and started preaching. I sometimes attended a church in Hong Kong made up largely of former drug addicts and their elderly mothers.

Such churches stood out because in East Asia, there was a strong positive correlation between education and Christian faith. The more books you read, the more likely you were to be a Christian. In Singapore, a person with a doctorate was many times as likely to believe as someone with a high school education, and also more likely than a mere college graduate. A six-story building owned by Campus Evangelical Fellowship hummed with activity on the popular Gong Guan strip across the street from Taiwan's most prestigious school, National Taiwan University. Most of the people I knew at the Baptist church I attended in Nagasaki, Japan were college professors, engineers, and scientists. On a flight across China, the man across the aisle from me turned out to be one of China's top scientists. He carried a complete Bible inside his jacket, and before he knew I was a Christian, began a Bible study (rather bizarre—he wanted to know why King David could have concubines and modern-day Christians couldn't). I ended up staying with him and his patient wife for three days.

The question, then, is not, "Why are 'brights' less likely to believe in God?" A better question would be, "Why do educated people in one culture accept Christianity less often than usual, while educated people in another culture (seventeenth-century Europe, twenty-first-century East Asia) accept it more often?"

Ask why a person thinks as he does, and two kinds of answers may suggest themselves. "Why does Keiko prefer green tea?" "Because she grew up in a small town near Kyoto, and drank it at every meal." "Because it contains catechin polyphenols, which she believes, as a medical doctor, inhibits the growth of certain kinds of cancer."

If scientists believe for nonrational reasons, then their lack of faith isn't relevant to the truth of religion. The word of an Oxford zoologist would be a mere celebrity endorsement, like Harrison Ford selling Kirin lager beer in a Japanese commercial. It's unreasonable to be swayed by a celebrity endorsement unless the celebrity knows what he's talking about!

To which category do the doubts of scientists belong?

One might argue that evolution makes atheism more plausible. Scientists know more about the age of the earth and evidence for change in biology, and therefore realize better than the common man that nature can be explained without need for the "God hypothesis."

Are there any nonlogical reasons why American scientists (at least) would be less likely to believe in God? I can think of seven, some of which seem to explain the phenomena better.

1. Hostility Toward Religion

There may be a "selective disadvantage" to believers in the American academy. On the last day of class, my anthropology professor, an atheist who helped on my research and chatted about such issues, told his Chinese religions class, as if continuing our private conversation aloud, that anthropologists may have it in for the Christian faith. Indeed, Huston Smith says, "The modern university is not agnostic towards religion; it is actively hostile to it." He traces this animus to the claim to control knowledge, competition with the church for influence, and positivism, the idea that only facts proven by science are worth much. He quotes historian George Marsden: "Younger scholars quickly learn that influential professors hold negative attitudes towards open religious expression and that to be accepted they should keep quiet about their faith."[15] According to Sam Harris, "Some propositions are so dangerous that it may even be ethical to kill people for believing them."[16] A little job discrimination would seem mild by comparison.

I'm taken aback by the case of Richard Sternberg. Biologist Stephen Meyer, a prominent proponent of Intelligent Design, published an article in the *Proceedings of the Biological Society of Washington* in August, 2004, arguing that the explosion of new body forms that appear in Cambrian rocks undermines evolution. The editor responsible for allowing this article to surface was shunned, lied about, and kept from doing research at the Smithsonian Institute. Milder forms of the same intolerance could act as a Darwinian mechanism by which people with "scandalous ideas" are kept out of the upper ranks in the United States.

My point isn't to build a case for paranoia or a class-action lawsuit. But it would be naive not to look at the question sociologically.

It's a seller's market for post-Christian ideas, especially if they can claim "scientific" endorsement. Many great modern schools of thought have been founded by virulent post-Christian thinkers: Marxism, Freudianism, Social

Darwinism, French existentialism, behaviorism, objectivism, postmodernism, postcolonialism—the list is long and painfully polysyllabic. What did their founders—Marx, Engels, Comte, Freud, Haeckel, Nietzsche, Sartre, Skinner, Wells, Rorty, Said, and so on—have in common? Not that they obviously contributed a great deal to science. All were "brights," as were most of their followers. Some were gifted writers or poets. Some grew up believers but abandoned their faith, usually in their late teens. Each claimed the mantle of science. Each wowed intellectuals by attacking the Christian view of nature, humanity, or morals. All adopted the Enlightenment story of scientific progress. Most of the schools they founded uncovered some fragment of truth "torn asunder," as Clement of Alexandria put it, "and each vaunts as the whole truth the portion which has fallen to its lot."

But quite a few of these folk threaten to go down in history as quacks. Nor were they all harmless quacks. Each invented or encouraged currents of thought that would be undermined by more careful investigation, often in ways that left Vatican spokesmen looking for gracious ways of saying, "We told you so."

Consider by contrast these influential modern Christian thinkers: Dostoevsky, Chesterton, Lewis, Girard, Solzhenitsyn, Robert Coles, Rodney Stark. These men were also among the brightest of the bright. Most lost their faith at about the same age as the skeptics—in high school or college. In the course of living and other forms of research, each ran into some set of facts that made the Enlightenment story ring hollow. They returned to faith.

Sorry if this sounds like stacking the deck. My point isn't that all unbelieving scientists are quacks and believing intellectuals are saints! (Dostoevsky, for one, was far from the latter.) Nor is it that atheism is inherently more fertile of new ideas, even of harebrained schemes for secular salvation (though without other gods, it is tempting to elevate science or state to that position).

What's the difference between the two lists? Psychologist M. Scott Peck (who belonged to the second) suggested an interesting theory. Peck described four levels of spiritual development (let's call them premoral, authoritarian, skeptical, and integrative). Some people grow up in a *premoral* environment, then find an *authoritarian* parent substitute; gang leader, bossy pastor, a drill sergeant. By contrast, young people who grow up in a strict atmosphere are educated, seduced, enticed, socialized—use whichever word you like—away from parental or church *authority* into accepting the *skeptical* Enlightenment myth that dominates intellectual life in the West. They often see themselves as rebels escaping the heavy hand of intellectual oppression.

A good example is the biologist Edward O. Wilson. He grew up in the South and was escorted by "Mother Raub" (not his real mother) to a Baptist church. Keenly interested, he was taken, dressed in Sunday best, "to announce my decision and to select a time for baptism." Wilson was disappointed to find the pastor dressed in flashy clothes and smoking a cigar (of which Mother Raub did not approve). The baptism itself was a let-down; he felt no epiphany. In fact it felt "totally physical." Wilson asked, "Was the whole world completely physical, after all?"

A "small crack" of doubt entered Wilson's mind, which widened as he was mentored in biological research. He read physicist Erwin Schrödinger and evolutionary biologist Ernst Mayr. Science became "the new light and the way." Perhaps even religion itself had a natural explanation.[17]

Wilson wasn't argued out of his faith. At 16, he hadn't studied the evidence for Christian beliefs and found it deficient. Nor did he understand life history very well—he wrote an "excited" essay on what he later recognized as the bogus ideas of Stalin's favorite biologist, Trofim Lysenko.

What seduced Wilson was a bigger story. He found a door out of cramped pieties into a life of intellectual discovery and adventure—like Bilbo Baggins setting off from the Shire in search of the dragon's gold.

By contrast, those on my list of Christians seemed to bloom a little later. After embracing the Enlightenment story and studying their corner of truth valiantly (and at first with excitement), they found things that made them question the new orthodoxy. They didn't so much abandon the modernist story as integrate their passion for discovery and appreciation of the scientific method into what they began to see as an even grander story.

The point is that "what we believe" (like "what we drink") is influenced by "who we hang around" and "what stories we are told." Education is a process of socializing young scholars into a "way" of seeing the world, as Wilson put it. It's not surprising if different educational cultures bias young minds in different directions. Whether or not that direction is toward truth cannot be judged simply by counting heads, bright as they may be.

2. Self-imposed Limitations

The scientist must bracket considerations not relevant to his research. This means assuming that God does not spike the petri dish (or, as biologist Ben McFarland told me, "You do another ten Petri dishes and publish what's repeatable!"). Just as a bone can turn into stone after years in the ground, "methodological naturalism" may fossilize into a philosophy. This doesn't mean we have "universal experience" against miracles, as David Hume assumed (how could he know that?). But the habit of setting miracles to one side may become hard to break.

3. Bias Against Miracles

Miracles involve unique experiences. They are not reproducible, and therefore offend what many see as the core of the scientific method. There is, of course, a distinction between "My job is to explain things naturally, and so far things have worked out," and "We haven't seen any miracles in our lab, so they don't happen." Miracles are a province of history, not science. Science is an adjacent province of history: Every experiment reported in a journal is, in the end, a historical report. But since scientists are not always philosophers, and every trade privileges its own, it may be easier for some scientists, or populists, to say, "Prove it to me scientifically, or I won't believe!"

4. Doubt Instead of Discernment

Scientists are rightly offended by the arbitrary and silly nature of many miracle reports. Many babies have been thrown out with that bathwater.

In *Jesus and the Religions of Man*, I argued that miracles are different from "magic" in five ways. Miracles invite verification, usually historical, while magic often flaunts its irrational character. Miracles are usually practical, while magic is showy—bleeding statues, levitation, Mary in a loaf of bread. Miracles enhance human dignity, while magic undermines our humanity—it makes us bark like dogs, or "[affect] Godhead, and so loosing all" in Milton's words. Miracles point to God; magic to something or someone else. Finally, miracles come in response to requests, while magic makes demands. Like a fireman "running red lights," miracles actually affirm the dignity and reasonableness of natural law. But to some onlookers, "the rules" are being broken and therefore cheating is going on.

When Christ healed the sick, he didn't stand with the credulous masses against the men in white coats, or vice versa. The gospel bridges the gap between blind faith and the "hermeneutics of suspicion." By offering reason to the masses, and faith to scientists, Christ makes us all more fully human.

5. Faulty Information

Some churches set young people up to lose their faith by teaching bad science. Sir Paul Nurse, 2001 Nobel Peace Prize laureate in physiology, says he abandoned religion in secondary school because his attempts to reconcile what he learned about life history to Genesis were squelched by his church.[18] Wilson also felt forced to choose between biology and Christianity.

As a teenager, I enjoyed a religious comic book that depicted a cursing scientist losing his temper when a student disproved radiocarbon dating. A mollusk was tested and found to be thousands of years old, "and the thing was still alive!" I snickered smugly. But the subtext seemed to say, "If radiocarbon dating were accurate, it would undermine your faith." I wonder if I would have kept my faith if that were the only kind of apologetics I was exposed to.

I don't want to be too hard on pastors or parents who make such mistakes. No one owns a crystal-clear picture of reality. A little humility and curiosity go a long ways. These are modeled in many Christian homes, as they were in mine.

6. Presumption

Few scientists take the time to become experts on God. Dawkins quotes Albert Einstein as writing, "The idea of a personal God is quite alien to me and seems even naïve." A Catholic clergyman responded that Einstein didn't know what he was talking about. "Some men think that because they have achieved a high degree of learning in some field, they are qualified to express opinions in all." Dawkins responded, "On the contrary, Einstein understood very well what he was denying."[19]

But how was this unnamed theologian wrong? His point was that the opinion of an expert in one field is of little value in another if he hasn't studied it. Dawkins ignores the point—perhaps because it is so relevant to his own case.

Leading scientists at research universities work long hours. How much time does an 80-hour work week leave to study arguments for the historical Jesus, talk to missionaries about answered prayer, research the role of Christianity in reform movements, or even soak in Jesus' words very deeply? Great scientists of the past were steeped in the biblical texts. They didn't need to search "evil Bible verses" (see chapter 7) on the Internet to make up their minds about the nature of the biblical revelation. One biologist told me:

> I actually think the "science game" is played such that if you don't idolize science you won't win the game. If you let other things in your life—God, a baby, or heaven help you, both—you are handicapped, and given the tenure process, probably tenure for life. I do kind of laugh at all the hand-wringing about women not going into academia. Some days, I just say to myself that means the women are smart, reasonable, free beings!

7. Ignorance

Scientists who take a radical stance against religion often reveal an ignorance of that which they speak about. Examples will appear throughout this book—though I will have space to cover only a tithe of the errors I found in the works of Dawkins, Dennett, and Harris (not to mention the anti-God writings of other part-time theologians). My goal is not to show disrespect to those dedicated to studying the natural world. But let's not engage in credulous hero worship, either. Knowledge in one realm does not transfer to another without careful, humble study. Those who assume it does often heap a large serving of crow for themselves, as we will see.

Science and Faith

We should be cautious, then, about moving too glibly between science and faith. Some scientists do believe, though it may be more difficult to do so in modern America. Many don't. A decline in faith among eminent scientists, while unfortunate (I think) for themselves and (we will see later) for society, is generally not a logically valid or emotionally persuasive reason to doubt. It may be that a nun in Calcutta knows more about God than a professor in Harvard or Oxford. If, as the apostle James wrote, "God opposes the proud but gives grace to the humble" (James 4:6), that would not be surprising at all.

The branch of study called *theology* attempts to look at the faith of nuns with the intellectual tools of professors. Oddly, Dawkins shows special dislike for theologians (perhaps he sees them as traitors). Consider the following clear statement on the Trinity by a third-century saint, Gregory the Miracle Worker, a disciple of Origen:

> There is therefore nothing created, nothing subject to another in the Trinity...the Father has never been without the Son, nor the Son without the Spirit: and this same Trinity is immutable and unalterable forever.

Dawkins quotes this, then comments sarcastically:

> Whatever miracles may have earned St. Gregory his nickname, they were not miracles of honest lucidity. His words convey the characteristically obscurantist flavour of theology, which—unlike science or most other branches of human scholarship—has not moved on in eighteen centuries.[20]

The quote seems both lucid and clear to me (especially compared to what I've read in many social science texts!). God is three in one, and has always been. What Dawkins seems to mean is he finds this lucid, honest statement incredible. Maybe it is. Certainly it is true that the Trinity has remained orthodox for a very long time.

But there are different kinds of "moving on." Some theologians "move on" in the sense that they lose faith in the Triune God. Despite the contempt Dawkins frequently expresses for theologians, he quotes such pioneers often and approvingly (indeed, Huston Smith suggests that religious studies professionals fully share the hostility of the university towards religion).[21] But learning new things doesn't need to mean leaving behind the basics in any field. Ancient astronomers found that the earth is round. Do modern ones need to prove it's a trapezoid to keep observatories from being turned into swimming pools? (as one British historian said should be done with the school chapel?). "Moving on" means building on prior discoveries, not abandoning them.

Augustine read the Bible and deduced that time came into being with the universe. Stephen Hawking credits him as the first person to realize what is now an element in the standard big bang interpretation.[22] In this and other cases, twentieth-century science has caught up with fourth-century theology. In other cases, theologians apply new discoveries in science and other fields to old beliefs, or use old insights to interpret new discoveries. Clement of Alexandria said, "Truth is one." Because that is so, as knowledge expands, so do the challenges and insights involved in thinking about God.

Scientists who become theologians, such as Polkinghorne, know how dynamic and intellectually challenging God-study can be. For a Christian, every breakthrough in science, every new reading in history, every discovery of a new culture, every philosophical insight casts new light on the nature of God and how he interacts with the world he made.

Does Evolution Make God Redundant?

"Philosophy is, in fact, the greatest possession, and most
honorable before God, to whom it leads us and
alone commends us...Knowledge being one, I wish to tell
why it has become many-headed."

—JUSTIN MARTYR

Icons of Evolution, an exposé of bad arguments for evolution by cell
biologist Jonathan Wells, draws controversy like a magnet draws iron.
In the copy I borrowed from the University of Washington library, a
previous reader had scribbled in editorial comments. When Wells
introduced Steven Jay Gould as "the world-famous expert," the reader
crossed out "expert" and wrote in "dogmatist." "Darwinian research" was
altered by similar point mutation to "Darwinian fraud." The Amazon.
com Web site for the same book contains angry reviews by scientists who
question, among other things, the author's honesty, writing style, religion
(he's a member of the Unification Church), institutional associations ("a
bunch of ideologues") and the credentials of anyone who agrees with him
("they seem to all be creationists, and therefore, hardly real scientists").

Most of the book argues the error of particular "icons": examples of
evolution you come across in textbooks such as peppered moths, Haeckel's embryos, Darwin's finches, and four-winged fruit flies. But in the final
chapter, Wells moved from evidence to attitude. He told the story of
teachers and scientists who have been persecuted for arguing against
evolution in public. Skeptics are denied funding, their articles rejected,

and "eventually the critics are hounded out of the scientific community altogether."[1]

Clearly, evolution is a contentious issue. Many worry that the theory undermines not only faith but also the ethical foundations of society (for reasons we will look at later). To many skeptics, arguments against evolution are an assault on science, pluralism, and democracy, not to mention foolish.

In their own way, Dawkins and Dennett have also become "icons of evolution." Dawkins's *The Selfish Gene* (1976) inspired a generation of biologists. In *Richard Dawkins: How a Scientist Changed the Way We Think*, eminent scholars such as Steven Pinker, Sir John Krebs, David Haig, and Daniel Dennett describe the revolutionary impact Dawkins's "relentless, uncompromising, and surgical application of neo-Darwinian thinking," as Krebs put it, had on their thought.[2] Others praise the rhythm, precision, and creativity of his prose. Dennett has worked to develop a philosophy built on similar principles. *Breaking the Spell* applies the evolutionary program to religion, as Edward Wilson's *Sociobiology* applied it to society as a whole and Marc Hauser's *Moral Minds* applied it to ethics.

Evolution, Dawkins famously said, allows one to be an "intellectually fulfilled atheist." Dawkins and Dennett hope it can do more: drive a stake through the heart of religion. They throw cold water on any attempt to reconcile God and Darwin, whether by skeptics such as Gould or believing scientists such as Francis Collins. The New Atheism agrees with the old creationism: evolution and faith are mutually exclusive. Choose you this day which you will serve.

I find things more complicated. Confucius said, "To know what you know, and know what you don't know—this is knowledge." I suspect that a lot of people on all sides of this argument—icons and ordinary mortals—know less than they pretend.

What do we know about the origin of the species? And what does that have to do with faith in God?

Answering these questions may feel a bit like stepping between wolves fighting over a bone ("bones of contention," as the human fossil record has been described). But the goal of Christian apologetics is not to shill for indefensible dogmas—that would be to "offer the unclean sacrifice of a lie to the Author of truth," as Francis Bacon put it. Christian thought means "faith seeking understanding," an attempt to relate truths known by different rational methods.

In this chapter I plan to look at points I think the New Atheists get right. In the next chapter I'll argue that at other points, they would do well to step more carefully.

Darwin Was a Great Scientist

Some Christians have taken to belittling Charles Darwin. This is both unfair and counterproductive. *The Origin of Species* is a brilliant piece of intellectual literature. One only has to read the book to see that Darwin was a remarkable naturalist: well-read, cautious, observant, informed, and aware of contrary evidence and of weaknesses in his theory. "The crust of the earth is a vast museum; but the natural collections have been imperfectly made, and only at long intervals of time."[3] This is good writing: economical, clear, and weighty. Darwin's description of how natural selection keeps the species fit was a huge discovery that has stood the test of time. His emphasis on variation has also proven deeply fruitful.

Darwin's bright young cousin, Francis Galton, soon applied Darwin's ideas to the *eugenics* (good breeding, or, one could almost say, good races) of man. Galton thought the human stock needed to be improved, writing of the "childish, stupid, and simpleton-like" nature of Africans.[4] Unfortunately, he made at least a partial convert of his famous relative. Darwin was a humane man. But as we will see, Social Darwinism would have a terrible history, set in motion by its own severe logic.

Evolution proved a "dangerous idea" (as Dennett calls it)—especially to society's outcasts. But natural selection shares a quality in common with the gospel: it is true. Knowledge is one, said Justin. All truth is God's truth, said Clement. With the rest of God's counsel in view, Darwin's idea doesn't need to be quite so dangerous. The Bible tells us creation is "groaning from its bondage to decay" (Romans 8:21-22). At least Darwin described the mechanism by which, even when individual bunnies go to the wolves, rabbits in general are kept from going to the dogs.

The World Is Old

St. Augustine was undeniably one of the greatest thinkers who ever lived. He was deeply in love with Scripture, and passionately committed to Jesus Christ.

Most non-Christians, Augustine admitted, know something about science, "the earth, the heavens, and the other elements of this world." How, he asked, would an educated unbeliever react if he heard a Christian, "presumably giving the meaning of Holy Scripture," making wild claims on these topics? Not only would the skeptic ("for whose salvation we toil") laugh at the believer; he would dismiss the Bible, too. If a Christian speaks foolishly about a field of knowledge his non-Christian friends know better, "how are they going to believe those books in matters concerning the resurrection of the dead, the hope of eternal life, and the kingdom of heaven?" "Untold trouble" is brought by "reckless and incompetent" preachers claiming on biblical authority what educated people know to be false.

If we say the earth is only 6000 years old, educated unbelievers are likely to respond as Augustine warned. Young Earth creationism denies the daily experience of scientists in many fields. Astronomers must believe there are no stars more than 6000 light years away. (Then what is the rest of the Milky Way, which is 100,000 light years across? Not to mention every other galaxy in the sky? Or did God create light in transit just to fool us?) Paleontologists are asked to believe the fossils in their hands were specially created to look old. Methods for testing the age of rocks, familiar to geologists as a thermometer or speedometer, must be delusional. Sam Harris remarked that young earth creationists ask historians to believe the world was created centuries after the Sumerians learned to brew beer! Setting the gospel up for such jibes is not a helpful way to reach skeptics with the gospel or to understand and appreciate the work of God.

True, an old earth presents certain problems for the Christian faith. One minor problem is the text of Genesis, which seems to describe a recent creation. When I say this problem is minor, I don't mean the meaning of Genesis is a trivial question. I mean it is easily answered by looking at how the text was meant to be read.

C.S. Lewis said he knew Genesis was inspired simply because (unlike other ancient stories it resembles) it "achieves the idea of true Creation and a transcendent Creator."[5] But that's just the beginning of the riches of this text.

The world has often quarreled with Genesis, and gotten the worst of it. Let me give some quick examples.

The Book of Beginnings says the universe came from nothing. We have tried alternative theories: everything from an egg, elephants all the way down, "cosmic crunch," "steady state"—but the biblical idea of a cosmic origin has now been vindicated.

"All humanity came from one man and one woman," we read. Greek philosophers, Gnostics, Hindus, the Nation of Islam, and some Social Darwinists said no, people are a mixture of free and slave, of spiritual, psychic, and physical, different parts of the body of Brahma, or separately evolved species. Genetics has settled the matter in favor of Moses. Francis Collins, head of the Human Genome Project, notes that one of the surprises from research into human genes is the discovery that people of all races on earth share 99.9 percent of their DNA. This is unusual, he added: most animals are far more diverse. We are, he concludes, "truly part of one family."[6]

Karl Marx convinced a third of the world, and many professors in the other two thirds, that money was the real problem. Communism then proved conclusively that people can hate one another in a cashless society.

Adam called Eve "bone of my bones, and flesh of my flesh" (Genesis 2:23). Attempts to mold corporate Amazons or to deny the humanity of women (or men) have proved disappointing.

Steven Hawking credited Augustine as the first person to realize that time began with the universe. Actually, Origen beat Augustine to this epiphany, also by meditating on Genesis. Genesis warns against pride, what C.S. Lewis called the "Great Sin." In the story of Cain and Abel, it reveals the danger of what one school of anthropology calls *mimesis*, or competitive imitation. It shows how love of knowledge can lead to loss of innocence.

If not God, some ancient shepherd got a whole lot spot on. One could write a history of the human race, utilizing the deepest psychological and anthropological insights, based on the first three chapters of Genesis. It's not hard for me to believe that God speaks through Genesis. The question is, What does he mean to tell us about origins?

The purpose of inspiration, according to the apostle Paul, is practical: "that the man of God may be thoroughly equipped for every good work" (2 Timothy 3:17). St. Jerome said Genesis was written "after the manner of a popular poet," which Lewis translates "mythically."[7] For Lewis, that didn't mean it wasn't inspired. If Jesus can use parables and farce (a camel going through the eye of a needle, mountains jumping into the sea) to get a point across, we should be cautious about telling God how he can or cannot speak. Even if the opening chapters of Genesis bear resemblance to what is loosely called myth, their unparalleled practical wisdom presents a powerful argument for the inspiration of Scripture.

A deeper problem is that if the Earth is old, then death, suffering, and disease long preceded the appearance of man. Why would God create a world in which there is so much suffering? Why would he make the worm 190 million years before Eve bit the apple? And the mosquito and flea 30 million years later? Could Satan have messed in biology millions of years ago? (Mission theorist Ralph Winter has made this suggestion.) Or can we somehow rationalize all this suffering away as part of a divinely ordered "circle of strife"?

This is one of the great riddles modern science presents the Christian faith. Philosophers such as C.S. Lewis, Richard Swinburne, Nicholas Wolterstorff, and Peter Kreeft have tried to answer it, professionally or personally.

Sam Harris is the only one of our troika who touches on this subject much. At times he writes with what looks like honest passion. "On a day when over one hundred thousand children were simultaneously torn from their mothers' arms and casually drowned," he writes of the great after-Christmas tsunami of 2005, "liberal theology must stand revealed for what it is: the sheerest of moral pretenses."[8] It is when Harris shouts at God for the deaths of children swept away in the tsunami, or tortured by sexual perverts, that I most respect his atheism. What honest believer doesn't sometimes want to scream, too?

Still, since truth is one, being honest doesn't mean looking only at one side of a question. Harris's arguments follow a consistent pattern. He never thanks God for the good, but only blames him for the bad. Nor does he pay any attention to answers that Christians (like those mentioned above) have offered.

Few animals (and of course, no plants) have the intellectual capacity to suffer. Higher animals can and do—though not, probably, as much as we think, looking at it sympathetically from the human point of view.[9] The Bible tells a story that explains some of that suffering, gives the oppressed hope, and (perhaps most helpfully of all) shows that God walks with those who carry a cross. Still, part of the Christian answer to this question can only be, as it has always been, "We see in a mirror dimly, but then face to face" (1 Corinthians 13:12).

Life Is Connected

In a famous debate at the Museum of Natural Science in Oxford (where Charles Dodgson would take Alice to see the remains of an extinct dodo a couple years later), Samuel Wilberforce (son of William Wilberforce) is supposed to have asked Thomas Huxley on which side of his family tree he claimed to be descended. I say "is supposed" because like many alleged incidents in the mythological "history of the warfare of science and religion," this story has been embroidered dramatically.[10] Huxley replied (the story goes) that he wasn't ashamed of his ancestry, but would be ashamed to use his intellectual gifts to obscure the truth.

If we find monkeys swinging from our family tree, should the relationship shame us, or undermine Christianity?

I see three reasons to think the "big picture" Darwin described may be true. First, while a surprising number of fossils remain missing, and the "missing links" that have been found often bring up more questions than they answer, the basic pattern of life history roughly follows Darwin's scheme. The earliest rocks from the Proterozoic Period contain single-celled creatures. No rabbits show up in pre-Cambrian rocks, to give the iconic example. Second, the bodies of man and ape do share many common structures. Third, DNA research seems to clearly reveal connections.

At first glance, our genetic coding seems troublingly makeshift. Michael Shermer asks why the "Intelligent Designer" put "junk DNA, repeated copies of useless DNA, orphan genes, gene fragments, tandem repeats, and pseudogenes" into the genome, "none of which are involved directly in the making of a human being."[11] Collins warns that it takes some hubris "for anyone to call any part of the genome 'junk,' given our level of ignorance."[12] Some of Shermer's questions might be answered as we come to understand DNA better. Fazale Rana and Hugh Ross, and Francis Collins as well, argue that much of this "junk" is useful after all.[13] The "junk" moniker is falling out of favor among biologists, who are making "constant discoveries," as biologist Ben McFarland told me, about its uses. Still, DNA does seem to suggest that life is more or less like a tree, and we are in some way related.

Ard Louis posed an interesting question to me: "Which would seem more remarkable? If you found Legos all put together in the shapes of cars and houses? Or if you found a box of Legos that snapped together into complex shapes on their own?" Organic life can be seen as a remarkable set of Lego blocks, and the universe a truly amazing place, if it really did self-assemble rabbits, rhubarb, Rembrandt, and Rasputin. Stark shows that in some ways, opposition between evolution and Christianity was "drummed up" by radical skeptics such as Huxley: Many Christian thinkers were inclined to see evolution as "God's way of creating." That doesn't mean, of course, that they were right.

Evolution Can Make You an Intellectually Fulfilled Atheist—If You Don't Ask Too Many Questions

If you were to survey the plant, animal, fungi, and various microbial kingdoms in 1850, you would have found an endless variety of complex and strange creatures, like the dodo. With a good microscope, you would uncover layer beneath layer of intricacy. As you observed workmanship and the relationship of parts, along with motion, adaptability, and grace (a cat climbing a roof, a fir swaying in a winter gale, a spider spinning a web), design would seem writ large across the fabric of life. Whether Darwin's theory succeeds or not, the mechanism he described gives a plausible account of how certain things could have developed (given the first life). An atheist who believes in evolution might reasonably conclude, "If Science [having earned an upper case "S," like Superman] explains so much, why not everything else, too? A solar system is a simple thing compared to a sea urchin."

The universe has grown. That's not a bad thing. Before beginning his scientific career, Robert Boyle wrote, "He whose Faith never doubted, may justly doubt of his Faith."[14] Swinburne is right. If God had wanted to leave no room for doubt, we might see his hand push the moon across the sky every day. Faith is reasonable, but without intellectual wiggle room, it might feel rather stifling.

The book of 1 Kings tells the story of how Elijah won a great victory against the pagan prophets of Baal, then became depressed. Holed up in a cave on a mountain, he sought God. A gale blew up, strong enough to send rocks careening down the slope. But God was not in the wind. An earthquake shook the peak. God was not in the earthquake. A brush fire began, but God could not be found there, either. Finally the prophet heard his creator speak in a "still small voice" (1 Kings 19:12 NKJV).

For some, evolution has shouted down the voice of God. For others, it allows them to hear that voice in a new and more subtle way.

Some Riddles
of Evolution

Do St. Bernards mourn the unsanctity of their fleas?
Do seagulls blush at their gull abilities?
Gold in pig's snout, so the soul in shorts and sleeves
I wonder at stars, and seas, and me.

—"THINKING OF AUGUSTINE AT THE BEACH,"
DAVID MARSHALL

Science helps some people disconnect from God. We find the universe much older than our ancestors did. Life appears in roughly the pattern Genesis describes, but over vast periods, and "red in tooth and claw." Charles Darwin's theory seems, at first glance, to fit the pattern even better. When we study the bones, muscles, and genetic molecules in different animals, they appear related. Is the problem of life solved? Can we say, with Edward Wilson, that religion was "just the first literate attempt to explain the universe," and science has superseded it?[1]

Thoughtful Christians who have responded to the New Atheism, such as Alister McGrath and Richard Swinburne, say the answer to the first question is yes, and the second no. I agree that the clearest evidence for the existence of God may not lie in biology. But I'm not quite prepared to admit Darwin entirely solved the mystery of life, and will now explain why.

Something Is Rotten in the State of Science

For most nonscientists, such as myself, the best reason to believe in evolution is that biologists agree it explains life. If a person has dedicated her life to a specialty, one wants to listen respectfully to what she has to say about it. Of course, if the subject is important—remodeling one's home, global warming, whether a lump is cancerous—a proactive person will read to evaluate expert opinion for herself, and after careful study, may even reasonably side with a minority view.

But trust is fragile and can be easily undermined. Any hint that scientists are too biased, any reaction that looks more like defending territory than seeking truth, is bound to undermine confidence in a theory. Reading up on evolution, one doesn't have to go far to come across troubling signs.

Dawkins wrote that Darwin devoted an "entire chapter" in *The Origin of Species* to difficulties with his theory. "It is fair to say," he added, "that this brief chapter anticipated and disposed of every single one of the alleged difficulties that have since been proposed."[2]

In fact, Darwin devoted *four* chapters to difficulties. But some central ideas in modern evolutionary theory, such as the role of mutations, wouldn't be developed for decades after his death. How could Darwin have "disposed of" objections to ideas he had never heard of? Darwin himself candidly admitted that some objections were "so serious that to this day I can hardly reflect on them without being in some degree staggered..."[3]

One of Darwin's arguments has, however, gained new life with debate over Intelligent Design.

Intelligent Design is the idea that life exhibits features that can't be explained by evolution alone, and show evidence of having been designed. One Intelligent Design concept is what maverick biologist Michael Behe calls "irreducible complexity." This is the claim that some living mechanisms are too complex to arise by short steps. Kenneth Miller argues, in response, that the parts of a complex organ may have been used for other purposes, stepping stones along the path to development. For example, says Gould, the stubby appendages that developed into wings might once have been used to keep big animals cool, or small animals warm, or help them walk, catch insects, or attract mates.[4] Darwin also wrote of "functional change in structural continuity."[5]

Theories, like deer, need predators to keep fit. In the best of worlds, Intelligent Design should be welcome to biologists who hope it will help keep evolutionary theory honest. But unlike Darwin, many on both sides of the controversy seem to go out of their way to insult opponents. A lot of social posturing goes on here in the name of science.

In June 1996, iconoclastic mathematician David Berlinski wrote an article called "The Deniable Darwin" in *Commentary* magazine. A who's who of disputants on both sides, including Dawkins and Dennett, responded three months later. Dawkins mocked Berlinski as a "creationist" (a charge Berlinski denied). Dennett described Berlinski's arguments in scatological terms. He also mockingly suggested that the paper was a scam to hoodwink "earnest creationists" into making fools of themselves.

The point in both cases was not scientific, but social: to draw a line between scientific "brights" and credulous, "creationist" dims. The two correspondents appealed to the atavistic fear of being picked by the wrong team. These responses were the mirror image of the book borrower who scribbled out "expert" and wrote "dogmatist."

In *The God Delusion*, Dawkins does offer arguments against Intelligent Design. But he seems to resent the idea of a challenge. The following quotes both appear on page 125:

> The creationists are right that, if genuinely irreducible complexity could be properly demonstrated, it would wreck Darwin's theory. Darwin himself said as much: "If it could be demonstrated that any complex organ existed which could not possibly have been formed by numerous, successive, slight modifications, my theory would absolutely break down."

> Searching for particular examples of irreducible complexity is a fundamentally unscientific way to proceed: a special case of arguing from present ignorance.

A hundred or so words, and a subject subtitle, separate these two statements. Were irreducibly complex organs to be found, Dawkins admitted in the first, evolution would be ruined. He quoted Darwin as saying the same (always a safe way to proceed), and implicitly challenged critics to find such organs. A few sentences later, he said the search for evidence both he and Darwin admitted would overthrow evolution is "fundamentally unscientific."

At times like this, the scientific community can resemble a tree fort with a sign affixed to the wall: "Gurlz Kepe Out!" Only instead of girls, the excluded party is identified as creationists, fundamentalists, or even (in one strange instance) Republicans.

In 2006, the U.S. House Committee on Government took up the case of Dr. Richard Sternberg. A biologist with the National Institutes of Health, Sternberg edited an obscure Smithsonian Institute journal, *Proceedings of the Biological Society of Washington*. In 2004, Sternberg made the mistake of publishing a paper (after vetting it with three other biologists) by Intelligent Design proponent Stephen Meyer. The article questioned the ability of evolution to explain the Cambrian Explosion, the sudden appearance of many distinct animals in the fossil record about 570 million years ago.

Another sort of explosion took place at the Smithsonian. Colleagues launched a campaign to smear and, if possible, get rid of Dr. Sternberg. Sternberg's boss hinted the biologist should quit. When Sternberg failed to follow this prompt, colleagues tried to force him out via numerous cuts and inconveniences: taking keys away, demanding extra paperwork, circulating rumors (was he a closet fundamentalist, or even a Republican?). One Dutch scientist e-mailed his support for the campaign:

> These people are coming out and invading our schools, biology classes, museums and now our professional journals. These people to my mind are only a scale up on the fundies of a more destructive kind in other parts of the world.[6]

Quite a night at the museum—all for the crime not of denying Darwin, but of allowing one skeptical paper (by a man with a doctorate in related research from Cambridge University) to see daylight.

One finds more subtle forms of the "sociological argument" for evolution. Alan Orr's challenge to Berlinski in *Commentary*, by contrast to Dawkins and Dennett, was a model of courtesy and fairness. He ended his own substantive critique by noting, "I know [Berlinski] well enough to know that he, unlike [other anti-evolutionists], is neither anti-scientific nor doctrinaire. His criticisms—like those from any good scientist—are, I think, both sincere and tentative."[7] Why did Orr feel the need to add this character reference? He knew that many interpret arguments against evolution as "antiscientific" (assaults on our club) and "doctrinaire" (carrying the odor of a rival, theological club).

When asked if he held creationist beliefs, Berlinski denied it. "My views of Darwinism [are] negative, but rational."[8] By accepting the implicit claim that religious views are "irrational," Berlinski was saying, "I belong to the scientific team as much as you do."

Hubert Yockey goes further and tries to turn the tables on the Dawkins crowd. Like Berlinski, Yockey is a mathematician who finds theories for the origin of life doubtful. The title of his discussion on Talk.Origins was "Belief in a Pre-Biotic Soup in the Early Ocean is a Religious or Ideological Belief,"[9] as if one only dares criticize evolution by first throwing a few ritual stones at the church. The idea that there ever was a primeval soup for life to emerge from, he argued, is "a doctrine of religion or ideology," not the result of "specific and detailed evidence." Therefore (Yockey doesn't suffer fools gladly), Dawkins and his ilk were the real religious fanatics.

Essentially, Yockey asked his colleagues to pick new teams. Science is not about coming to "orthodox" conclusions, but about openness to evidence.

As if this weren't enough to ward off the "creationist" bogey, Yockey ended his letter curiously. First, he pointed out that his argument applies only to the origin of life, not evolution. Therefore, "creationists should take no pleasure in this post," since "there is no scientific need for special creation, especially 6000 years ago." Then he adds whimsically, "Long live the memory and work of Charles Darwin."[10]

Why would an eminent scientist append a statement of faith in a nineteenth-century naturalist to a discussion about twenty-first-century microbiology? Why do Yockey, Berlinski, and their defenders underscore that they have not "gone native" among the fundamentalists? Dawkins tells us the Intelligent Design argument is "lazy and defeatist."[11] Dennett dismisses critics as "frauds and charlatans."[12] The prematurely triumphal tone of University of California law professor Phillip E. Johnson, who helped found the Intelligent Design movement, sometimes strikes a similar note.

None of this helps us think clearly.

Implicit social threats should make us more, not less, determined to think through questions about faith and science honestly. Nor should we pay attention to people who waste time debating whether Intelligent Design or evolution are "real science" or not. David Bohm once defined science as "openness to evidence."[13] The best scientist—or theologian— is not someone who shouts, "Heresy!" when he hears strange views, but one who listens carefully and responds with reason and evidence. When it comes to ultimate questions, "openness to evidence" is the definition that counts.

No One Knows How Life Began

The origin of life has not been explained, long research and bold claims aside.

Dawkins assures us that considering the vast size of the universe, the origin of life is no problem. With the air of an heiress tossing gold coins to gutter snipes, he asks, What if the "spontaneous arising" of a DNA-like molecular code were so "staggeringly improbable" as to occur just once on a billion planets? He calls this "the most pessimistic estimate," adding that he doesn't believe the origin of life was really so touch-and-go. The universe holds more than a hundred billion galaxies, each with a hundred billion or so stars. The "magic of large numbers" makes it likely that even on such a "pessimistic" scenario, a *billion* planets in the universe host life! This argument, Dawkins tells us calmly, "completely demolishes" any need for design to explain the first living creature.[14]

This move, which Dawkins also made 20 years earlier in *The Blind Watchmaker,* is a staggering bit of magic, pulling a rabbit (or its ancestor) from the cosmic hat.[15] Actually, the "most pessimistic" estimates of the origin of life from nonlife by natural processes are a lot more pessimistic than that. Some researchers have concluded that "something equivalent to DNA" simply can't arise by chance, even if every atom in the universe were itself a universe, stewing and frothing for a hundred times the wait since the big bang. Francis Crick, co-discoverer of DNA, said it was "almost impossible" to give a probability estimate. Francis Collins, who took over from Crick as head of the Human Genome Project, admits that no plausible mechanism has even been found yet.[16] Paul Davies called the spontaneous self-assembly of DNA "ludicrously, almost unthinkably—small," adding that "the origin of life remains a mystery."[17] Biologist Fazale Rana notes that modern cells require for some 300 different proteins, a source of sugars, nucleotides, amino acids, and fatty acids to all be placed together in working order.[18] Probably not all of these would be needed for the first life, but much of it likely would.

Fred Hoyle and Chandra Wickramasinghe did suggest a number for the random coming together of the simplest organism: one in ten to the forty-thousandth power. (Imagine every atom in the cosmos expanding to the size of the cosmos. Then every atom in those cosmos expanding again. Do that *500 times*. At the end of that, you just might have a chance of obtaining a living molecule from nonlife. And then hope the pool it forms in doesn't dry up and end its run of luck!)

To get around the immense improbability of anything like the simplest modern life mixing up out of the primeval brew by chance, researchers suppose early molecules also evolved. But it has remained incredibly difficult to imagine (in detail) how this could have happened on its own.

Yockey is scathing about proposed scenarios. Citing Dawkins as an example, he writes, "People who do not understand probability often say that extremely improbable events occur frequently."[19] He argues that no scenario explains even one fact about life chemistry: that proteins are "left-handed," and sugars in DNA and RNA "right-handed." For Yockey, a refrain from early biology, "*Omne vivum ex vivo*—life must come only from life," sums up what origin of life research has discovered so far.[20]

Yockey's response to one scenario, that the first biochemicals came together in sea foam to form life, is delightfully incredulous:

> The credibility of this scenario is supported by the authority of Hesiod (Theogony c. 700 B.C.), who tells us that Aphrodite (her name means foam-born) arose from the sea foam on the island of Cythera. From there she was wafted on Homer's "wine dark sea" to Cyprus...The goddess, being immortal, was able to escape the effect of the intense ultraviolet light on the Earth at the time and that would have exposed mortal organisms to a lethal dose in less than 0.3 seconds...[Aphrodite] is still widely worshipped today, especially near colleges, universities, and army camps. Nevertheless, as far as the emergence of mortal beings is concerned, one must be a little more skeptical about this mode of origination...[21]

Berlinski, who wields an equally acerbic pen, in another *Commentary* article wrote a brilliant short description of the many problems involved in getting life out of death. He then commented:

> At the conclusion of a long essay, it is customary to summarize what has been learned. In the present case, I suspect it would be more prudent to recall how much has been *assumed:* First, that the pre-biotic atmosphere was chemically reductive; second, that nature found a way to synthesize cytosine; third, that nature also found a way to synthesize ribose; fourth, that nature found the means to assemble nucleotides into polynucleotides; fifth, that nature discovered a self-replicating molecule; and sixth, that having done all that, nature promoted a self-replicating molecule into a full system of coded chemistry.
>
> These assumptions are not only vexing but progressively so, ending in a serious impediment to thought...All questions about the global origins of these strange and baffling systems seem to demand answers that the model itself cannot by its nature provide.[22]

Ask me why my car runs, and I'll say, "I turned the key!" Dawkins's gloss on the origin of life sheds little more light than that. "Once the vital ingredient—some kind of genetic molecule—is in place, true Darwinian natural selection can follow."[23] One might compare this to the "all you need is love" theory of marriage. Berlinski argues that a coded molecule is not all you need to make life.

Both Yockey and Berlinski mention the problem of homochirality, the fact that all amino acids in living tissue are "left-handed." Nature produces left and right-handed acids in about equal numbers, and the wrong kind interfere with reactions. How did the first life gather only southpaws for its team? Organic chemist William Bonner admitted, "I spent 25 years looking for terrestrial mechanisms for homochirality and trying to investigate them and didn't find any supporting evidence."[24] Other biologists continue the search. In honor of such long labor, if nothing else, it's too glib to glance at the stars and declare the problem solved.

I am not making a "God of the gaps" argument. Not that there is anything unscientific about such an argument. To paraphrase Deng Xiaoping, it doesn't matter if a cat wears a lab coat or a bishop's robe, so long as it catches mice. Gaps in the power of a hypothesis to explain facts need to be filled, and some wounds in the surface of nature may be too large for anything but God. But the usual picture is of gaps narrowing as science progresses. Primitive man sees a bolt of lightning, and thinks Zeus is quarreling with Hera. Then Ben Franklin comes along and we learn about static electricity and paths of ionized air.

Here the situation is reversed. Earlier generations believed "simple" life could spontaneously generate from nonlife. Francesco Redi discovered in 1688 that worms do not come from meat itself but from eggs laid in it. Louis Pasteur found that not even microbes come from nonlife. The gap between inanimate chemicals and the simplest bug—which turns out not so simple—was expanded into a Grand Canyon by science.

Will scientists cross this canyon, or enlarge it? Only time will tell.

In the meanwhile, I'm not offering an argument for God. I'm pointing out that no one knows how life arose, including Richard Dawkins. Let's not pretend otherwise.

Creative Mutations Are Hard to Find

The origin of the species is generally explained as follows. Creatures bear young. Sex distributes genes in a "white elephant" fashion, causing offspring to differ. As descendants struggle to survive and propagate, variations are sorted out to the advantage of candidates more fit in a given environment. The most profound differences—those that lead to the innovation that made Noah's Ark the wild place it was—are introduced by more or less random copying errors, or *mutations*. This theory, we are told, is the central, unifying truth of biology.

But can mutations pull their weight in it? They're being asked to produce the innovations that created all life, from squirrels to squid. Dennett says mutations don't even occur once in a trillion "copyings."[25] Actually, it's more like one in a hundred million. But it's extremely hard to find mutations that make an organism more complex and fit. Italian geneticist Giuseppe Sermonti says baldly, "Their effect in all instances is to demolish...transgressions of the kind needed by Darwinian evolution have never been documented."[26]

Mutations can be found that make an organism more likely to survive. For example, certain bacteria mutate to become resistant to drugs. Even Intelligent Design proponent Michael Behe admits that single "point" mutations that confer resistance to drugs occur so frequently that some drugs are rendered useless before they are marketed. But according to physicist Lee Spetner, such a mutation may make the bacteria simpler. It is like filling a keyhole with mud. A house can become more secure because the lock has been smashed and is now harder to pick. The house is harder to break into, but daubing mud isn't how the house or the lock came into being in the first place. In the same way, the bacteria may become secure against the drug—which attaches key-like to the bacterial surface—by losing genetic complexity.[27] Complex indentations are "paved over" with a daub of protein.

Spetner echoes Sermonti: "There aren't any known, clear examples of a mutation that has added information."[28] Many biologists heatedly disagree, and he's debated the question quite a bit online. Some claim to have found bacteria which, having lost the ability to wiggle to food, regain it by a second mutation. Others find evidence for past productive mutations in the genome. But at least it seems painfully hard to find favorable new mutations that add information even to viruses or bacteria, and more so among multicellular organisms. (I am following with great interest the debate over Michael Behe's book *The Edge of Evolution* [New York: Free Press, 2007], which focuses on the known history of pathogens responsible for malaria, HIV, and food poisoning. So far, of his many passionate critics, I have seen none claim that in the relatively well-known history of these pathogens, any have in fact managed to evolve into anything strikingly new.)

Look at the fruit fly, the most abused "big" creature on the planet. Since 1908, when Thomas Morgan discovered that its large chromosomes are handy for genetic research, like a little Rasputin, the creature has been irradiated, electrocuted, scalded with chemicals, frozen, and otherwise assaulted. Morgan won the 1933 Nobel Prize for his work. His student Hermann Muller won in 1946 for discovering that X-rays could induce mutations in the fly. Edward Lewis, Christiane Nüsslein-Volhard, and Eric Wieschaus won in 1995 by inflicting further discomfort. Scientific inquisitors have forced all kinds of confessions from the creature's jumbo chromosomes. By 1938, Calvin Bridges compiled a dictionary of fruit fly mutations more than 200 pages long. The book would make gloomy reading for insect rights activists, full of terms such as "sterile," "viability poor," and "homozygous lethal."[29]

Where are the helpful mutations? With millions of mutations over a century, why hasn't science built a better fruit fly yet? Or turned one into a moth? Surely there would be a Nobel Prize in *that*.

Or look at a larger species—Homo sapiens. This is a creature known for such maladaptive behavior as channel surfing, ordering sauerkraut, driving 50 miles to "save" four dollars at a sale, and climbing into the death zone of Mount Everest "because it's there."

Since the nineteenth century, some three million generations of E. coli bacteria have reproduced, tuberculosis perhaps a tenth as many. Since hominids began chipping flint, by contrast, less than 200,000 generations have passed. Over those generations, if what we're told is correct, our bodies have developed in remarkable ways. To name a few:

- Faces shortened
- Arms shortened
- Legs lengthened
- Spines curved at the base to spring while walking
- The spinal column moved from back to center of the skull base
- The rib cage widened into a barrel shape to allow arms to pivot more freely
- The pelvis sunk lower and broadened out so we could walk upright
- The knee was restructured
- Muscles and ligaments were altered all over the body
- Neck muscles became smaller, since they no longer needed to support the head horizontally
- Inner ear bones changed to balance so we could walk upright, water-ski, and wait tables
- Ladies grew in proportion to men
- We learned to walk[30]

- Brains more than doubled in size—the brain became asymmetrical, and chemistry, size, and function of regions in the brain changed dramatically

- Eighteen changes occurred in a gene that operates late in the first trimester, especially in brain development—this gene had only experienced two changes in the prior 300 million years

- We learned to sing, swear, lie, pray, and make bad puns

- It occurred to us that if we thought, we must be

- The Tao was spoken

Linguist Noam Chomsky called the problem of language "far from trivial: how can a system such as a human language arise in the mind/brain, or for that matter in the organic world, in which one seems not to find anything like the basic properties of human language?"[31] With language, wrote Walker Percy, something radically new entered the universe:

> The old arrow route, the six-billion-year-old chain of causal relations, the energy exchanges which had held good from the earliest collisions of hydrogen atoms to the responses of amoeba and dogs and chimps, that ancient circuit of causes, my troop of arrows, had been short-circuited.[32]

To the extent that the difference between man and chimps is genetic, where did the information that coded for all the needed changes come from? Mutations? To say the word and think the problem is thereby solved turns common concepts of faith and science on their heads.

It's often said people and chimps share 98.5 percent of their DNA. The actual figure appears to be 96 percent.[33] Still, that represents thousands of useful changes. All of them took place when the number of people on Earth was a tiny fraction of what it is today. The human race is thought to have passed through a "genetic bottleneck" of some 10,000 individuals before leaving Africa. Even if our evolving population was a hundred times larger on average, that means the numbers alive today are a hefty proportion of the pool from which all these changes are supposed to have come. In 40 million years, a hooved wolf is thought to have evolved into a slinky crocodile-like aquatic beast, then into sperm, humpback, killer, and blue whales, living in small numbers and having few calves.

Evolution doesn't know its work is done. It doesn't know it shouldn't turn us into whales, teach us to eat grass like cows, or to glide like flying squirrels. For any direction evolution might take, given all it achieved when numbers were small, one might expect hundreds of useful mutations in every generation, fitting us for many new tasks.

Where are those mutations?

You might expect innovations to show up first among athletes. They specialize in new "adaptive roles": throwing a screwball, tackling punters, holding feet still while swimming upside down to music. What mutations have appeared to help out? Did Gaylord Perry have special sweat glands on his hands that allowed him to throw a spitball without artificial lubrication? Did Pelé have mutant bone structures on his forehead that let him send a "header" into the goal? A web between fingers and cow-like skin on the hand might allow a baseball player to catch balls without a glove—and find reproductive opportunities in every major league town.

Lynne Fox has set all kinds of records for swimming in cold water: three miles in the Bering Strait between American and Soviet islands, in Lake Baikal, Glacier Bay, even a mile in the Antarctic. Doctors say her veins constrict blood flow to peripheral parts of the body well. Her body fat is high and well-distributed, like an internal wet suit. Was any of this due to mutations?

Has a new generation of gifted sportsmen and women emerged from the radioactive grounds of Chernobyl in recent years?

I don't mean to be silly, certainly not to mock. After all, the behavior of our genetic libraries can be very eccentric at times. Sometimes single bits of genetic material are altered in copying. Occasionally nucleotides or regions of DNA are copied double, omitted, or even flipped backward. But it does surprise me that something so fundamental as the mutations thought to have created us must be spoken of so vaguely. In the anthology titled *Human Populations, Genetic Variation, and Evolution*, Howard Newcombe noted:

> While it is recognized that mutations may occasionally be beneficial, and that evolution must have occurred in the past through a process of selection for such beneficial effects by means of differences in fertility and mortality, such selection must be regarded as costly in terms of human suffering.[34]

Notice the words "must have." That's about all that is given. While examples of the billions of helpful mutations that "must have" coughed up ourselves and every other plant, animal, and mushroom on the planet may be forthcoming, in the meanwhile this sort of talk makes me feel a bit as I do when reading the Gnostic theory about 72 archons that sub-contracted to build the human body.

The Origin of Complex Organs Could Still Use Explaining

Richard Dawkins, like Darwin, takes issue with the argument from irre-ducible complexity. This is the idea that some organs require a minimum number of parts to work—if there is just one less part, nothing good hap-pens. Michael Behe believes such organs are a problem for evolution. He finds it hard to imagine mutations suddenly creating several new struc-tures and fitting them together in a complex system. Dawkins replies:

> "What is the use of half an eye?" and "What is the use of half a wing?" are both instances of the argument from "irreducible com-plexity."...But as soon as we give these assumptions a moment's thought, we immediately see the fallacy. A cataract patient with the lens of her eye surgically removed can't see clear images with-out glasses, but can see enough not to bump into a tree or fall over a cliff. Half a wing is indeed not as good as a whole wing, but it is certainly better than no wing at all.[35]

This answers the wrong riddle. The question isn't what happens when half the complete *structure* is missing. The question is what happens when half its *parts* are missing. What good is an eye without an optic nerve? Or an optic nerve that connects only halfway? An example of the problem is a series of mutations in a poor fruit fly that produces an extra pair of wings. Ed Lewis found if he saved one generation of freaks and bred them, he could link three mutations to form a fruit fly with two pairs of wings.

The problem is, without muscles, the extra pair of wings doesn't move. The clever "design" that linked three mutations helped scientists understand embryonic development and helped Lewis win a Nobel Prize, but did nothing at all for the flies. The little Frankenbugs would find life in the unforgiving air space around an apple tree "solitary, poor, nasty, brutish, and short."[36] In any case, two wings are probably optimal. Even if the extra wings worked, they would probably just get in the way.

The irreducible complexity argument, which Darwin himself seemed to see as legitimate, cannot be disposed of so simply, or by calling any-one who offers it a creationist and invoking separation of church and state. A better way to decide whether it can be disposed of at all (say, by positing intermediate uses for new organisms) is to read both sides of the debate. Miller and Behe have dueling articles online as well as in the book *Debating Design: From Darwin to DNA* (Cambridge University Press, 2004). My point is not that Behe is right, only that Dawkins should follow his Darwinian instincts: that sort of argument deserves to be heard respectfully.

Even If It Works, Evolution May Reveal Purpose

Children are "native teleologists," Dawkins tells us. This seems to be one of the strongest conclusions of the school of cognitive psychology and anthropology that the New Atheism draws upon. Young humans see purpose in nature. "Clouds are 'for raining.' Pointy rocks are 'so that ani-mals could scratch on them when they get itchy.'"[37] Olivera Petrovich found that even Japanese children raised in nontheistic societies often ascribed natural objects to a creator. Unfortunately, Dawkins comments, not all children "grow out of" this tendency. Some become theologians who think nature actually *is* intended.

But Dawkins's argument also implies purpose. Apparent design, he tells us confidently, can be explained by mutations tested by natu-ral selection, creating the "appearance" of design. Many evolutionary thinkers compare this biological process to a computer program. But why assume that the appearance of purpose in biology is an illusion? Even if evolution can do all it's cracked up to do, how do we know nature isn't itself a design program? The apparent design astronomers see, Dawkins says, can be explained by the anthropic principle. If the environment didn't suit us, we wouldn't be here to complain. So no matter how long the odds against the sun and the moon and the stars being as they must for us to live, so it must be, or we wouldn't be alive to notice.

In that case, on what grounds do we tell the child who sees purpose in nature she's deluded? Dawkins sees the evidence for design, too. The child takes appearances at face value; Dawkins chooses to deny them. For all he knows, this universe (or multiverse) was created precisely in order to snap chemical Legos into clouds for rain, granite rocks for bears to scratch themselves on, or pebbles for children to skip across the surface of ponds. Science offers no grounds whatsoever on which to rebuke four-year-old teleologists—even if they grow up to be G.K. Chesterton and thank God for the gift of legs to put in his Christmas stockings.

Does Evolution Disprove God?

So what can we say about evolution and God? Certainly not that evolution disproves Christianity.

Even plants defend their territories with chemical warfare. Among humans, words often become "holy ground," and we fight over them like cats and dogs. The issue of origins isn't just an abstract game of one-upmanship, a struggle between scientists and theologians to assert "alpha male" priority. As a boy, I got it into my head that dinosaurs were an invention of "evolutionists." I still get the shivers when I think of the swarming ancient trilobites in illustrations of early Earth: The place seemed creepy.

Jesus said, "You will know the truth, and the truth will set you free" (John 8:32). His followers invented science, quoting Solomon, "It is the glory of God to conceal a matter, to search out a matter is the glory of kings" (Proverbs 25:2). Why let secularists have all the fun?

I come to the question of origins and design with mixed bias, and I think a pretty open mind. On the one hand, I'd probably prefer to find clear fingerprints of God in biology (though Dr. Louis's image of self-assembling Lego blocks is also attractive). Most conservative American Christians are skeptical of the story of evolution, as usually told, and that's my spiritual home. On the other hand, Christian biologists are often confident of evolution: I have heard engaging and brilliant ideas as they verbalize "faith seeking understanding." If I'm irritated with the arrogance of Dawkins, I also find myself bothered by the logic-chopping Phillip E. Johnson sometimes seems to engage in, and feel the scientists (that is what they are) at Discovery Institute could be more forthcoming on, for example, their Theory of What Really Happened. Both sides discredit themselves at times by forcing all science into a theological cage that depends on what great Christians thousands of years ago already saw as a naïve reading of Genesis, and some atheists by "No Bleevurz Aloud"-type postings on the doorpost of *Le Club Scientifique*.

So what is my Theory of What Really Happened? My theory is I don't know, and neither (perhaps) does anyone. Darwin was a great scientist, but the origin of the species remains rather mysterious. The pattern of evidence roughly resembles the days of Genesis, and roughly resembles Darwin's theory. But it is also unlike what either Christians or atheists expected. Species do not, for example, change as gradually as Darwin anticipated—something dramatically new appears, then remains much the same for long periods.

Some things we can be fairly sure of. Life is old. It appears related, but mutations seem a clumsy instrument to explain that relationship. Scientists are human, and therefore sapiens, but also sometimes full of hot air.

Biology doesn't provide a knockout blow for or against God. Fossils offer an overview of a grand progression in life, broken by many lacunae. (Breaks in a story build suspense!) If anyone is confident that this strange story was told without a bard, I wonder how he knows that.

I'll come back to the story of life in the final chapter. Let's look now at the even stranger, and I think more revealing, story of man.

5

Did God Evolve?

"All Chinese pagans believe in God."

—Lin Yutang[1]

In 1512, Michelangelo completed a painting on the ceiling of the Sistine Chapel in Rome: God reaching down to create Adam. But is that what really happened? Or did the creative spark fly the other way? Did Adam, or the selective forces by which he evolved, create God? One of the goals of evolutionary philosophy is to revise Genesis in the latter direction. In *Breaking the Spell*, Daniel Dennett depicts God as a work of human and evolutionary art.

Dennett's book is interesting because, while Dawkins vaguely refers to the evolution of religion, Dennett offers ideas about how it could have happened. Borrowing pigments from anthropologists Scott Atran and Pascal Boyer, psychologists Paul Bloom and William James, and the early work of sociologist Rodney Stark, Dennett paints the origin of religion.

This work, I will argue, fails badly. At its best social science sketches a recognizable outline of man, missing perhaps a few appendages. But even in describing human nature, the hindsight of social science often proves muddier than the foresight of Michelangelo's teachers, such as Paul and Augustine. When it comes to God, Dennett and his informants fail to see what stands above them in plain sight, holding out his arm to give life.

Where Does Religion Come From?

Breaking the Spell is not an academic exercise—it's an exorcism, an attempt to free believers from delusion. While Dennett tries to be diplomatic, his goal is as radical as that of Dawkins, Harris, or Hitchens: to "break the spell" of belief. In his *Philosophical Lexicon*, Dennett defined *church* as "a tightly constructed, heavily defended medieval place of worship, now primarily a tourist attraction." His goal is to make this definition come true.

In C.S. Lewis's fantasy *Out of the Silent Planet*, the scientist Weston, thinking that the natives of Mars are about to sacrifice him, defiantly explains the "scientific perspective." Dennett comes on the same mission. Describing himself as a "revivalist preacher" of "democracy, justice, life, love and truth," and an "ambassador" of science[2] and supposing, I guess, that believers oppose these things, Dennett writes to an audience he expects to be hostile and maybe a bit dim. Diplomacy is called for. Dennett credits believers with "uncounted good deeds,"[3] and admits that faith may be good for your health. The problem, Dennett patiently explains, is that whatever benefits it may bring, religion is *untrue*.

The best way to undermine religion, Dennett assumes, is to show that it can be explained as a natural but superfluous result of the evolutionary process. Tell a better story of religion, and belief will be rendered illogical:

> It might be that God implants each human being with an immortal soul that thirsts for opportunities to worship God...The only honest way to defend that proposition, or anything like it, is to give fair consideration to alternative theories of the persistence and popularity of religion and rule them out by showing that they are unable to account for the phenomena observed.[4]

In other words, if you want to prove God exists, read naturalistic theories of religion, and show they don't explain him. That's the program I'll follow in this chapter.

Let's not assume, however, that explaining a state of mind really does explain it away. If you hit your head on a beam and say, "I see stars," your doctor probably won't get out a telescope and look for the Andromeda Galaxy in the ceiling joist of his clinic. On the other hand, if Dennett is right, the perception that "two and two make four" must also have an evolutionary origin. Natural selection, presumably, makes all mental states possible, including the state of believing in evolution. If evolutionary roots explain one idea away, they explain them all away. In that case, and if there is no God to whom we can fall back on, skeptical philosophy (and all other thinking) is a lost cause. That may be why William James warned of "medical materialists" who "use the criterion of origin in a destructive instead of an accreditive way."[5]

But let's follow Dennett's argument and see where it leads. We may, after all, find that social science can't explain faith in God.

Dennett thinks religion derives (like a perfect storm) from several mental faculties that evolved separately. Our ancestors chanted, sang, and used ritual to help remember tribal lore. They learned to sniff out freeloaders, people who want rewards without work, like the lazy member of Lord Shackleton's crew who refused to help row from Elephant Island to South Georgia. They found that acting "morally" paid off, and developed a conscience. They gained a "sweet tooth" for stories, which helped them look at problems from more objective perspectives. Figuring out what others were up to developed into a complex art.

Sniffing out the intent of others, what Dennett calls the "intentional stance,"[6] was crucial, the "irritant around which the pearls of religion grow."[7] Anything that moves in a complex way, we tend to see as having "agency," or intent.[8] Hear a rhythmic creak at night, and we say, "It's just a branch scraping the gutter." But patterned, unscheduled bumps make us sit up in bed, suspecting a leopard, thief, or ghost. Notice how that last word sneaks in. Fear of "bumps in the night" was a useful survival mechanism. Our brain extrapolated by creating "virtual images" of unseen beings, and the first haunting occurred.

In the nineteenth century, British anthropologist Edward Tylor proposed a theory about how religion evolves (which remains popular in Communist countries, and became the "common ancestor" of many modern theories). Tribes "low in the scale of humanity" dreamed dreams, saw visions, and remembered the dead.[9] They came to believe that every tree, rock, or mountain was "animated" by the sort of things that appeared in dreams. These "spirits" became gods. Then one wrested the throne of Olympus and became the Supreme, Almighty Creator.

Animation is also central to Dennett's theory. Our minds, he says, are wired by evolution to "ping" at the sign of animated motion. Natural objects—clouds, currents, wind—don't trigger our "intentional agent" motion detector directly. But who pulled the child into the whirlpool? Who brought rain when the shaman danced? It seemed that the god who rode the cloud wasn't the cloud itself, nor was the sacred stream the spirit that haunted it. Nor was every common willow tree "old Willow-man" (as Tolkien called him).

When someone dies, an image of the deceased remains with us. We develop rituals both to remove the corrupt body and release his "spirit," a "virtual person created by the survivors' troubled mind-sets,"[10] to another world.

I find this phase of the story (which Dennett has adapted from Pascal Boyer and Paul Bloom) interesting and fairly plausible.

During the Obon "ghost" festival in Nagasaki, Japan, each family that lost a loved one during the previous year builds a bamboo float. The last day of the festival, families escort the floats, and spirits, down the city's many hills to the harbor, scattering firecrackers in the streets. On one hill I found a tiny float to Aiko, a deceased pet dog. Having just lost a dog ourselves, memories of it "haunt" our yard—the porch where it pawed to come in, the river where it swam heroically after sticks. One night I dreamed the dog had been out wandering and I found him in the parking lot at a grocery store. So much more may deceased family members remain with us.

But this can't be the whole story even of "primitive" belief. What about out-of-body experiences? Miraculous cures? Answers to prayer? When I asked 77 longtime Christians why they believed in God, 42 of them (54 percent) circled the answer, "I have had a supernatural experience that taught me the reality of the spiritual world." I have, too. And while under examination, in some cases *miracle* is probably used as a synonym for *amazing or mysterious event*, I've also heard many firsthand stories that, if true, pretty much rule out materialism as a possible explanation for reality.

A friend's father was deathly ill in a hospital in Tennessee. One morning his friend in another city prepared to visit, not knowing how sick the father was. Just as she was about to set out, she saw a light. Sensing it had to do with him, she asked, "Jim?" An audible voice replied, "Yeah?" She said, "Go in peace." Later she learned he had died within five minutes of the experience.

My point at the moment isn't to argue that such experiences are real. It's that primitive man must have had them, too. Even so experienced a psychologist as Scott Peck met patients whom he became convinced were literally possessed. Surely earlier generations had an excuse to make the same diagnosis! Apart from William James, the social scientists Dennett relies on generally ignore such experiences. But we can't ignore them if we want to understand the origin and basis of "primitive" religion.

Nor, I think, does Dennett seem sufficiently startled by the portrait of man social science has sketched. Clearly, far more has changed in us than meets the eye. Do gorillas tell ghost stories in the jungle at night? Do chimps see King Kong in the clouds? When Fido is unfaithful, does he do penance? Why does a monkey in a wedding gown make us laugh? If evolution saw fit to make us moral, nuptial, praying, ghost-seeing, story telling, socially hypersensitive creatures, why only us? As evolutionary theorists describe the many complex developments they suppose gave Homo sapiens a soul, man looks less like one beast among many, and more a "monster" as Chesterton called him (the only hopeful monster), standing alone in the Garden with a frown on his brow.

Not only does the attempt to depict man as just another animal serve to highlight how different he is, the "scientific, evolutionary portrait" of man turns out strangely familiar.

Madam, I'm Still Adam

"What is man?" Richard Dawkins asked at the opening of *The Selfish Gene*. He dismissed all pre-evolutionary answers in a single short burst from zoologist G.G. Simpson: "All attempts to answer that question before 1859 are worthless...we will be better off if we ignore them completely."[11]

Why, then, do so many strokes of Dennett's brush seem so familiar, yet also a bit amateurish?

Dennett warns against "over-attributing intentionality" to inanimate objects. That sounds a lot like what the prophets said when they warned against worshipping stone or beast. He says religion encourages us to repeat "incomprehensible elements."[12] Two millennia ago, Jesus warned against "meaningless repetition" (Matthew 6:7). Dennett assures us we should be free to question God: "Perhaps the most shocking implication of my inquiry," he breathlessly concludes, is that "unquestioning faith" in poorly credentialed preachers is a bad idea.[13] Doesn't he know the prophets have been saying that for thousands of years?

In fact, in his own warning against creepy gurus, one primitive rabbi showed mastery of several of the very principles Dennett thinks social scientists just discovered.

Some ways of saying things, Dennett tells us, "catch" in the mind better than others. We focus on animated motion. We have built-in "alarm systems" for predators, and share a "sweet tooth" for stories. We remember things well if they stand out in just one way (a two-headed monster is the fit subject of a fairy story, but a two-headed monster who cheats on taxes is just irritating).

As an eminent philosopher, Dennett duly notes these cognitive propensities, recognized by experimental science, and writes a 400-page book against credulous belief. He's a good writer, and when he forgets to talk down to the natives, the book has its moments. But even Dennett seems unsure if it'll much break the spell of religious credulity.

Jesus took a quick shot at the same problem. "Beware of the false prophets, who come to you in sheep's clothing, but inwardly are ravenous wolves," he said (Matthew 7:15). In that simple sentence (16 words in the original Greek text), Jesus also sought to break the spell of credulity. To do so, he told (1) an (implied) story involving (2) a predator that (3) was unusual in just one way, (4) warned us to watch out for religious con men (5) in graphic (6) and few words. His followers still remember at least the gist of this pithy formula (as I did, when I first wrote this quote down). Jesus didn't naively think his warning would "break the spell" forever—crowds still gather around a Grigori Rasputin, Bhagwan Rajneesh, or Vladimir Lenin just as snow crystalizes around specks of dust. Jesus didn't threaten our freedom to make fools of ourselves. But he made the danger eternally clear to anyone who would listen.

Dennett is never so orthodox as when he thinks he's original. Nor is he the only one. Often, as social science puts the final touches on some new heresy, the crowning insight of the latest research magically transforms into bulky footnotes to words a blue-collar Hebrew tossed out twenty centuries ago. Psychologist Ernest Becker, in his Pulitzer Prize-winning book *Denial of Death*, described his amazement at finding Søren Kierkegaard (translating old Sunday school lessons into philosophical argot) anticipating the conclusions of Otto Rank: "Such a mixture of intense clinical insight and pure Christian theology is absolutely heady. One doesn't know what kind of emotional attitude to adopt towards it."[14] Another Pulitzer Prize laureate, Robert Coles, described his long, fruitful career in child psychology as a "return to the Sermon on the Mount."[15]

So much for the "worthless" character of pre-Darwinian insights about man. There's cause for humility here, a humility that might bring healing to brights who are willing to listen.

Even more so since when it comes to memes, Dennett falls into the very traps he warns against, and is seduced by the animistic impulse.

Are Memes Out to Get Us?

A complete theory of religion should explain not just the instincts that give rise to perception of the divine, but how religious ideas develop, spread, and are preserved. Here, *The Selfish Gene* seemed to help. Dawkins proposed a "gene-centric" story of origins. The way to understand evolution, he said, isn't to look at the creatures that scurry and sweat and scum for mates, but at the coding molecules discretely tucked into cell nuclei. Genes are the real actors. Dawkins waxed poetic as he described how genes use our bodies as surrogates, "survival machines" in the grand evolutionary struggle:

> Now they swarm in huge colonies, safe inside gigantic lumbering robots, sealed off from the outside world, communicating with it by tortuous indirect routes, manipulating it by remote control. They are in you and in me; they created us, body and mind; and their preservation is the ultimate rationale for our existence. They have come a long way, those replicators. Now they go by the name of genes, and we are their survival machines.[16]

The prose is brilliant, though some see these images as a bit over the top. Physiologist Denis Noble responded in *The Music of Life*:

The "selfish gene" view, is a metaphorical polemic: the invention of a colourful metaphor to interpret scientific discovery in a particular way. It has provided valuable insights and these have been used to advance biological science in novel ways. I am not one of those critics of 'the selfish gene' idea who deny its impact and value. But it is nevertheless a metaphor. It is not a straightforward scientific hypothesis.[17]

Noble illustrated his point by reversing the metaphor, looking at genes not as powerful genies that control organisms, but powerless hostages used by organisms for our selfish purposes. Noble was careful not to overplay his hand, but concluded that "It does seem to me more natural, and certainly more meaningful" to talk first about survival of organisms, not genes.[18]

But *The Selfish Gene* was a hit with both popular and scientific audiences, offering a gripping "myth" that shed an intriguing new light on biology.

Late in the book, Dawkins threw off a suggestion about cultural evolution that also gained (as they say) a life of its own: "meme theory," or *memetics*.

A *meme* is a "unit of cultural transference," an idea, habit, "clothing fashion, way of making pots or building arches," or set of verbal signals we acquire not genetically, but by copying others.[19]

Both Dawkins and Dennett, who adopted "memetics" with enthusiasm, write as if memes ("living structures, not just metaphorically but technically") are "intentional objects." They "propagate" themselves. They "parasitize my brain, turning it into a vehicle for the meme's propagation."[20] Like genes, they work "unobtrusively, without disturbing their hosts any more than is absolutely necessary."

All this seems pretty poetic for a scientific hypothesis. The meme sounds as if it were conscious and plotting, like Mr. McGreedy's chickens.

Ideas have their own logic, "free-floating rationales" Dennett calls them, natural goals towards which evolution gropes blindly, like a computer search engine. A religion that says God will punish anyone who doubts helps itself, whether or not it helps the believer.

But Dennett seems to forget the danger of projecting life onto inanimate objects. Memes "acquire tricks"[21] "exploit" romance, "proliferate," and "benefit" from adaptation. They "conceal their true nature from their hosts." Like body snatchers in a low-budget sci-fi film, "once allegiance is captured," an unwilling host "is turned into a rational servant."[22] Wily religious memes teach "submission" (Islam) and love of "the Word" (Christians) over life. This explains why religious ideas, once created by all those new mechanisms in the mind, evolve and "propagate." Thus Dennett takes what he calls a "sketchy but non-miraculous and matter-of-fact stroll" from "blind, mechanical, robotic nature to the passionate defense and elaboration of the most exalted ideas known to humankind."[23]

Or has he reinvented the devil?

In his *Philosopher's Lexicon*[24] Dennett satirized Christian philosopher Alvin Plantinga with this definition: "*alvinize*, to stimulate protracted discussion by making a bizarre claim. His contention that natural evil is due to Satanic agency alvinized his listeners." One feels "alvinized" at the pointy-eared shape materializing in the brain as one reads Dennett's theory. In an effort to explain God, his invisible memes conceal, exploit, benefit, outwit, even possess their innocent hosts, the meme machine Homo sapiens, sapiens in name only. The devil makes us worship God.

The problem with memetics is not just that it's "meaningless metaphor," as Steven Jay Gould complained,[25] nor that, as Phillip E. Johnson argued, if natural origin discredits religious ideas, it undermines antireligious ones, too (*Origin of Species* would be one giant "meme-plex"). The deeper fallacy lies in confusing subject and object, just as Dennett (and the Bible) warns. Our "built-in love for the intentional stance" encourages Dennett to see "invisible agents" as "secret puppeteers behind the perplexing phenomena."[26] The problem isn't that Dennett finds the demonic in man, but that his demonology (this was Cotton Mather's problem, too) wrongly ascribes creative power to forces that consume and destroy. It *is* hard to understand why people fall for bizarre beliefs! But blaming the ideas themselves, rather than the people who buy and sell them, subverts human choice. As the ingratiating devil-figure Art Immelmann explained in Walker Percy's *Love in the Ruins*, "We never never 'do' anything to anybody. We only help people do what they want to do."[27]

Dennett may believe in the devil, but not in God. The creative spark, he thinks, passed the other way. Because the literature of social science is based on observation, a recognizable outline of the god-fearing, duplicitous, idolatrous, storytelling, jumpy, curious shape of Adam does appear on the ceiling, along with drips, smudges, and holidays. But which way did the charge really pass? Here, Dennett needs to read his own sources more carefully.

Did Man Create God?

Does Dennett's theory explain God? Really, it doesn't even explain poltergeists. God, it just ignores.

Three hundred years ago, philosopher David Hume claimed that "north, south, east, west," all mankind was polytheistic, with "not a single exception." If the clever Greeks worshipped many gods, as a deist Hume thought it unbelievable that "ignorant and barbarous" savages could have known the one true God.[28] E.B. Tylor also developed his theory of the evolution of religion on the assumption that early man was ignorant of God.

Dennett agrees. As human creations, "the gods" came first, "God" afterwards. He writes of "the historical process by which polytheisms turned into monotheism." He finds a "dramatic deformation" between ancient and modern religious ideas. If we even tried talking about God with ancient man, a "chasm" would open up.[29]

And this, Dawkins and Dennett think, is a good reason to think there is no God. For Dennett, explain religion in evolutionary terms, and you prove it false. Dawkins seems even more confident of the facts and what they imply:

> Not surprisingly, since it is founded on local traditions of private revelation rather than evidence, the God Hypothesis comes in many versions. Historians of religion recognize a progression from primitive tribal animisms, through polytheisms such as those of the Greeks, Romans and Norsemen, to monotheisms such as Judaism and its derivatives, Christianity and Islam.[30]

Dawkins doesn't say which historians he has in mind, nor are they named in his bibliography. Dennett mentions several well-known writers who have written on this subject, including Karen Armstrong (*History of God*), Rodney Stark, and Emile Durkheim. But read these sources carefully, and this argument against God backfires, rolls down the hill, and threatens to crush its makers.

One gets a hint of this, first, by a close read of Durkheim's classic *Elementary Forms of the Religious Life*. Durkheim, an unbeliever, noted that beliefs have "varied infinitely." Like Dennett and Dawkins, he concluded from this that none "expresses (truth) adequately."[31] But earlier in the same work, he noted that among Australian tribes, one idea—the Supreme God—was "fundamentally the same everywhere." God was always "eternal," "a sort of creator," "father of men," "made animals and trees," "benefactor," "communicates," "punishes," and was "judge after death." The aborigines "feel his presence everywhere."[32] This idea didn't come from one culture alone. Tribes separated by long distances worshipped the Supreme God by names that showed no linguistic connection: Bunjil, Daramulun, Baiame, Nuralie, Kohin, Mungan-ngana, Altjira.

If inconsistency shows all religions are false, what should we think when scattered tribes agree in so much detail about God? Shouldn't that make us suspect that one religious idea is true? Or does the argument work only when it favors atheism?

Durkheim isn't the only one of Dennett's sources to come across such evidence. In his early work, eminent sociologist of religion Rodney Stark argued (as Dawkins does) that as societies become "older, larger, and more cosmopolitan," each divine being takes on a broader portfolio, and people worship "fewer gods of greater scope," until God is left (plus the devil).[33] Later, however, Stark examined the work of Andrew Lang and Wilhelm Schmidt, who showed that primitive peoples are often aware of what Stark now refers to as "the One True God."

During the late nineteenth century, anthropologists and missionaries found that a surprisingly consistent concept of a Supreme God was held by primitive tribes not only in Australia, but elsewhere, too. In 1896, these observations were written up by a student of E.B. Tylor's, Andrew Lang, most famous nowadays for his books of fairy tales (*Lang's Red Book of Fairy Tales* inspired one young reader, Ronald Tolkien, to a lifelong love of dragons!).

In the twentieth century, the Austrian anthropologist Wilhelm Schmidt built on Lang's ideas. He wrote a series of books making the case that the earliest peoples believed in a Supreme God very like the Christian deity. While some have argued over the details (or the apologetic use to which he put them), eminent scholars of religion such as Stark, Paul Radin, and Mircea Eliade admit that the "Sky God" phenomena is widespread—and not just in Australia. John Mbiti described the Supreme God as worshipped among hundreds of African tribes. Much of what he said sounds like it comes from the Old Testament of the Bible, or like the characteristics Durkheim ascribed to the Australian God. Radin found belief in the Great Spirit among some American and Polynesian tribes, though he thought tribal "intellectuals" invented Him.

The early Chinese believed in a Supreme God a lot like the God of Australia, Africa, and America. I describe the evidence for this in my book *True Son of Heaven*.[34] The greatest nineteenth-century student of China in the West, James Legge, concluded, "*Ti* (Shang Di) was to the Chinese fathers, I believe, exactly what God was to our fathers."[35] In 1898, a year after his death, tortoise shells used for divination in prehistoric China were excavated, with the name "Shang Di" (which Chinese still use for God) prominent.

Dennett says a "chasm" separates us even from the ancient Greeks. But missionaries who cross that chasm often find "primitive man" waiting with arms outstretched on the other side. "We as a people have been waiting for you for centuries," Lahu tribesmen in Myanmar told Baptist missionary William Young. They'd even built houses for them.[36] When the white man failed to render himself too odious, missionaries often met with a similar reception.

Much of the intellectual drama behind these movements was played out within a few minutes' walk of Dawkins's office. Tylor was curator of the Pitt River Museum in Oxford (the totem poles he contributed from British Columbia are still on display). Lang was his student, then taught at Merton College. Legge was Oxford's first professor of Chinese language and literature. In the library of the China Studies Institute hangs a photo of the chalkboard Legge wrote his last lesson on, the day before his death. *Jesus* and *sheep* (an animal used by both Jews and Chinese for sacrifice, in ceremonies that Legge related to the death of Christ on the cross) are almost the last words he wrote.

Karen Armstrong, another of Dennett's informants, begins her *History of God* by mentioning Wilhelm Schmidt's work. Having gotten that out of her system, she then ignores all traces of the God whose history she is supposed to be telling outside the West. Some of our elite seem to superstitiously suppose that if they give God an ethnic name—*Yahweh, Shang Di, Allah*—that will rob him of power in "our world." Rather than "Judaism" or "theism," Armstrong thus writes of "Yahwehism," as if to quarantine God in the Hebrew dictionary. But even the "savage" Australians (to use Hume's adjective) understood that the true God knows no boundaries.

So did the Chinese. When Jesuit missionaries arrived in Beijing at the end of the sixteenth century, they borrowed an old Chinese term for the Supreme Being, *Tian,* meaning "Heaven," and added the suffix *zhu,* or "lord," to create the cognate "Lord of Heaven." They also used the ancient term *Shang Di.* The Kang Xi emperor, perhaps the greatest ruler in all China's long history, recognized the Jesuit term as a valid name for the Supreme Being the founders of China had worshipped. Christianity spread fairly quickly.

But the Vatican refused to leave well enough alone. God was a Western idea, they assumed, so these heathen words couldn't possibly refer to Him. A missionary named Maigrot took it upon himself to explain to Kang Xi that the Jesuits were wrong, the ancient Chinese didn't know the true God. Grilling Maigrot, the emperor found his Chinese language skills weak. Kang Xi explained (you can almost hear the impatient tap of his foot) that when people wished him "eternal life" (*wan sui,* or "ten thousand years") they were speaking figuratively. He added: "Well, learn from that! The true meaning of Chinese words does not always coincide with their literal meaning."

Kang Xi inscribed yet another name for God on a plaque which hung over a Catholic church: "True Source of All Things." One illustrious convert, the official Xu Guangqi, explained, "The Creator is called *Deus* in Western countries and is translated here as Master of Heaven." Xu found at least six ancient Chinese names for God. A modern Jesuit scholar lists 13 terms used in ancient Chinese writings, many of which early Chinese Christians saw as synonyms.[37] So Kang Xi was right, and Maigrot, Armstrong, and Dennett are wrong. What matters isn't names (Yahwehism), geography (Western) or culture (Judeo-Christian), but the reality to which words may point. And in many cultures, different words seem to point to one and the same Reality.

Note the irony. The "central tenet" of all religions, Harris informs us, is that competing religions are all "mere repositories of error" or at least "dangerously incomplete."[38] This is why, if the names of God or Allah don't follow Apollo and Baal into oblivion, they'll likely doom the human race.[39] Harris has this backwards: Faith in God made our world, while unbelief almost undid it—as I'll show in due course. But in truth it is hardcore atheists such as Harris and his allies who see all religions as "mere repositories of error." The Jesuits who came to China—like Christians from the apostle Paul to Pope John Paul II—found profound truth in non-Christian religions. I will argue that the gospel even finds truth in atheism.

Hume said all peoples north, south, east, and west were polytheists. More than a thousand years earlier, Augustine predicted that believers in the true God would be found in all directions. Looking at the discoveries of modern anthropology, who can say that Augustine (and Paul, whose teachings he followed) was wrong?

A Willful Ignorance

So the attempt to explain God away through social science backfires. No idea about man written before 1859 has value? How absurd. Dennett climbs the highest peak of social science and victoriously raises the Darwinian flag, trying valiantly to ignore a herd of theologians sipping lattes in glacial caverns on the summit. He echoes Jesus and the prophets by warning against idols, vain repetition, and predatory religious teachers. He reinvents a crude devil. In an effort to destroy the idea of God, he calls ideas irrational forces, forgetting that evolution is an idea, too. He argues that the inconsistency of religion proves it false. Then he quotes researchers who found the Christian God at all stations of the compass.

There are moments, wrote Chesterton, when "the motley mob of gods and goddesses [sink] suddenly out of sight and the sky Father [is] alone in the sky."[40] That, as we will see, is often how He breaks the spells of idolatry, ideology, misogyny, scapegoating, oppression, and demonology, and sets humanity free.

PART TWO

WORD
AND
FLESH

Is the Good
Book Bad?

"And the Word became flesh, and dwelt among us."

—JOHN 1:14

The world's most famous book may be its most unusual. Written by dozens of authors in three languages over more than a millennia, the Bible has been translated (at least in part) into 2400 languages, read by billions of people, and influenced almost every person alive today in many ways. In it you find an ode to a hippo, a sensual love poem, the legal code of a confederation of ancient Semitic tribes, an account of Mediterranean shipping, a note asking a slave owner to be kind to a returning slave, apocalyptic fantasy in service of political satire, and what the Greeks called *bioi*, four biographies about the man whose life hinges "the Book"—and history.

Christians see all 66 documents as (in some sense) one work, with one Author. Historians see it as the text that, more than any, has made our world.

Is its author God or the devil? Or was an ad hoc team of Iron Age poets, mystics, and fishermen entirely responsible for its contents? The Bible is called "holy" because millions think God had a hand in its production. It is read by yam farmers in New Guinea wearing penis gourds, ex-gangsters in Japan with flowers tattooed across their chests, AIDS patients in India, and congressmen in Washington, D.C. Christians in early Rome and the Soviet Union copied it by hand and risked death to keep it safe.

The New Atheists find the popularity of this book unfathomable. Did God really tell the Jews to torch Canaanite villages? Did he inspire the psalmist to write lyrics about dashing the heads of Babylonian babies on rocks? In *Letter to a Christian Nation*, Harris quotes several of the most juicy such passages at length, assuming that to publish is to promote doubt. Dawkins finds the Bible as a whole "just plain weird."[1] The book may have made sense in Iron Age Galilee, but not in twenty-first-century north Oxford. Yet strangely enough, colonies of biblicists thrive within yards of Dawkins's front door. One such colony is Wycliffe Hall, a haven for evangelical scholars named for the fourteenth-century head of Balliol College John Wycliffe, who first translated the Book into English.

But why should a zoologist object to strangeness? Have you seen a squid put on a light show to scare away predators? Now that's strange. Dawkins has made it his life work to study the natural world and look for patterns. If some of his neighbors find patterns in the Bible they think help explain even deeper mysteries, shouldn't that provoke curiosity rather than contempt?

But Dawkins has little patience for this book or its fans. As we saw, "petty," "vindictive," and "unjust" were his kindest words for the Old Testament God.[2] And the New Testament, with its doctrine of eternal damnation, may be even worse.

If the Bible is so bad, it's a wonder there are so many Christians, and that the Jewish people survived so long with such an albatross around their necks!

Dawkins offers four critiques that are popular among modern secularists: (1) The biblical God is cruel. (2) The Bible has nothing to teach enlightened society about right and wrong. (3) It presents women as "property." (4) The book is not even coherent, but a "chaotically cobbled-together anthology of disjoined documents."[3] Like a tour guide dragging a gaggle of gawking Baptists through Amsterdam's red light district, Dawkins takes his readers on a tour of the Bible's "wild side" to make these points.

Let's tag along. Rather than just gawk at sights, however, let's look for the patterns Dawkins misses. Curiously, the very passages he cites to prove the cruelty of the biblical God can often be seen—even beg to be seen—as landmarks in human progress.

My goal won't be to explain away difficulties or deny "weirdness." In fact, I think the Bible is even odder than Dawkins perceives. Like a glove that fits that five-headed monster, the hand, the problems it solves are complex, asymmetrical, diverse, and yes, "just plain weird." It may be that oddness is a prerequisite of any book that would explain or help that oddest of all creatures, yourself (and me).

I'll argue that some of the very passages easiest to jeer at turn out, on closer inspection, to have made the world a better place. Furthermore, once you get off the infidel tourist trail, it's easy to see why Western civilization called this collection "the Good Book." There's something here for everyone, emphatically including "brights." Yes, there are also difficulties. At the end of the chapter, we'll look more closely at the Bible through the eyes of two other Oxford boys: C.S. Lewis and Nicholas Wolterstorff, whose Wilde Lectures in Natural and Comparative Religion there are instructive.

Touring the Wild Side of the Bible

Dawkins carries us on a breezy gallop through the Old Testament, stopping to see sites that illustrate the theme of the tour. He tells the story of how residents of Sodom tried to rape angels, and Lot offered his daughters instead. "Whatever else this strange story might mean, it surely tells us something about the respect accorded to women in this intensely religious culture."[4] Actually, the story took place in Sodom, which was about to become an object lesson for sin, not for unbridled religiosity. But it's true women had few rights in most of the ancient world.

This is better illustrated at Dawkins's next stop, the horrific story of the man who set his concubine outside to be raped and murdered in his place, then cut her in pieces and sent them to the 12 tribes of Israel (Judges 19–21). "Let's charitably put it down again to the ubiquitous weirdness of the Bible,"[5] Dawkins suggests.

Why not put it down to the ubiquitous weirdness of people? One might as well blame Darwin for finches dying in the Galápagos. Dawkins seems under the strange assumption that the author approves of these episodes. He makes the same assumption with the story of the foolish Jephthah, who won a military victory, then sacrificed his daughter (Judges 11): "God was obviously looking forward to the promised burnt offering."[6] But the last verse of the book sums up the author's true editorial position: "In those days there was no king in Israel; everyone did what was right in his own eyes."

One should credit, not blame, a writer for reporting harsh facts. The author of Judges knew that when everyone does what is "right in his own eyes," a lot will look pretty wrong to anyone who's right in the head. We don't blame historians of the twentieth century for writing of children packing bombs onto buses, dictators making films while people starve, or lampshades made of human skin.

Indian philosopher Vishal Mangalwadi has described how surprised he was when he began reading the Old Testament. What impressed him was that, unlike Indian chronicles, it makes kings, prophets and "chosen people" all look bad! In Egyptian chronicles, too, almost no one dares reprove the king.

The Hebrew Scriptures "speak truth to power." The oracles of God flatter no one—kings, priests, prophets, the rich, or the democratic mob. The Old Testament is full of surgically precise indictments of social evil. They are in that sense the ancestor of Oliver Twist and (in its glory years) 60 Minutes.

What's going on in Judges is far more interesting than Dawkins realizes. The Bible is chronicling a crucial historical transition.

The Old Testament doesn't deny the value of civilization. Savages were seldom noble, even if they failed to invent weapons of mass destruction. The Hurons burned and cut captives through the night until regretfully putting their lives to an end in the morning. The Yamonamo raped and murdered enemy villages wholesale, saving only a few women. But tribal peoples had one clear advantage: They were free.

Most ancient empires operated under the theory that "bigger is better": the more ants, and the more they're controlled, the higher you can build pyramids, the longer you can build Great Walls, the more flowers you can hang in your hanging garden, and the more soldiers you can conscript into your army. The challenge has been to combine civilization and liberty.

Judges describes the classic tradeoff between tribal freedom and the violence it allows, and the systematic oppression of a controlled agrarian society. The Old Testament is ambivalent about "progress" from one to the other. As we'll see, that ambivalence ultimately helped Western civilization keep the best of both worlds. Here roads diverge: one leads to the Aztecs and their bloody pyramids, the other to Oxford. Whatever the virtues of the former, or vices of the latter, only a fool would deny that there are huge differences between the destinations. Dawkins is too busy looking down his nose at the ancient Hebrews to have an inkling what they did for him.

One morning many years ago, I lined up with a crowd on the communist Chinese side of the border with Hong Kong, then a British colony. Customs opened at 8:00. As soon as the signal sounded, the crowd surged forward like a flash flood through a canyon. A tourist, not used to the rush-hour consciousness of the Cantonese, and maybe in danger of losing her footing, turned towards the torrent and yelled in irate Australian, "WHAT is the MATTAH with you people?"

Dawkins and Harris are equally perplexed by the ancient Jews. Faced with the fact that "these people" don't act like proper Anglo-Saxons, and unaware of how their books civilized Anglos and Saxons in the first place, they shout, "What is the matter with you people?" Yet this is the current that carried us into that most unusual thing, a free civilization.

Missing the Point Better

In the children's story *The Voyage of the Dawn Treader*, we learn of Dufflepuds, a race of invisible dwarves who always agree with their chief.

> "Why, bless me, if I haven't gone and left out the whole point."
> "That you have, that you have," roared the Other Voices with great enthusiasm. "No one couldn't have left it out cleaner and better. Keep it up, Chief, keep it up."[7]

Like the chief of the Dufflepuds, Dawkins does not merely miss the point: he leaves it out cleaner and better than a man of lesser talents could manage.

In misreading the Bible, Dawkins doesn't merely mistake narrative for editorial (one can hardly blame a reader of the *New York Times* for that!). Sometimes he misses the point of the story in a spectacular way, like the little old lady on *Saturday Night Live* who spoke up for "sax and violins" in schools (what's *wrong* with jazz, or classical music?).

God told Abraham to sacrifice his beloved son, for whose birth he had waited all his life. Isaac carried wood up a mountain in "the land of Moriah" (Genesis 22:2) and an altar was built. Father placed son on the altar. Just as he was about to plunge a knife into the boy's heart, an angel appeared. Dawkins explains, "with a last-minute change of plans: God was only joking after all."[8] Dawkins tells us this "disgraceful story" records an act of horrendous "child abuse," "bullying in two asymmetrical power relations," and the "first recorded use of the Nuremberg defense: 'I was only obeying orders.'"

Perhaps, Dawkins adds, believers will explain the story away as allegorical. "Allegory for what?" Dawkins responds preemptively. "What kind of morals could one derive from this appalling story?"

As someone who has tried to protect girls from being sold into prostitution, I appreciate the passion behind the question. But if you ask a serious question, you should listen to serious answers.

Christians and Jews have long seen Isaac's harrowing experience on the mountaintop as a turning point in history. In two historical senses, Dawkins's own argument depends upon it.

What kind of morals can we derive from this story? First of all, God was saying, "No more human sacrifice!" This dramatic scene marked the end (in the causative sense) of ceremonial religious murder. True, as Dawkins points out, there are two later instances in the Old Testament of men promising to sacrifice the first living thing they see when they come home from war, which turns out to be their children (one carried out). This kind of morality tale, common in Greek tragedy, was probably a way of warning people not to make rash promises. Again, there is no suggestion that the two men who did this were heroes.

The Old Testament rails against abuse of children. The Canaanites were driven out of their land because of sin, the greatest of which was to "burn their sons and daughters in the fire to their gods" (Deuteronomy 12:31)—this is thought to have been carried out as a "foundational sacrifice" to bless new buildings). Yahweh warned the Hebrews that if they repeated the crime, they would suffer the same penalty. A radically different sort of "sacrifice" was demanded:

> With what shall I come to the LORD...Shall I present my firstborn for my rebellious acts, the fruit of my body for the sin of my soul? He has showed you, O man, what is good; and what does the LORD require of you but to do justice, to love kindness, and to walk humbly with your God? (Micah 6:6-7 NIV).

The psalmist generalized the lesson:

> Let the mountain bring peace to the people, and the hills, in righteousness. May he vindicate the afflicted of the people, save the children of the needy and crush the oppressor...For he will deliver the needy when he cries for help, the afflicted also, and him who has no helper...He will rescue their life from oppression and violence, and their blood will be precious in his sight (Psalm 72:3-4,12,14 NIV).

Such passages, far more common than the ones Harris and Dawkins favor, are the source of a river that would bring life to the world.

Christians have always seen an even deeper meaning to the text about Abraham and Isaac. Read on:

> "Do not lay a hand on the boy," [the angel] said. "Do not do anything to him. Now I know that you fear God, because you have not withheld from me your son, your only son." Abraham looked up and there in a thicket he saw a ram caught by its horns. He went over and took the ram and sacrificed it as a burnt offering instead of his son. So Abraham called that place The LORD Will Provide. And to this day it is said, "On the mountain of the LORD it will be provided."
>
> The angel of the LORD called to Abraham from heaven a second time and said, "I swear by myself, declares the LORD, that because you have done this and not withheld your son, your only son, I will surely bless you and make your descendants as numerous as the stars...and through your offspring all nations on earth will be blessed" (Genesis 22:12-18).

Does that sound familiar? An only son, to be sacrificed on a mountain? A lamb dying in his place?

Forget our Judeo-Christian heritage for a moment. This was written thousands of years ago in a small, obscure nation surrounded by mighty empires that have since disappeared with barely a trace. Atheists assume that the Jewish God is the God of the Jews—a tribal deity, perhaps descended from a primitive god of war. But here Yahweh promises to bless not just Jews, but "all nations on earth." Did Mars ever do that? Guan Di? And when does God make this promise? After Abraham has offered his son, his "only son," as a sacrifice.

According to Jewish tradition, Mount Moriah was close to, and perhaps identical with, the hillock Romans would later call Golgotha, the "Place of a Skull" (Matthew 27:33). Here, Christians believe, the Lamb of God would die in our place and bring a blessing to all the nations of the world.

Why does Richard Dawkins so often overlook the point of the passages he discusses? He's an intelligent man. He may be a bit glib about origins, but he has shown himself capable of subtle argument. The problem seems to be theoretical. As Lewis put it, it's hard to see something above you when you look down your nose at things. Dawkins assumes that no description of human beings written before 1859 is worth anything. It therefore becomes impossible for him to notice what the Bible holds for him.

Does the Bible Teach Us to Do Good?

Having visited such horrors, Dawkins gathers the tour group around and generalizes the lesson as follows. All right, he says, some parts of this book may be fine, but obviously others are less so. How do Christians pick and choose? They must have some other criterion by which to sort good apples from bad. If they have that superior criteria, what do they need the Bible for?

In *The Selfish Gene* Dawkins admitted that "we should not derive our values from Darwinism, unless it is with a negative sign."[9] More recently, an interviewer asked whether we should obey our "selfish genes," and Dawkins replied, "Scientific facts about the world do not translate into moral shoulds."[10]

But sometimes this goes out the window as Dawkins seems to suggest that evolution may furnish an objective criteria by which to judge morality. If morality, like sex, derives from evolution, then science should find universal values that cross geographical, cultural, "and also, crucially, religious barriers." Harvard biologist Marc Hauser used Internet surveys to ask people of different or no religions how they would resolve certain moral dilemmas. Hauser found that regardless of religion or lack thereof, people agreed that one shouldn't sacrifice an innocent person for the convenience of others, and that one should save a drowning child. From this, Dawkins (and Hauser) concluded, "We do not need God to be good—or evil."[11]

I find the argument doubly astounding. The criteria by which Christians read the Bible is supposed to be a mystery? Note the first six letters of the word *Christian*: C-H-R-I-S-T. That Christians see the life of Jesus as the interpretive principle by which to read the Bible shouldn't come as a surprise to anyone who has wandered into a church and glanced at a stained glass window!

The naivete displayed by Hauser's questionnaire is even more remarkable. Can a Harvard professor writing about morality have never heard of Natural Law theory? Christians (and others) have been talking about it for thousands of years.

That moral awareness is universal has always been a theistic dogma. The first man and woman, Genesis says, came to know good and evil. Paul wrote explicitly, "When Gentiles, who do not have the law, do by nature things required by the law, they are a law for themselves...since they show that the requirements of the law are written on their hearts" (Romans 2:14-15 NIV).

In the Christian tradition, this concept is called Natural Law. Even if we've never seen a Bible, our hearts "now defend, now accuse us," as Paul put it. In *The Abolition of Man*, C.S. Lewis listed eight universal values: "General Beneficence," "Special Beneficence," "Duties to Parents, Elders, Ancestors," "Duties to Children and Posterity," "Justice," "Good Faith and Veracity," "Mercy," and "Magnanimity." These made up what he called the Tao (borrowing the term accurately from Confucius). Lewis quoted precepts from Plato, Confucius, Cicero, Babylonians, Egyptians, the Norse, and American Indians, along with the Old Testament, to illustrate the Tao. John Cooper offered a similar summary of universal moral truths:

> The peoples of the world, however much they differ as to details of morality; hold universally, or with practical universality, to at least the following basic precepts. Respect the Supreme Being or the benevolent being or beings who take his place. Do not "blaspheme." Care for your children. Malicious murder or maiming, stealing, deliberate slander or "black" lying, when committed against friend or unoffending fellow clansman or tribesman, are reprehensible. Adultery proper is wrong, even though there be exceptional circumstances that permit or enjoin it and even though sexual relations among the unmarried may be viewed leniently. Incest is a heinous offense. This universal moral code agrees rather closely with our own Decalogue taken in a strictly literal sense.[12]

Rather than read the books that have nourished the human conscience for millennia, and engaging with this ancient tradition, the New Atheism brings us back to square one. For all his wit and intellect, Dawkins is essentially a child asking the simplest questions in the catechism. But maybe that's the place to start if one brings a child's innocence as well.

While it's good to see scientists at Harvard and Oxford rediscover universal moral intuition, chillingly, Dawkins finds it hard to explain why we "ought" to obey it. Dawkins and Hauser seem to see morality as one more bit of data about the evolution of a particular species. I may *feel* it is immoral to let a child drown. But if I see that feeling as an accidental product of evolution, like my appendix, what if I want it out? And if I'm late for work, and the child belongs to a competing race—threatening not just jeans, but selfish genes—it's hard to see how evolution furnishes any argument for saving her. After all, infanticide and human sacrifice have been practiced on every continent.

What does Dawkins mean by "universals"? If he means all people share certain moral values that are hardwired in us, then yes, I would expect cognitive research to back up the apostle Paul and the Natural Law. But if he means that values are universal in the causative sense— effective on all human agents—that doesn't follow. One could conclude, as some have, "So evolution gives us guilty feelings when we steal candy from children. Now that I understand the blind forces that produced this emotion, and the fact that it has no transcendent value, I'll take what I want." Evolution doesn't help at all.

Dawkins mires us in an even deeper problem, from which the Bible rescues us.

We know what's right. We "can't not know," as moral philosopher Jay Budziszewski put it. We share what he calls the witness of "deep conscience," "design as such," "our own design," and "natural consequences."[13] But knowing doesn't make us *do*. We argue with our conscience, defend swiping the extra pie, flick the good angel off our shoulder. The more we abuse or oppress others, the more zealously we justify ourselves.

Dawkins's exaggerations aside, the Old Testament helps first by strengthening the grip of the good angel. Here again, the Bible's book of Proverbs provides good, simple examples. "Do not be wise in your own eyes" (3:7). "Do not withhold good from those to whom it is due, when it is in your power to do it" (3:27). "The lips of an adulteress drip honey... She does not ponder the path of life" (5:3,6). "Go to the ant, O sluggard, observe her ways and be wise" (6:6). "Hatred stirs up strife, but love covers all transgressions" (10:11-12). What university faculty wouldn't benefit by meditating on a few such proverbs every day?

The Bible also forces us to confront the devious internal machinations by which we elude moral truth. It does this by confronting us with our sin in story form, which, as Dennett recognizes, is so helpful. It does this further by giving examples of something better.

The heart of the Bible, and the filter through which Christians read the whole, is Jesus. The crowds around him said, "Never has a man spoken the way this man speaks" (John 7:46). Many of the greatest moral thinkers agree. So to answer Dawkins's question, the criterion by which Christians interpret the Bible, and understand right and wrong, is truth planted in the human heart—as Christianity has always taught—and modeled and taught by Jesus and his disciples.

Does the Bible Tell Us to Love Our Group Only?

Dawkins's most astoundingly wrongheaded reading of the Bible may be his claim that care for others is only meant for "a narrowly defined in-group." Here he borrows liberally from an article in *Skeptic* magazine by "physician and anthropologist" John Hartung, entitled "Love Thy Neighbor: The Evolution of In-group Morality."[14] According to Hartung, the Hebrew command "Love your neighbor as yourself" just meant "love another Jew." "Thou shalt not kill" meant "Don't kill other Jews." Foreigners were fair game. Dawkins even claims that the humanity of women and of other races is "deeply unbiblical," an error we are only beginning to rise above. Quoting Hartung, "The Bible is a blueprint of in-group morality, complete with instructions of genocide, enslavement of outgroups, and world domination." Even Jesus, Dawkins argues, "limited his in-group of the saved strictly to Jews."[15] Hartung admits this points to a general dilemma: "Evolutionists have not been able to devise a model for converting in-group morality into general morality."

Neither man can have read either the Old or New Testaments carefully. If they had, they might find the answer to this dilemma.

The concept of salvation for all peoples runs through the Bible from Genesis to Revelation. The history of Israel is bloody at times, like most histories. And it's true that God is shown commanding violent acts—which may be why the Jews survived. But the overall plan was always for the good of the nations. This comes to the fore in the New Testament, which is explicitly and dramatically a set of blueprints for blessing all humanity. Anyone who cannot see this may have moved his eyes across but has not really ever *read* the Bible.

True, the Old Testament does emphasize the Jewish responsibility to look out for other Jews. But there are also many references to caring for, loving, being kind to, or reaching out somehow to non-Jews. "Let the nations be glad and sing for joy" (Psalm 67:4). "Are not you Israelites the same to me as the Cushites? declares the LORD. Did I not bring Israel up from Egypt, the Philistines from Caphtor and the Arameans from Kir?" (Amos 9:7 NIV). "They will hammer their swords into plowshares and their spears into pruning hooks. Nation will not lift up sword against nation, and never again will they learn war" (Isaiah 2:4). Keeping Jews from getting killed has always been a tough job. But God's plan to bless all peoples is a strong balancing counternarrative, which began with the very first Jew, Abraham, and his son, Isaac.

When it comes to the New Testament, the error committed by Hartung and Dawkins is stark indeed. "Jesus limited his in-group of the saved strictly to Jews,"[16] says Dawkins. Hartung credited, or blamed, the apostle Paul for the universalism of Christianity: "Jesus would have turned over in his grave if he had known that Paul would be taking his plan to the pigs."[17]

As we will see, Sam Harris says the New Testament was written by people who hated Jews. Hartung and Dawkins say Jesus hated Gentiles. That covers everyone! The New Testament must be a very hateful book. So how did so many verses such as, "Love your enemies" and "Pray for those who persecute you" (Matthew 5:44) slip past such a fine net of vitriol? In fact, the NIV Bible contains $6^{1}/_{2}$ pages of verses containing the word "love" or its cognates—over 700 references!

Here, New Atheists part company even with radical New Testament scholarship, not to mention anyone who has ever read the Book with an open mind!

Even skeptical Bible scholars say the most consistent theme not just in Jesus' teachings (as you might get from having him take an e-poll), but in his actions, was to tear down barriers between people. Robert Funk, founder of the radical Jesus Seminar, noted that all through the Gospels, Jesus "privileged" the poor, sick, infirm, women, children, tax collectors, and foreigners. Liberal colleagues such as Marcus Borg, John Crossan, and Walter Wink underline this point repeatedly. "In a society ordered by a purity system, the inclusiveness of Jesus' movement embodied a radically alternative social vision," Borg argued.[18] Funk wrote:

> In contravention of the social order, Jesus was socially promiscuous: he ate and drank publicly with petty tax officials and "sinners," yet did not refuse dinner with the learned and wealthy. He was seen in the company of women in public—an occasion for scandal in his society. He included children in his social circle—children were regarded as chattel, especially females, if they were permitted to live at birth—and advised that God's domain is filled with them.[19]

Ironically, Dawkins hones in on the phrase "love thy neighbor" to illustrate his belief that Jesus only cared about the "in-group." But there was a particular moment in history when "neighbor" emphatically stopped meaning "another Jew" and came forever to mean "anyone you meet." Dawkins should recognize that moment, for he twice uses the term *Good Samaritan*.

A young Jewish man asked Jesus, "Who is my neighbor?" (Luke 10:29). Jesus responded by telling the story of the Good Samaritan, perhaps the most famous story ever.

A Samaritan was not a Jew. He was a despised half-breed. He was an improbable hero for a rabbi in an era when the always nationalistic Jews were chafing under foreign occupation. That is precisely, Funk points out, what made the Good Samaritan so typical a hero in a story by Jesus.[20] The sheer absurdity of accusing Jesus, of all people, of "exclusiveness" seems almost inspired (by whom, I leave the reader to consider).

How did we really discover our common humanity?

Aristotle held that "from the hour of their birth, some are marked out for subjection, others for rule." He even claimed it was better for the "lower sort" to be ruled by masters, since they were "by nature slaves." Gnostics said some were naturally incapable of being saved from this "lowest region of all matter." According to the Rig Veda, the four great castes proceeded from the mouth, arms, thighs, and feet of Brahma.

With a few kindly allies such as Confucius, the Bible taught us racial unity. It has always been a theistic dogma that humans are alike in nature and dignity as the image of God. In one of the earliest Old Testament documents, Job said, "If I have denied justice to my menservants and maidservants...what will I do when God confronts me?... Did not he who made me in the womb make them?" (Job 31:13-15 NIV). Paul wrote, "There is neither Jew nor Greek, there is neither slave nor free, there is neither male nor female; for you are all one in Christ Jesus" (Galatians 3:28). Augustine thus rebutted Aristotle: Whatever society may do to us, no one is a slave by nature. There was a great future in that insight. But there was also a great future in the response by Social Darwinist Hermann Klaatch: "The humanitarian nonsense which grants equal rights to all on the premise of the unity of humanity, is to be condemned from the scientific standpoint."[21]

Does the Bible Demean Women?

Feminism is a core value of our age. Not surprisingly, the New Atheism swallows the popular myth that the Bible enslaves women. Thus, Dawkins tells us, "women are no longer regarded as property, as they clearly were in biblical times."[22] He cites that weighty authority, *Ken's*

Guide to the Bible, to point out that the 144,000 elect in the book of Revelation "did not defile themselves with women." So none of the saved *were* women. "That's the sort of thing we've come to expect," he sniffs.[23] (The New Atheists are often more wooden in their hermeneutics than the most literal fundamentalist. One could answer that argument on its own level by supposing half the saved were heterosexual women or chaste lesbians!)

In the Old Testament, women acted as prophets and queens, and took the initiative for good and ill. Two Old Testament books bore the names of women—Ruth and Esther—and neither lady is a drawing room daisy. The Song of Solomon expresses frank female sensuality:

> May he kiss me with the kisses of his mouth! For your love is better than wine...My beloved responded and said to me, "Arise, my darling, my beautiful one, and come along. For behold, the winter is past, the rain is over and gone" (1:2; 2:10-11).

Proverbs ends with a vivid portrait of an entrepreneurial, multitalented girl, the daughter-in-law of a mother's dreams. She "extends her hand to the poor," buys real estate, invests in grape cultivation, makes clothes, and "opens her mouth in wisdom." "Charm is deceitful and beauty is vain, but a woman who fears the LORD, she shall be praised" (31:30).

One notes, ominously, that the Old Testament does not appear in Dawkins's bibliography.

It's even less plausible to describe the women of the New Testament as "property." Gender roles are complex, and the pure wind of feminism does not blow as cleanly through Paul as some would like. But Paul tells husbands to "stop depriving" their wives of sexual pleasure (1 Corinthians 7:5—no female circumcision?). He assumes women will worship (unlike lawn chairs). He tells husbands to love their wives and give their lives for them (Ephesians 5:25-28).

Walter Wink summarized the gospel data: "In every single encounter with women in the four Gospels, Jesus violated the mores of his time... his behavior towards women...was without parallel in 'civilized' societies since the rise of patriarchy roughly three thousand years before his birth."[24]

Dawkins thinks morality ages, like wine. But compare Jesus with a gangster rapper or two, or movies that pander to evolutionary libido. Observe how the sexes treat one another among the most promiscuous post-Christian segments of modern society. What Martin Burber calls the "I-It" relationship, the view of woman or man as property, spontaneously generates in pure secular society. Jesus' teachings are the cure, not the disease.

Is the Bible Disjointed?

The final charge we'll consider is that the Bible lacks coherence. Little wonder, you might think. Why should 66 writings, written over more than a millennia in three languages, by fishermen, tent-makers, shepherds, kings, doctors, and tax collectors, in different moods, for different purposes, cobbled together by who knows who or why, coalesce into one book?

Yet like billions of other readers, I do find unity (within diversity) in the Bible. True, I'm fond of sprawling Russian novels with lots of subplots and characters ranging from hunting dogs to emperors. Dawkins is captivated by the biosphere, which is held together by biochemical laws and structures, and exhibits endless diversity as it unfolds in (as is thought) a single narrative, with countless characters and subplots. The Bible is the sort of thing a zoologist should love: oddities, as in the Amazon rain forest or deep blue sea, alongside soaring beauty, terror, and characters as odd as denizens of Dickens or a coral reef, deep perplexity and unanswerable riddles. And that's just the book of Job.

Where do Christians find unity in this collection? Why did George Frideric Handel write songs about the birth of Jesus from Isaiah? How did gargoyles find their way onto houses of worship? How were Søren Kierkegaard, George Handel, Fanny Crosby, and William Booth inspired by the very same volume? Those are the kinds of questions Dawkins ought to ask. Maybe we are deluded in finding unity here. But like nature, for us, these texts prove strangely alive and creative.

Literal or Symbolic?

Dawkins is impatient with "apologists" who claim an "inside track" to interpreting the Bible correctly. "They cannot get away with it," he warns, "not even if they employ that favorite trick of interpreting selected scriptures as 'symbolic' rather than literal. By what criteria do you decide which passages are symbolic, which literal?"[25]

I don't want to play tricks. I commend Dawkins for asking questions; it's a pity he doesn't listen to answers.

There *are* answers. The most important is that in our tradition, Christ is the center of faith, and therefore the lens through which we "read" Scripture.

Symbolic and *literal* are the daily coin of literary discourse. Because the Bible is literature, we can't escape trying to answer what for Dawkins appears to be just a rhetorical question. If Dawkins finds the difference between standard literary categories "tricky," he should stick to biology. To tell Bible experts (theologians) they can't use such terms would be like asking biologists to confuse us no more with foolish chatter about species or phyla, genes, or chromosomes.

What Dawkins is getting at is the question of how Christians understand God to speak through the Bible. There are different ways of answering that question. My goal here is not to argue for "my position" against that of other Christians. But the New Atheists tend to assume only the most wooden interpretation of the Bible is valid. Consider the ideas of C.S. Lewis and Nicholas Wolterstorff, two very serious Christians, by contrast.

Reflections on Divine Discourse

Philosopher Gottfried Leibnitz (1646–1716) incautiously described ours as "the best of all possible worlds." In the novel *Candide* Voltaire responded by putting those words in the mouth of the glib and forlorn Pangloss, who continued to preach this philosophy after being beggared, enslaved, hung, infected with syphilis, and losing an ear, eye, and nose.

As Harris's list of difficult scriptures shows, the "inerrancy doctrine" is vulnerable in a similar way. The Quran claims to have been dictated by God in "clear Arabic," like a letter dictated from heaven. Harris assumes that's how Christians think the Bible arrived: "for reasons difficult to fathom," God "made Shakespeare a far better writer than Himself." As a literary judgment, I think that's pretty crude. Even Nietzsche thought Luther's Bible the best thing in German. I agree with the *National Review* that, compared to the teachings of Jesus, even Shakespeare is "shallow stuff." But set Dawkins or Harris on an errancy hunt, or comparing Leviticus to Hamlet, and they'll miss truth under their very noses, like cranky tourists from Ann Arbor who find nothing in Europe but leaky toilets and poorly cooked cheeseburgers.

The deeper problem with Harris's remark is the Islamic view of inspiration it betrays.

The apostle Paul says Scripture is "inspired by God" and useful for "teaching, for reproof, for correction, for training in righteousness," to prepare believers for "every good work" (2 Timothy 3:16-17). So whatever inspiration means, it's practical. The focus is on changing lives.

In ordinary conversation, a simple statement may be meant in different ways: literally and directly, literally but indirectly ("*Could* you pass the salt?"), with metaphor, irony, or hyperbole. Children's movies provide a good example of speaking on different levels. When we watch *Chicken Run*, my children laugh at the cockney rats dancing in sunglasses. I laugh at the slapstick, too, but even more at the reference to the Blues Brothers. Shouldn't divine speech be at least as rich as *Chicken Run*? Why shouldn't a Gandhi, Tolstoy, or Girard discover what a single verse in the Sermon on the Mount "means," and change the world?

Wolterstorff describes the Bible largely as human "discourse" that God "appropriates" for his own purposes.[26] The Scriptures come to us through the thoughts, emotions, and writing styles of human beings. God takes up humanity and speaks through it, rather than overthrowing human personality.

The Bible isn't an inkblot on which to project our fancies. But revelation is progressive. God guides readers as well as authors. Often, what is implicit in the Scripture—Trinity, the wrongness of slavery, political freedom, science—grows over time, like trees from seeds. Wolterstorff explains, "Additional discernment is always possible; the activity of discerning the divine discourse is forever incomplete."[27] While "divine compulsion" inspired the prophets to speak directly in God's name, Lewis agreed that God guided the author of Genesis more subtly. The natural is "raised by God above itself," for new and better purposes. He added:

> I take it that the whole Old Testament consists of the same sort
> of material as other literature—chronicles (some of it obviously

pretty accurate), poems, moral and political diatribes, romances, and what not; but all taken into the service of God's word.[28]

What is God saying through Scripture? Nothing, to those who put hands over ears. Those who read humbly "will gain new strength; they will mount up with wings like eagles" (Isaiah 40:31).

Lewis goes further than most conservative Christians might feel comfortable:

> The human qualities of the raw materials show through. Naivety, errors, contradiction, even (as in the cursing Psalms) wickedness are not removed. The total result is not "the Word of God" in the sense that every passage, in itself, gives impeccable science or history. It carries the Word of God; and we (under grace, with attention to tradition and to interpreters wiser than ourselves, and with the use of such intelligence and learning as we may have) receive that word from it not by using it as an encyclopedia or encyclical but by steeping ourselves in its tone or temper and so learning its overall message.[29]

We might prefer a more cut-and-dried Letter from Heaven, in clear Arabic. But Lewis saw advantages to this sort of communiqué.

The Scriptures are alive not in the sense that some would make the U.S. Constitution a "living document," meaning whatever we want it to mean. Rather they live because the God who inspired them is alive, and speaks to those who read and humbly attend to his voice through these documents. That, we will see, is how the world is changed.

The Foundation of Civilization

Some places are better to visit, others are better to live in. The New Atheists approach the Bible as tourists, looking for thrills by cruising among cannibals. But the Bible is the ground on which their civilization was built.

The issue, some will reply, is not the literary or even moral value of the Bible, but its authorship and effect on humanity. Of course a book can be great without being the Word of God, or even making the world better. Nietzsche was a great writer, and Wagner a great composer, and the Nazis among their biggest fans.

Later chapters will answer this challenge indirectly not by proving that God inspired the Bible, but by showing how the Judeo-Christian revelation has changed the world for the better. How odd if a "disjointed" book from the Stone Age about the "most unpleasant character in all fiction" managed to liberate the human race! You might just suppose the skeptics have overlooked something. But first, let's look at Jesus, the heart and center of biblical revelation.

What Should an Atheist Do About Jesus?

"Despite this apparent variety of extraterrestrials, the UFO abduction syndrome portrays, it seems to me, a banal Universe…Not a single being presented in all these accounts is as astonishing as a cockatoo would be if you have never before beheld a bird. Any protozoology or bacteriology or mycology textbook is filled with wonders that far outshine the most exotic descriptions of the alien abductionists."

—CARL SAGAN[1]

"I also ascribe to this unreasonable theology precisely because of its unreasonableness. Moses, Buddha, Lao-Tse, Muhammed, were all reasonable men, wise and sensible. Jesus, too, was wise, but he was also *weird*. I do not know how to explain him in purely human terms… No one could have made up the man described…"

—M. SCOTT PECK[2]

Some places are so desolate that the few creatures that can stand them have them almost all to themselves. Emperor penguins waddle freely across Antarctic wastes because there are no "south polar bears" or "Antarctic wolves" to eat them. Camels carried Arab armies to victory across North Africa because they were the only beast of burden with a built-in water supply. By contrast, no one has a monopoly on the jungle: Every square inch is contested.

First-century history is more a jungle than a desert. From almost the day Jesus began to preach, people have offered competing theories of his life. Contemporaries called him mad, demon-possessed, sinner, and (as bad if not worse) a Samaritan. In the second century, Celsus suggested

Jesus was a magician who learned the craft in Egypt. Gnostics saw him as an incarnation of Adamas, a "righteous angel" or a spirit who didn't really die on the cross. According to the tenth-century Muslim ascetic Abu Talib al-Makki, Jesus said to the world, "Away from me, you pig!"[3] The *Gospel of Barnabas* made Jesus a forerunner of Mohammed. Hindus describe him as a yogi[4] who died to save his devotees (and no one else) from karma.[5] Others say Jesus went to India or Tibet to learn the Vedas, to South America to preach to the Indians, to Aomori in northern Japan, where he married and raised three daughters,[6] or, of course, to France with his sweatheart Mary Magdelene.[7] Over the past 200 years, "serious" theories about Jesus have blossomed just as profusely. Thomas Jefferson and Leo Tolstoy wrote Gospels without miracles to fit their Deistic worldview. David Strauss portrayed the Gospels as largely myth. Albert Schweitzer described Jesus as an apocalyptic prophet. John Crossan and Burton Mack saw him as an "Augustan hippy in an age of yuppies" or "cynic sage" who worked a Palestinian crowd with clever one-liners. Jesus Seminarians call him an aphorist and story-teller who challenged the political conventions of his day, as they hope to challenge ours, and spoke up for the poor and marginalized. With the dawning of the Age of Aquarius, the Gospels were exposed (like fruit flies) to the exotic radiation of New Age thought. Elaine Pagels and Marcus Borg see Jesus as a second Buddha or "spirit person" who "[subverts] conventional ways of seeing and living."[8] Kenneth Leong portrays him as a Zen master.[9]

Like hunter and gatherers foraging in the New Guinea jungle, Dawkins and his tribe cultivate no original "Jesus theories" of their own, but pick from among these gleanings.

The Gospels, Dawkins tells us, are "legends," written "long after the death of Jesus" and copied over many generations by scribes with their "own religious agendas." No one knows who those scribes were, but they "almost certainly" never met Jesus. The first four books of the New Testament were chosen "more or less arbitrarily" from a dozen or so candidates, including "Gospels" of Thomas, Peter, Nicodemus, Philip, Bartholomew, and Mary Magdalen (Dawkins offers an endorsement of these alternatives by no less than Thomas Jefferson). But all "Gospels," Christian or Gnostic, were "made up from start to finish."[10]

Jesus was one of many such "charismatic figures" of the day, around whom legends accumulated.[11] The Christian story was borrowed from other religions and stitched together by Paul of Tarsus.[12] Jesus probably never claimed divine status. Even if he did, he may have been "honestly mistaken."[13] Harris agrees:

> There is no evidence whatsoever, apart from the tendentious writings of the later church, that Jesus ever considered himself as anything other than a Jew among Jews, seeking the fulfillment of Judaism—and likely, the return of Jewish sovereignty in a Roman world.[14]

In my last three books, I surfed all three waves of "Jesus spin": premodern, modern, postmodern. They all fall flat, I concluded, not because those who propose them are stupid or lack creativity. The problem is the Gospels themselves.

The Gospels do three things to disarm all such criticism. First, they pass strict historical interrogation with flying colors. (N.T. Wright's acclaimed Christian Origins and the Question of God series may be the best material on this.) Second, they portray a person who convinces those with the most acute insight into human nature that, as M. Scott Peck put it, "no one could have made up the man described."[15] Like fingerprints on a windowpane, the Gospels reveal the complex and unforgable identifying marks of a unique mind. And third, as we will see in the following section, they have changed the world for the better.

It would be futile to try to summarize all the evidence for the historicity of the Gospels in one chapter. Dawkins challenges the New Testament picture of Jesus. He is poorly informed, as we'll see, and his blows often land wildly. But the questions he raises show why it's hard to "spin" Jesus, and why the Gospels do in fact give us cause to believe God is real.

Are the Gospels Late and Legendary?

Each of the Gospels, Dawkins supposes, was "copied and recopied, through many different 'Chinese Whispers generations' by fallible scribes who, in any case, had their own religious agendas."[16]

Some New Testament scholars seem to agree. The founder of the Jesus Seminar, Robert Funk, wrote that "oral tradition" circulated for two decades "by word of mouth" before anyone began to write it down.[17] Harvard historian Paula Fredriksen claimed Gospel stories were "told and retold—by those of the original generation during their lifetimes; by the later, intervening generations for theirs" before gaining "the relative stability of writing."[18] John Crossan wrote of the "stratification" of the Gospel narratives, as if describing the buildup of sandstone columns along the Colorado River.

But look at the dates. Two decades? I just attended my uncle's fiftieth wedding anniversary, at which stories were not circulated, but told firsthand, about events that happened *six* decades ago. Fredriksen claimed the Gospels were written 40 to 70 years after the events they describe. Most skeptical scholars say Mark was the first Gospel written, about 40 years after the fact. Other scholars put the dates a bit earlier.

Most wandering countercultural movements are made up of young people. Jesus' followers were probably in their twenties or teens. Those who dodged the brisk scythe of the Grim Reaper could easily have lived decades after the writing of the first Gospels. I still recall my grandmother's account of the great influenza epidemic after World War I, almost 90 years ago now. Almost every extended family preserves such memories.

Christopher Hitchens, writing almost 40 years after Martin Luther King was assassinated, noted that the speech King gave the night before was a "transcendent moment" that left a heavy imprint on the memory of those who were there. "Nobody who was there that night has ever forgotten it," he notes.[19] Two millennia ago, before TV was around to rot people's brains and accurate memorization was the primary means of recording things, the even more dramatic and traumatic events of Jesus' life were seared into the minds of those who had witnessed them.

Many of Jesus' first followers would have been alive, and ready to talk, when the Gospels were written. Nor would it have been hard for Luke (say) to track them down: The Christian community was a compact, highly social group, like an extended family. Everyone knew who the elders were, and who had walked with Jesus. In such a tight-knit community, it would have been child's play to look them up.

Dawkins claims the Gospels were "written long after the death of Jesus."[20] From the perspective of a child waiting to open Christmas presents, the wait might be called "long." But as ancient accounts go, they weren't. Richard Fletcher notes that despite slight discrepancies, "No one has ever doubted" that the Bede's account of the baptism of Edwin, the king of Northumbria, more than 100 years before he wrote it, took place.[21]

Not only were the Gospels written while eyewitnesses were still alive, they sound like eyewitness reports. Read a few paragraphs at random. You can cut the tension with a knife. Jesus is subject to nitpicking, entrapment, barbed comments, and catcalls. "Is not this the carpenter?" (Mark 6:3). He's accused of low status, sin, breaking the law, failing to pay taxes, lack of education, madness, and black magic. Find me a hagiographer who writes like this. As Peck put it, most of the Gospels "reek of authenticity."[22]

The Gospels give names, surprising replies, and facts about Jerusalem only an inhabitant or archaeologist would know, like the details about the pool of Siloam or Jacob's well.

Furthermore, Jesus' words are easy to remember. "Whoever seeks to keep his life will lose it, and whoever loses his life will preserve it" (Luke 17:33). "Do not let your left hand know what your right hand is doing" (Matthew 6:3). "Many who are first will be last" (Mark 10:31). Reports of the debate between Thomas Huxley and Samuel Wilberforce differ on many details but generally get the gist of Huxley's response to the "Your grandfather was an ape" comment roughly correct, though written 40 years later. What seemed to aid memory was the combination of high drama and witty a repartee, which is also present throughout the Gospels.

How does Dawkins know that the four evangelists never met Jesus? Mark and John implicitly claim to have. The dates work. John knew first-century Israel, for he describes objects from the Jerusalem before A.D. 70. When the author implicitly claims to have met his subject and would have had every chance to do so, and the text breaths immediacy and realism, why contradict him so dogmatically? Did Dawkins have CCTV cameras with face-recognition software following the disciples?

It's true that the evangelists had their own agendas. So does every scholar, even if only tenure. And ancient biographers all liked to preach.

That's one reason history is an art, not a science: we deal with people here, like the ones we rub elbows with every day. But there are critical methods by which one can test historical texts. Are the authors honest enough to tell about embarrassing incidents? Do they confirm one another on basic facts, even while showing independence? Do the sayings of Jesus clash sometimes with earlier and later party lines? Does he make sense as a Jew, and as the founder of Christianity, even though his teachings are distinct from both? Apply these criteria to the Gospels, and you find multiple layers of strong internal evidence for the historicity of the Gospels. It becomes clear that the evangelists' primary agenda could only have been to tell the truth.

What about "alternative Gospels"? Since Elaine Pagels's *The Gnostic Gospels* (1979), Gnostic texts from the second and third century have become standard critical tools for deconstructing the Gospels. "Why the orthodox texts and not the Gnostic ones?" we're asked. Dawkins doesn't overlook this "good trick."

How Many Gospels Have Been Found?

Modern research supplies the New Atheists with what may seem at first a promising check on Gospel accounts: ancient manuscripts that offer radically different stories about Jesus. Bookstores overflow with new translations and interpretations of the *Gospel of Thomas*. Major magazines promote the Gospels of *Mary* and *Judas* at Easter, which tell about a Jesus who didn't die or rise again and who cursed the God of the Jews. *The Da Vinci Code* helped make these works a cultural phenomena, claiming that more than 80 gospels were considered for the New Testament.

Dawkins swallows what I call the "neo-Gnostic myth" hook, line, and seaweed. The Gospels were chosen "more or less arbitrarily," he tells us, from a sample of a dozen or more including such "Gospels" as "*Thomas, Peter, Nicodemus, Philip, Bartholomew,* and *Mary Magdalen.*"[23]

Thomas probably comes first in his list because radical scholars consider it the best potential source of alternative "Jesus material." *Thomas* is not, however, a Gospel in any important sense. Analyzing the work line by line, I found Thomas shares only four to seven characteristics out of 50 that define the Gospels. It was less a Gospel than any other ancient work I studied—even China's kung fu epic, *Journey to the West*.

Gospel means "good news" (Greek, *euangelion*). At a minimum, a Gospel should therefore tell a story. Dawkins is under the impression that this work does. "The *Gospel of Thomas*," he writes, contains "numerous anecdotes" about Jesus abusing magical powers "in the manner of a mischievous fairy," turning playmates into goats or mud into sparrows, or miraculously lengthening a beam for his father the carpenter. To pre-empt the expected retort, he adds, "It will be said that nobody believes crude miracle stories such as those in the *Gospel of Thomas* anyway."[24]

What needs to be said is that the Oxford professor of the public understanding of science and his reputable publisher have got the wrong book! These stories are found not in the *Gospel of Thomas*, but in the *Infancy Gospel of Thomas*. The former contains no stories at all, which is one reason it isn't a Gospel. And this kind of sloppiness is one reason Dawkins is not a historian.

Nor was there anything arbitrary about the selection of the four first-century Gospels in favor of their second, third, and even fourth-century "competitors." They can be found easily online; read one or two. What the Gnostics called "Gospels" are to the real Gospels as *The Barbecue Bible* is to the real Bible. Read Pagels or Karen King carefully, and you find that even historians who have grown fat off the popularity of the Gnostics only pretend to take them seriously as historical texts.

The most remarkable such admission comes from the Jesus Seminar. This group of radical scholars promotes the Gnostics heavily, in particular the *Gospel of Thomas*. Their most famous publication is *The Five Gospels*, which offers a new translation of the canonical four, plus *Thomas*. But look carefully, and you find the Jesus Seminar doesn't believe its own propaganda. Seminar fellows could point to only two unimportant sayings in *Thomas* they suggest may be historical. It took three votes for them to whip up that much enthusiasm.

The other works Dawkins lists are taken even less seriously by serious scholars. There is no *Gospel of Mary Magdalen*. There is a *Gospel of Mary*, which Karen King (the work's most prominent scholarly fan) admits (once in an entire book on the subject) is ahistorical. Some scholars like the text because in it, Jesus rebukes Peter for showing disrespect to Mary. They read that (implausibly) as a protofeminist rebuke of orthodox Christianity for disrespecting women.

Dawkins's ineptness with these texts is underscored yet again with his "blurb" from Thomas Jefferson: "It is these additional gospels that Thomas Jefferson was referring to in his letter to his nephew...'You should read all the histories of Christ.' "[25]

Jefferson was a talented man. Some people, in their interpretation of the U.S. Constitution, lean heavily on a private letter he wrote about the "wall of separation" between church and state. In his book *Civilization*, almost the only artwork from North America that Kenneth Clark features are Jefferson's designs for the University of Virginia and Monticello. But Jefferson did not, I think, claim the gift of prophecy. That would have been required for him to refer to *Thomas, Mary*, or *Philip*, which were lost in the Egyptian desert at the time Jefferson allegedly recommended them to his nephew.

My point isn't just that Dawkins often gets his facts wrong. We all make mistakes. But why quote Einstein and other scientists on theology, and Jefferson on history? The argument to authority, when properly used, can be a useful tool of rational thought. But such muddle is the sign of an excluded middle. Those who idolize the scientific method often seem to lose the art of careful historical reasoning.

Plainly, Dawkins is no historian. Was Thomas Jefferson? What both exhibit is the hubris of "brights" who think a high IQ and a cynical attitude trump the insights of ordinary, humble readers, and even the work of more modest and careful historians.

Was Jesus a Legend?

As our initial review showed, many people feel more comfortable with a Jesus who can be placed in some well-defined category. But readers of the Gospels disagree over where to place him. Was he a Jewish rabbi? A cynical Greek sage? A teacher? Demon? Samaritan? Revolutionary? Or perhaps—the list grows—aphorist, prophet, bodhisattva, yogi, sadhu, feminist, apocalyptic fanatic, faith healer, storyteller, or Messiah? Strangely, a case can be made from first-century records for most of these hypotheses! Some overlap, but others contradict one another.

Perhaps the Vatican should invite proponents of all these theories to a party to say thanks. You can't make a living, breathing elephant from the parts described by the blind men. But you can begin to realize how extraordinary the creature really is.

To Dawkins, Jesus was "one of many such charismatic figures who emerged in Palestine around his time, surrounded by similar legends."[26] Since David Strauss's *Life of Jesus* in 1835, it has been common to say the stories in the Gospels are full of mythological or legendary elements.

This business of being "surrounded by similar legends" sounds ghostly. Who are the ghosts? John Crossan compares Jesus to two "legendary" Jewish rabbis: Honi the Circle Drawer, and Hanina ben Dosa. In fact, Honi is the only rabbi from the time of Jesus or before to whom anything vaguely miraculous is attributed. It's said that once, during a drought, he drew a circle and stood inside it, asking God to send rain or he wouldn't leave the circle! Hanina ben Dosa lived after the time of Jesus, and stories about him were recorded hundreds of years later. It's said he knew when his prayers for the sick would be answered, and that a lizard once bit him and he didn't get sick. Others compare Jesus to Apollonius of Tyana, a pompous windbag (his part best played, I have suggested, by Steve Martin)[27] who, according to a second-century tale, chatted up local kings, then went off to India and witnessed levitating Brahmins, pepper-growing monkeys, and crested dragons.

Many efforts have been invested in finding legends that look like Jesus. The search has come up spectacularly empty. The failure of informed, intelligent scholars to find any parallel that is even remotely believable is really a success—like the failure to find jackrabbits in the pre-Cambrian. Reality has been greatly illuminated by all this vain mucking about.

Nor is it possible anymore to call the Gospels "legends." In *What Are the Gospels? A Comparison with Graeco-Roman Biography*, Richard Burridge proved that the Gospels closely conform to the genre of *bioi*, or ancient biography (though I argue that they are far better-attested).[28] Dawkins is free to refute the arguments that have established these facts, or the painstaking historical reconstructions of scholars such as John Meier and N.T. Wright. But the "legend" interpretation of the Gospels is best maintained by avoiding contrary arguments like the plague. Reading Dawkins's bibliography, it appears this is precisely what he has done.

But Don't the Gospels Copy Myth?

One of the latest crazes in Jesus spinning, developed by a few serious historians but more often in Internet conspiracy pages and the books that derive from them, is that the Gospels borrowed from earlier myths. Dawkins plucks this fruit readily: "All the essential features of the Jesus legend" are borrowed "from other religions."[29]

That is a historical claim, which requires historical evidence. Stolen money can be traced by serial numbers. But how do we know if an idea or pattern of action has been borrowed from an earlier source?

Just finding similar stories in two places doesn't prove copying. If I say, "The neighbor dog growled," how do you know the claim wasn't borrowed from the legend of Cerberus, the three-headed canine that guards the gates of Hades? Or perhaps Buck in *Call of the Wild*, or Levin's dog in *Anna Karenina?* The literary growls came first. As Joseph Campbell shows in *Hero with a Thousand Faces*, motifs crop up in widely scattered cultures. Real life can "copy" myth, and myth can "copy" real life. Plato's story of the cave is echoed by many great modern leaders who descended into some subterranean hovel (Gandhi, Aquino, Solzhenitsyn) to bring "liberation." As skeptics often remind us, people are "pattern-seeking" animals. It's probably impossible to write a biography that doesn't resemble myth in some ways.

The claim that the Gospel writers borrowed from pagan sources was never based on much, and was historically refuted by Ronald Nash's *The Gospel and the Greeks: Did the New Testament Borrow From Pagan Thought?*[30] Glenn Miller writes a great summary of the evidence against this position in his article "Was Jesus Just a Copycat Savior Myth?"[31] In their eagerness to prove the Gospels depend on other works, otherwise serious scholars often commit the sin of anachronism—relying on stories that show up in later material as "sources" for ideas that appear in the Gospels first. Nash writes:

> Far too many writers use this later source material to form reconstructions of the third-century mystery experience and then uncritically reason back to what they think must have been the earlier nature of the cults. This practice is exceptionally bad scholarship.[32]

Marcus Borg compares Buddha and Jesus and finds them much alike. You can indeed find a bit of Buddha (moral teachings, psychological insights) the cynics (one-liners) and fourth-century Jewish miracle workers (miracles) in the Gospels. Columbia historian Morton Smith liked the idea of Jesus as a magician so much that he forged a Gospel (*The Secret Gospel of Mark*) to support it!

But if anyone were to find a document outside the Bible that really looked like a Gospel, they would be richer and more famous than Dan Brown by now. The utter inability of skeptics to find serious parallels to the life of Jesus is what forces them to pass off such works as the *Gospel of Thomas* and *Apollonius of Tyana* as startling documents that "threaten the foundations of Christianity," as one young man said after hearing Elaine Pagels speak. The vast army of scholars who have scoured the ancient world for parallels have, ironically, established the Gospels more firmly than ever as utterly unique. There is no other Jesus.

What Do Scholars Say, and What Is It Worth?

Dawkins's argument against the Gospels is based on an appeal to authority. "Scholarly theologians have made an overwhelming case," he writes, that the Gospels don't tell us what really happened.[33] Jesus probably lived, he believes, but "reputable biblical scholars" don't see the New Testament "and obviously not the Old Testament" as a reliable record of what happened.[34]

Despite Dawkins's frequent jibes against theologians, when he likes their arguments, he does quote them.

He can do so because "reputable" first-century historians come down on all sides of the question of how much of the New Testament is historically accurate. Differences can often be traced to differences in bias, methodology, and most of all, philosophy. Many renowned scholars (Strauss, Renan, Bultmann, Funk, Fredriksen, Sanders, Crossan) have said the Gospels can't be true because these scholars don't believe in miracles. This leaves the "argument from authority" in an awkward state. Here we have a zoologist who confuses Gospels and relies on an eighteenth-century statesman and "scholarly theologians" (a category he has denigrated) who base their own historical views on philosophical assumptions! That's what happens when you let positivists do history.

Historians in general are usually careful about giving any text, ancient or modern, "carte blanche": no text is "reliable" in the sense of "beyond question." The fact is, many reputable biblical scholars think the basics of what the Gospels say really did happen.

Dawkins doesn't name the "reputable biblical scholars" on whom he relies, but he does mention four writers who belong to modern and post-modern waves of Jesus criticism. Aside from Robert Gillooly, who argues that the Gospels borrow from myth, in ascending level of seriousness, the other three are Dan Brown, A.N. Wilson, and Bart Ehrman.

The Da Vinci Code is brought in more as a jab in the ribs than with serious intent: "Dan Brown's novel...is indeed fabricated from start to finish: invented, made-up fiction. In that respect, it is exactly like the gospels."[35]

This comment ought to be less frivolous than it obviously is. If the Gospels were made up "from start to finish," fictional works that look like them ought to be easy to find.

But compare the story of Jesus turning mud into swallows in the *Infancy Gospel of Thomas* to a miracle in the Gospel of Mark:

> When this child Jesus was five years old, he was playing by the ford of a stream; and he gathered the flowing waters into pools and made them immediately pure. These things he ordered simply by speaking a word. He then made some soft mud and fashioned twelves sparrows from it...[Joseph asked] "Why are you doing what is forbidden on the Sabbath?" But Jesus clapped his hands and cried to the sparrows, "Be gone!" And the sparrows took flight and went off, chirping.[36]

Another boy then grabbed a stick and messed up Jesus' clean waters. Jesus called him an "unrepentant, irreverent idiot" and cursed him so he "withered" and became like an old tree.

Now look at Mark 3:

> He entered a synagogue again, and a man was there who had a withered hand. So they watched Him closely, whether He would heal him on the Sabbath, so that they might accuse Him. And He said to the man with the withered hand, "Step forward." Then He said to them, "Is it lawful on the Sabbath to do good or to do evil, to save life or to kill?" But they kept silent. And when He had looked around at them with anger, being grieved by the hardness of their hearts, He said to the man, "Stretch out your hand." And

he stretched it out, and his hand was restored...Then the Phari-
sees went out and immediately plotted with the Herodians against
Him, how they might destroy Him (verses 1-6).

Who can't tell the difference between these two stories? The second
was written within the lifetime of Jesus' first followers. This simple scene,
from "naive" Mark (as even his fans call him) is psychologically convincing. Jesus does a miracle, but still comes across as human and believable.
The story is set within the context of first-century debates about cleanli-
ness and the Sabbath, in which "physical wholeness was associated with
purity, and lack of wholeness with impurity," as Borg explained.[37]

Dawkins's second named source, A.N. Wilson, shares his skepticism,
but feels the realism of the miracle narrative in the canonical Gospels
intensely, and is therefore unable to dismiss them wholesale as Dawkins
does.

Like most modernist critics, Wilson denies miracles, which makes it
difficult for him to accept the Gospels. Most skeptics think John is the
latest Gospel, and the most "mythological." But Wilson isn't so sure.
"The cumulative effect of reading his words is to be confronted by a
wholly distinctive view and voice—distinctly Jewish, distinctly of its
time, but distinctive," he points out. John is full of "little details"—the
five porticoes at the sheep gate, the name of the town in Samaria where
Jesus met the woman at the well, the name of the slave whose ear Peter
cut off, the sponge full of sour wine—odd and compelling vignettes, not
quite in sync with later theology, that bring us face to face with a real
person. Wilson states, "The realistic details are too many, and too odd,
for me to be able to accept that they were all invented by some unsung
novelistic genius of the first century of our era..."[38]

It's not that Wilson accepts most of the account. His worldview has
no room for it. My point is that "subjective" evidence within the Gospels compels even honest unbelievers far beyond where Dawkins glibly
remains. But how far can it take us? Can little details add up to evidence
for the Gospels that can be compared to the fruits of rigorous scientific
inquiry?

Fingerprints and DNA also involve little details. But both betray the
presence of an individual. Despite themselves, even the biggest fans of

the scientific method show implicitly that they recognize that words also reveal pattern and personality.

How Do You Know I'm Here?

At an Amazon.com discussion site for *The God Delusion* I suggested, "Historical claims can and must also be 'tested,' though not in the same way as scientific claims. Each field has its own proper epistemology." A skeptic responded by saying Christian historical claims "would not survive the rigor of scientific scrutiny. Scientific results can be tested over and over again, claims dating back 2000 years cannot." Having read some of my other postings, he added, "You believe in God, and you feel a compelling urge to ground your belief on a rational foundation. You know science won't help you there, so you reach for the next best thing: human testimony..."

How is believing in Jesus any different from believing in alien abductions, he asked? After all, there is a "wealth of human testimony" for the latter. He added, "A little evidence would go far to establish your reputation in this forum."

At that point I had to laugh. All the talk about how scientific evidence alone was worthwhile had been betrayed. The positivist had shown, as most do, that he knew better than his theory.

The theory is that "only scientific evidence counts." But what is one to think when the theorist then tells the believer, whom he's never met, that he believes in God, is "compelled" to ground his faith in rationality, and "knows" science won't help him? How does he know all this? Perhaps the believer is a committee posting in one name, Siamese twins, or an alien from outer space? My discussion partner hadn't placed me in a test tube or even lain eyes on me. He hadn't weighed my brain, isolating neurons that spark for "faith in God." He hadn't conducted reproducible experiments that left my beliefs as a residue on a copper wire. Yet somehow he felt he had met a person through a series of dark marks on a screen: thought and expression, feeling, even a sense of humor.

And he was right, therefore wrong. His guesses about me were not particularly accurate; we had only started to talk. But you can get to know a person through postings, even if they are 2000 years old. Human beings are the most complex and therefore identifiable objects in the visible universe. Aside from identical twins, no two people share the same fingerprints, pattern of blood vessels in the retina, or DNA. And not even identical twins share a character.

We're social, "pattern-seeking" creatures.

A baby emperor penguin goes to sea for months. When he returns, his father picks out his squawk above a cacophony of other little birds.

A sheep, Jesus said, knows its shepherd's voice. Even the skeptical founders of the Jesus Seminar can hear (at times) the voice of the Shepherd. The distinctiveness of Jesus' voice is just one of many evidences for the Gospels. So far as I know, no such evidence has yet been gathered about space aliens. As Sagan points out, that kind of report—like the Gnostic Jesus, or the Book of Mormon Jesus tends to be "banal."[39] Fake Jesuses are less interesting than any real person I know, when they ought to be more interesting. I'd rather meet Steve Martin than Apollonius of Tyana, or Saint Peter than the Gnostic Adamas. The Jesus of the Gospels, by contrast, remains outside all the boxes people try to place him in. He is the most interesting person on Earth.

Consider the trouble skeptics have with women in the Gospels. Both secularist and neo-Gnostic scholars take it as an article of faith that the authors of the Gospels were patriarchal and wrote the Gospels to assert male interests. Elaine Pagels, Karen King, and Marvin Meyer insist that the evangelists undermined Mary Magdalene in favor of Peter (absurdly, since the stories they accuse the Gospel writers of "obscuring" wouldn't be written for decades afterwards).

But notice how Jesus treats women in the Gospels. He invites Mary to join a theological discussion when her sister wants her in the kitchen to help make dinner. He banters respectfully with the Samaritan woman at the well, whom most Jews would have shunned. He heals sick women. He rescues, from stoning, a girl accused of adultery. When a female "sinner" crashes a dinner party, he treats her with more respect than his host.

There are only two possibilities. One is that the authors of the Gospels were themselves feminists of the most radical feather. The other is that Jesus did these things, and his followers reported what they saw, however embarrassing it was. There are all kinds of reasons to favor the second and simpler hypothesis.

Did Jesus Claim to Be God?

Aside from miracles, one of the most difficult things about the Gospels for many skeptics is how Jesus sees himself. "Heaven and earth will pass away, but My words will not pass away" (Mark 13:31). "Blessed are you, Simon Barjona, because flesh and blood did not reveal this to you, but My Father who is in heaven" (Matthew 16:17). "If you knew the gift of God, and who it is who says to you, 'Give Me a drink,' you would have asked Him, and He would have given you living water" (John 4:10).

Did Jesus really say such things? How would it alter what we think of him—or of God—if he had?

Harris claims there is "no evidence whatsoever" that Jesus saw himself as more than a Jew waiting for God's kingdom, despite the "tendentious writings of the later church."[40] Dawkins critiques an argument, "attributed among others to C.S. Lewis (who should have known better)" known as the "Trilemma." Lewis made this argument during World War II on the BBC, in talks that were later rewritten as *Mere Christianity*. This is the idea that, having claimed to be God or the Son of God, Jesus must have been either right or wrong. If he was wrong and knew it, he was a terrible liar. If he didn't know it, he must have been crazy. So the choice (as Lewis put it) comes down to lunatic, liar, or Lord.

In response, Dawkins offers a fourth possibility "almost too obvious to need mentioning." Was Jesus just mistaken? "Plenty of people are."[41]

But people are not often "honestly mistaken" about being God. "Sorry! I thought I had the right to forgive other people's sins. I expected to come on the clouds with the angels, at least metaphorically speaking. I thought I had existed forever. I planned on dying for the sins of the world, then rising again. I must have confused myself for someone else. Care for some barley loaves?"

No. The Gospels force a choice. What Jesus said, how he said it, the sheer chutzpah with which he reconfigures the world of those whom he meets again and again make us wonder, as those around him did, "Who is this man?"

But Lewis's argument is incomplete, and Dawkins points out where it falls short.

In his original notes, Lewis briefly addressed a fourth "l," the theory that the Gospels are "legendary." He dismissed it with the comment that the "legend" theory "saddles you with twelve inexplicable lunatics instead of one."[42] In other words, all first-century Christian sources, in and out of the New Testament, present Jesus as divine. And as we have seen, these are not the writings of the later church, but writings from the shores of Galilee, from people who had seen the risen Christ. So close to the facts, could they have been honestly and innocently mistaken? A lot of screws would have to come loose in a lot of heads. And people with loose screws don't write the Sermon on the Mount.

So the difficulty remains, despite all attempts to purge the Gospels of qualities that offend the postreligious ear.

Does the Passion Make Sense?

The death of Jesus on the cross is, as Paul admitted, "foolishness" to the Greeks (1 Corinthians 1:23). Many moderns share that sentiment, including Richard Dawkins:

> So, in order to impress himself, Jesus had himself tortured and executed, in vicarious punishment for a symbolic sin committed by a non-existent individual? As I said, barking mad, as well as viciously unpleasant.[43]

Dawkins isn't mad, but does bark viciously sometimes. This is looking at things through the wrong end of the telescope. Ask instead: Is loving self-sacrifice so evil a quality to attribute to God? Were Augustine, Aquinas, Alfred the Great, Bach, Bede, Chesterton, Dostoevsky, St. Francis and Farraday, Gregory the Great, Johnson, Kepler and Kierkegaard, and so on, all "barking mad" to believe what Dawkins cannot? Faced with contrary opinions on this and so much else by so many wise men and women, wouldn't it be more cautious, as Confucius taught, to simply say, "I don't understand"?

During a debate with Francis Collins, Dawkins commented:

> I don't see the Olympian gods or Jesus coming down and dying on the Cross as worthy of that grandeur. They strike me as parochial. If there is a God, it's going to be a whole lot bigger and a whole lot more incomprehensible than anything that any theologian of any religion has ever proposed.[44]

Perhaps God is bored with being "big" and "incomprehensible." Maybe he would rather be small and hang out with the simple, just as Jesus made himself available to children, the sick, sinners, and the marginalized. Maybe he prefers barrios in Rio to ivory towers in Princeton (maybe the music is better!). Or maybe Christian doctrine really is "incomprehensible" to Richard Dawkins. Lao Zi said of the true sage, "It is because he did not contend that no one under heaven can contend with him." The apostle Paul added, "God has chosen the foolish things of the world to shame...the things which are strong" (1 Corinthians 1:27).

Let's see how that works.

PART THREE

TRUTH
AND
CONSEQUENCES

Is Christianity
a Blessing?

"I am, alas, not myself a believing Christian. I wish I were. But one thing I can say with the most utmost sincerity, and that is that I grow evermore convinced that the Christian gospel was the most wonderful thing that has ever happened in the world; that it represents the nearest to ultimate truth that has yet been revealed to mankind; that our civilization was born with it, is irretrievably bound up with it, and would most certainly perish without it."[1]

—MALCOLM MUGGERIDGE

Nature is indeed a strange place. A crumb-like male saltwater worm is eaten by its mate, then impregnates her from within. A freshwater protozoan forms rods of silicon hydrate, from which it weaves little "lobster pots" and captures bacteria to dine. We're used to pinecones, squirrels scampering up trees with bushy tails waving, pumpkins growing like lanterns out of dirt, the wag of a dog's tail, the monthly crescent fading of the moon. Look closer, and a "planetary system" circles a proton and neutron "sun," held together by a tiny flash of lightning. Smaller yet, and you fall into a Wonderland where particles a galaxy apart are joined and contrary, like Tweedledee and Tweedledum. If nature and the Bible share "weirdness" in common, is it because God is the author of both, as early scientists believed?

Despite its quirkiness, biology is bound by two things: a code, and a story that began with a microbe and ended (so far as physical changes go) with man and woman walking hand in hand in a garden. Here the Bible begins: with another story, and a code of life called the Gospels.

Elsewhere, I have argued that the Gospels are like DNA in one way: They can be used to identify someone. My point was that the unique qualities of a remarkable person can be found, like fingerprints or DNA, all over the Gospels. Matthew, Mark, Luke, and John are therefore strong evidence for the life and character of the historical Jesus.

Perhaps this is more than an analogy. Maybe the Gospels are literally "genetic codes." They are written in code—marketplace Greek, with a few words of Aramaic. They are also "genetic" in that they claim to "code for life." Jesus said, "I came that they may have life, and have it abundantly" (John 10:10). I will argue in this chapter that through these words, God's promise to Abraham to bless all the peoples of the world is indeed progressively fulfilled.

In *The Music of Life*, Denis Noble points out that the life of the cell is not directly determined by its genes.[2] The cell "reads" the genome and creates a panoply of structures for many purposes at different times—like picking keys on a piano to play ragtime, rock, or opera (except that each genetic "key" can play many notes).

Robert Hooke, who sketched the microscopic honeycombing he found in cork, borrowed the word *cell* from Christian monasticism to describe what he saw: "these pores, or cells, consisted of a great many little Boxes, separated out of one continued long pore."[3] Let me borrow the term back. Like DNA within the biological cell, the Gospel accomplishes nothing alone. Men and women called by God "play" the chords of the Gospel to make, mend, catalyze, and move things to where they belong in society. Of course believers often strike "wrong" cords, or right cords out of key. From such discords arise inquisitions, witch hunts, and crass religious come-ons. But when Christians act on Gospel teachings in tune with the Holy Spirit to respond to the needs of the world, a higher-order "music of life" emerges.

How Should We Judge?

How can we evaluate the influence of religion? Should we count corpses, bound feet, manacled hands, and notches in guillotines? Judging beliefs by the crimes they commit seems a dreary task, but justifiable: Ideas, like people, need to be held to account. But a quick glance at history shows that no faith or antifaith that gains power remains unspotted. That power corrupts needn't surprise anyone: both evolution and Christian theology predict it.

Kindness is something else. As Hauser and Dawkins admit, it's hard to squeeze out-group altruism from the evolutionary rocks. So where does moral progress come from?

Richard Dawkins thinks morality ticks upwards automatically, no thanks to the Bible:

> We have all moved on, and in a big way, since biblical times. Slavery, which was taken for granted in the Bible and throughout most of history, was abolished in civilized countries in the nineteenth century...women are no longer regarded as property, as they clearly were in biblical times. Any modern legal system would have prosecuted Abraham for child abuse.[4]

In what sense has the world "moved on"? Slavery has mostly ended, as Dawkins points out (with some 15 million exceptions). Women have become more equal. Most unbelievers would also agree, I think, that science, universal education, the spread of democracy, the erosion of caste in India and foot-binding in China have been among the biggest steps forward.

What if the Christian faith lay at the heart of each of these great reform movements? And what if radical, God-inspired compassion for members of the "out-group" turned out to be the engine of human progress?

We begin the story in India.

Jesus, the Tiger of Bengal

Both Dawkins and Harris are atheists. Yet they look to India, perhaps the world's most religious country, to argue the moral fatuity of the Christian message.

Dawkins claims that even though Martin Luther King was a Christian, "he derived his philosophy of non-violent civil disobedience from Gandhi, who was not."[5] Perhaps not, but Gandhi did believe in God! In *The End of Faith*, Harris writes enthusiastically about Buddhist meditation and compassion. He argues that "Jain fundamentalism" would "improve our situation immensely."[6] In *Letter to a Christian Nation*, Harris adds that "with a single sentence" Mahavira, the Jain patriarch, "surpassed" the moral teachings of the Bible: "Do not injure, abuse, oppress, enslave, insult, torment, torture, or kill any creature or living being." The world would be a better place if only Christians found that verse in their Bibles and obeyed it![7] As for Mother Teresa, the most famous Christian in India, Harris quotes Christopher Hitchens:

> She spent her life opposing the only known cure for poverty, which is the empowerment of women and the emancipation of them from a livestock version of compulsory reproduction.[8]

To give him credit, even Harris seems uncomfortable with this. What Mother Teresa spent her life doing, of course, was comforting the dying. But the quote, and Harris's use of it, reveals a profound ignorance of Indian history on the part of both men.

We face three charges here. First, Indian morality—in particular, Jainism—would have done the world more good than biblical teachings. Second, the most famous American reformer of the twentieth century had to go to India for inspiration presumably because he couldn't find it in Christianity. And third, the most famous modern missionary—and by implication, the rest too—left Indian women in the lurch.

The truth could hardly be more different.

With due respect to Mahavira (if he lived—sources are late), his teaching did not much help India. Jains taught that every animal, plant, and particle of wind has a soul. Mahavira stripped off his clothes, plucked out his hair, never bathed, and refused to harm the lice and fleas that colonized him. While the idea of injuring no living thing sounds good, taken literally, it proved a bitter pill. Scholar John Farquhar explained the program: "Twelve years of severe ascetic practice were necessary to win release. After that a Jain monk was allowed to starve himself to death, if he chose to do so."[9] Nor did Jainism end the terrible social evils of India.

Martin Luther King said, "I went to Gandhi through Jesus."[10] In a way, so did Gandhi.

It would be unfair to ascribe Gandhi's teachings part and parcel to Jesus, given his love of Indian scriptures. Gandhi was a syncretist, a Hindu, and a big fan of both Buddha and the Jains. Some of what he taught was at odds with Christianity. Even Harris finds his advice to the Jews of Europe—commit mass suicide to shame Hitler—too much. "Gandhi's was a world in which millions more would have died in the hopes that the Nazis would have one day doubted the goodness of their Thousand Year Reich,"[11] Harris comments, adding, "Ours is a world in which bombs must occasionally fall where such doubts are in short supply." On this point, Harris agrees with the Christian "just war" tradition. He entirely forgets to ask, "What would Mahavira do?"

But Gandhi was deeply influenced by Jesus in three ways. First, though offended when a convert in his area began insulting Hindu gods and drinking English booze, later he read the New Testament, and changed his mind about Christianity. The Sermon on the Mount "went straight to my heart."[12] Jesus' words about turning the other cheek "delighted me beyond measure," he said, and Gandhi began trying to unify the Bhagavad Gita, the story of Buddha, and Jesus' teachings. Gandhi also read and was deeply influenced by two thinkers whose minds were steeped in those teachings: Ruskin, and Tolstoy.[13] Finally, Gandhi was also touched by Christ indirectly, through profound intellectual changes the Gospel brought India.

It is ironic that Christopher Hitchens should berate Mother Teresa for not helping Indian women. Before missionaries arrived in India, it was common for upper-caste Hindu girls to be burnt to death after their husbands died (a practice called *sati*). Girls were seldom educated, and were taught not only to obey, but worship their husbands as *patidev*, patriarchal gods. If they were obedient enough, they might be reborn as men themselves and gain salvation.

The gospel began to change this. Missionaries were horrified by *sati*. With political allies like William Wilberforce, they harangued the British government to protect widows. The "brights" of the British empire had better things to do, says Indian philosopher Vishal Mangalwadi. The East India Company was a "gang of public robbers." British generals saw India as "territory to be conquered." Humanitarians and intellectuals "tended merely to respect and romanticize the 'customs and wisdom of the natives.'"[14]

It was Christian preachers who snatched the women of India off the funeral pyre. They set up thousands of schools to educate both sexes. They gave the lower castes medical training. Christian nurses, doubly scorned as women and outcastes, spread across India and the Middle East. Even today, many south Asian nurses are Christians from the state of Kerala.

Mangalwadi tells how missionaries fought English planters who exploited indigo laborers. Prices for indigo were kept artificially low, and growers starved. The landlords bought off the police, and anyone who protested was beaten. A missionary named Schurr stirred up a political stink, but the state sided with the planters. Missionaries then began to agitate in England. One missionary, James Long, was thrown in jail for "libel," which he accepted cheerfully. In part because of such examples, by the end of the nineteenth century, "Jesus had become the central issue in India."[15]

Nor did the influence of the gospel spread solely through Christians. On the west coast of England, on a hill above old Bristol, stands a statue of India's first great indigenous reformer, Ram Mohan Roy. Roy has been called the father of modern India. He was founder of the reformist movement Brahmo Samaj and one of the premier figures of the Bengal Renaissance (the first missionaries were based in Bengal). In 1820, Roy put together a selection of gospel quotations with a title that stated his views (as a Hindu) quite clearly: "The Principles of Jesus, the Guide to Peace and Happiness." In the preface he explained:

> This simple code of religion and morality is so admirably calculated to elevate men's ideas to high and liberal notions of one God...and is also so well fitted to regulate the conduct of the human race in the discharge of their various duties to God, to themselves and to society, that I cannot but hope the best effects from its promulgation in the present form.[16]

Keshab Chandra Sen, the third leader of the Brahmo Samaj movement, was also deeply influenced by the teachings of Jesus and the remarkably broad and ambitious social agenda of the missionaries. Like Roy, he believed in one God, opposed the caste system, child marriage, and polygamy, and set up women's education and vo-tech schools. He wrote,

> Christ has been my study for a quarter of a century. That God-Man—they say half God and half man—walks daily all over this

vast peninsula, from the Himalayas to Cape Comorin, enlighten-
ing and sanctifying its teeming millions. He is a mighty reality in
Indian history...He permeates society as a vital force, and imbues
our daily life, and is mixed with our thoughts, speculations and
pursuits.[17]

A third great Indian reformer was a rare female Sanskrit scholar,
Pandita Ramabai. Pandita agreed with Roy and Sen about the role
Jesus should play in India—in fact, she became a Christian. She also
wrote against polygamy and child marriage, and in 1889 founded Mukti
("freedom") Mission, which aided widows, orphans, and the blind. She
appeared on an Indian postage stamp a century later.

So Jesus began to deeply challenge the Indian status quo long before
anyone had heard of Gandhi.

The aftershocks continue. Last fall, an upper-caste Hindu friend
explained frankly that Christianity and Hinduism "are not the same."
Both talk about moral duty, but Christians actually help poor people in
his village—and not poor people alone. Even his aunt had become a
Christian. With fetching honesty, the Dalai Lama (a longtime resident
of India) noted in his autobiography how Christians of "all denomina-
tions" help others, adding that he hoped Buddhists would follow their
lead: "I feel that Buddhist monks and nuns tend to talk a great deal about
compassion without doing much about it."[18]

Perhaps Harris, as an admirer of Buddhism, should listen to the Dalai
Lama.

Jesus Touches the Untouchables

Mohatmas Gandhi tried over his long career to grapple with the problem of caste. Not all his ideas on this subject were helpful. Dr. Bhimrao
Ambedkhar, "outcaste" leader and drafter of the Indian Constitution,
rebuked him sharply for waffling:

> To the Untouchables, Hinduism is a veritable chamber of hor-
> rors...the iron law of caste, the heartless law of karma and the
> senseless law of status by birth are to the Untouchables veritable
> instruments of torture which Hinduism has forged against the

Untouchables. These very instruments...are to be found intact and untarnished in the bosom of Gandhism.[19]

Gandhi tried to overcome caste prejudice. He treated members of the lower castes kindly, boarding them at his home, even losing his temper when his wife refused to clean for one. And he tried to bring India to see outcastes as children of God.

But such reforms began long before Gandhi. From 1876–1879, a terrible famine struck India. Missionaries raised funds, gave work to the poor, and did what they could to help. After the famine, thousands of dirt-poor outcastes began pouring into the church, were educated, and began to make better lives for themselves. Others realized that the oppression they suffered under was not karmic necessity. One group petitioned the government,

As British subjects we cannot, we should not submit to ordinances which are entirely foreign to British ideas of public justice and public honor. We are sick of the bondage which the barbarism of Hindu customs imposes upon us...shall not that nation which emancipated the Negro at infinite self-sacrifice...condescend to give us a helping hand?[20]

Indians who saw themselves as Hindu but (like Roy and Sen) worshipped one God noted with alarm the growth of Christianity, and began to rethink the status of the outcastes. The Arja Samaj, a monotheistic reform movement founded in 1875 that looked to the ancient Vedas (often closer in tone to Christian thought than Advedic Hinduism), was the first to make the move.

Just consider for a moment what Christian missionaries are accomplishing in India, though they come here from the remotest part of Europe. They beat even the Arya Samajists, in spite of their preaching the indigenous faith of the country. The reason is that the Arya Samajists have not yet learnt to work among the masses who form the backbone of India. It is high time for us to realize that the future of India lies not in the hands of the higher classes but of the low caste people..."[21]

Christianity thus began to shatter the oppression of caste in India. It did so, like a hammer breaking glass, not by directly touching every Indian, but by breaking the facade of a tyrannical system with a series of sharp blows. Rural India still has a ways to go—and shamefully, some churches have given in to the caste system themselves. But as with the birth of science, once the gospel of Jesus brought truth clearly to mind, this "meme" went to work. It was Jesus, the first to "touch untouchables," who inspired this reform.

I've had the privilege of knowing Drs. Paul and Margaret Brand, two missionaries who played a role in the mission enterprise in India. Paul was a famous hand surgeon who made discoveries about the nature of leprosy, and rehabilitative surgery to correct its disfigurements, that ultimately helped millions (including diabetes patients). Dr. Brand was awarded membership in the Order of the British Empire, was a consultant with the World Health Organization, and served as professor emeritus at the University of Washington. Former U.S. Surgeon General C. Everett Koop once paid Paul the remarkable compliment of saying that when he daydreamed about living someone else's life, he most often thought of Dr. Brand. Margaret is an ophthalmologist who treated thousands of south Indians, and is quite a match for her late husband.

Paul's parents went to the hill peoples of south India a century ago as missionaries. They started nine schools and many clinics, treating bubonic plague, cholera, small pox, polio, typhus, and leprosy. They planted mulberry and citrus groves, coffee, sugarcane, and tapioca, and taught carpentry and tile making. His father escorted a delegation of poor tenant farmers who had a dispute with their landlords to make a case to the government.

One man opposed their work: a priest of the indigenous religion. But when he became sick with influenza, the priest found that the only ones available to nurse him (and others) were his foreign "enemies" (who failed to understand the etiquette of "in-group morality"). As he was dying, he bequeathed to Paul Brand's parents his daughter, and Paul gained a sister, Ruth. "My son was to be priest after me," he explained, "but no one in my religion has cared enough to help me. I want my children to grow up as Christians."[22]

The Brands lived in a small "cottage" (they're British) overlooking Puget Sound. On a visit, I noticed Margaret kept a bird feeder outside her kitchen window, and we talked a bit about birds (the Brands were great nature-lovers). A woman from southern China came in to clean, towing a little girl behind her. As I watched them interact, she almost seemed like one of the family. The woman's husband in Canton was disabled, they told me afterwards, and they were looking for work for her. Could my father use some help with his apartments?

That's the kind of people the Dalai Lama likely ran across in his subcontinental travels.

India is the wrong place to go to prove the moral vacuity of the Christian faith. I assume Dawkins and Harris chose this battlefield out of ignorance, or because a polytheist country seemed a particularly sharp stick with which to beat Christianity. But that probably wasn't their worst choice.

Jesus Frees Slaves

The outlawing of the slave trade was a huge milestone in history. Dawkins, Harris, and Hitchens all pin their criticism of the Bible on its failure to condemn this institution. For Harris, this is inexplicable. Isn't it obvious that a slave is a human being who suffers and enjoys like all of us? Every reasonable person understands that treating people "like farm equipment" is "patently evil." Harris argues, "It is remarkably easy for a person to arrive at this epiphany." Yet it had to be spread "at the point of a bayonet" in the pious American South.[23]

Only a historically sheltered child of the West and the product of a politically correct public school system could achieve such breathtaking and uncritical naivité.

Slavery was obviously not wrong to Aristotle. The equality of humanity was denied by Greeks, Gnostics, Indians (Asian and American), Africans, Chinese, and countless smaller tribes. Enlightenment figures such as Hume, Voltaire, Locke, and Jefferson favored slavery, either in word or deed. Some nineteenth- and twentieth-century Social Darwinists saw blacks as a distinct species, and Australian aborigines "at least two grades below the African negro."[24] Ernst Haeckel, the foremost evolutionary thinker in Germany (and a good friend of Darwin) did in fact compare some folk to farm (or jungle) animals: "lower races...are psychologically nearer to the mammals (apes and dogs) than to civilized Europeans," so "we must assign a totally different value to their lives."[25]

No great civilization arrived at the "epiphany" Harris thinks so obvious until the rise of Christian Europe. The great Islam scholar Bernard Lewis points out that while reform movements did arise in Islam, "None of these movements ever questioned the three sacrosanct distinctions establishing the subordinate status of the slave, the woman, and the unbeliever."[26] A few voices were raised against caste in India (in the Sikh religion, for example), but the system shook them off.[27]

Harris rests his argument against Christianity largely on the fact that the Bible didn't immediately end slavery. But the Bible did end slavery—twice.

Not many people know about the first abolition movement. But as soon as the church began disentangling itself from the wreckage of Rome (and where it did not become entangled with Islam), slaves began to trickle out from bondage. Christianity spread in northern Europe through the aristocracy. Already by the fourth century, an upper-class woman convert set 3000 slaves free. Early in the seventh century, the monk Aidan took donations from the rich to buy slaves, liberate them, and give them an education. Later in the same century, Queen Balthild (wife of Clovis II) worked to free Christian slaves (at least) and stop the slave trade. In A.D. 960 the bishops of Venice tried to prohibit Venetians from buying and selling people. By the eleventh century, "no slaves to speak of" remained in entire regions of Western Europe, and soon after, in England.[28] When the Normans conquered England, rather than enslaving enemies, as was the custom, they set thousands of slaves free.

Slavery didn't die in Greece or Iberia, however. As historian Richard Fletcher explained, "peripheral outsiders tend to model themselves upon the hegemonic power on whose flanks they are situated."[29] In the long grudge match with the more obviously civilized Moors, Visigoth kings "emulated Muslim behavior" and enslaved (rather than killed) their enemies.[30] With slavery an accepted institution, and warfare a way of life, as they became more "civilized" themselves, it was natural for the Portuguese and Spanish to go into the trade on a massive scale in Africa and the Americas. The English, French, and Americans followed their lead.

Hitchens claims that "this huge and terrible industry was blessed by all churches and for a long time aroused absolutely no religious protest."[31] He's wrong. Many popes protested, beginning in the fifteenth century. In 1639, Pope Urban VIII "condemned slavery absolutely."[32] In the eighteenth century, Pope Clement XI demanded an "end to slavery."[33] Generally speaking, such calls fell on deaf ears: Whatever the pope (or sheltered twenty-first-century grad students) thought, gentleman farmers knew that human beings make uncommonly handy farm equipment.

A second and more radical abolition movement began among the Quakers. One winter day a hunchback named Benjamin Lay near Philadelphia saw a slave hanging naked and dead, executed for trying to escape. Lay used the method of the Hebrew prophets to raise consciousness. He stood outside a Quaker meeting house with one leg half-buried in snow. When people passed on their way to church and expressed concern, he replied, "Ah, you pretend compassion for me, but you do not feel for the poor slaves in your fields who go all winter half-clad."[34]

Evangelical Christians led the movement against slavery in England and America, and England led the world. Rodney Stark chronicles Christian work to free the slaves in rich detail. In both England and America, "the movement was staffed by devout Christian activists, the majority of them clergy."[35] Fifty-two percent of "traveling agents," and 75 percent of "local agents" for the American Anti-Slavery Society were ordained ministers. Why did those so deep in the grasp of the "God delusion" go to this trouble if the Bible is so gung ho for human bondage? The New Testament implicitly undermines slavery in many ways: by affirming the nobility of manual labor (Jesus was a carpenter!), teaching the essential equality of humankind, and talking eloquently and frequently about liberty. All that talk about loving one's neighbor may have even registered in a few skulls. The abolitionists saw humanity as equal because they called a Jewish carpenter "Lord"—not because abolition was "obvious."

Harris tells us that Christian theologians who argued against slavery "lost" the argument. How so? Does Harris presume to know how the Bible should be interpreted better than Thomas Aquinas, at least four popes, John Wesley, Samuel Johnson, John Newton, Charles Finney, and

Edmund Burke? Wesley, founder of Methodism, passionately opposed slavery from early on. His letter to William Wilberforce, who did more than anyone to make the word *progress* mean something, should be memorized by school children:

> Unless the divine power has raised you up to be as *Athanasius contra mundum*, I see not how you can go through your glorious enterprise in opposing that execrable villainy which is the scandal of religion, of England, and of human nature. Unless God has raised you up for this very thing, you will be worn out by the opposition of men and devils. But if God be for you, who can be against you? Are all of them together stronger than God? O be not weary of well doing! Go on, in the name of God and in the power of his might, till even American slavery (the vilest that ever saw the sun) shall vanish away before it.

Wesley quotes the Bible five times here. How theologically illiterate he must have been not to realize that the Bible supports slavery! But as the movie *Amazing Grace* beautifully shows, Wilberforce's "delusion" that God had raised him to make slavery "vanish away" changed the course of history. Christian abolitionists won the argument, and liberated much of humanity.

Dawkins believes a "shifting Zeitgeist" carries humanity ever upwards.[36] Aside from "local and temporary setbacks" (the Bush administration is the example he gives), "the whole wave keeps moving." The "vanguard" of the nineteenth century is behind the "laggers" of more recent times.

Nonsense. In 1774 Wesley described Africans as "of a quiet and good disposition," "well instructed in what is right," hardworking, generous to the old and blind, "ingenious" at metallurgy and other crafts, "sociable," and prone to "become excellent astronomers" given the right instruments. A century later, social Democrats introduced ideas that (we will see) led to cruelty even worse than what Wesley and Wilberforce decried. The modern "vanguard" is now talking not just about late-term abortions, but infanticide and euthanasia. "Zeitgeists" do shift, but sometimes the wave is more destructive than any tsunami.

It took a powerful spiritual force to free the slaves. Few serious historians (and I've heard the subject discussed by a roomful of very serious historians within minutes of Dawkins's office) deny that that force was the gospel and those who put it into practice. The fight continues today in red-light districts around the world, in south Asia, in the Sudan. While I am correcting gratuitous slanders, let me risk this comment from Donna Hughes, women's studies professor and modern antislavery activist:

> President Bush has been the crucial factor. He has created a political climate in which all of us, from local activists to high-ranking political appointees, could do this work...by supporting the abolitionist work against the global sex trade, he's done more for women and girls than any one other president I can think of. And he seems to have done it because it's the right thing to do, not because of pressure or favoritism.[37]

Jesus Liberates Women

We've already seen how the gospel helped women in India. Such stories could be multiplied around the world.

During the Song Dynasty (960–1279), the Chinese began to wrap up the feet of little girls to make their mature waddle more "sexy." For the rest of their lives, women hobbled on crippled feet. (This also made it harder for them to walk off, an important concern in a polygamous society!) The movement to ban foot-binding was begun by Christians, though their role is often obscured.[38]

The status of women in a society may even be a function of how strongly the gospel has influenced that society.

I deal with this in more detail elsewhere. Note the United Nations's *Population Briefing Paper*.[39] Researchers ranked the status of women in 99 countries by employment, education, marriage and children, and health. In all four categories, the ten countries in which the status of women was highest had a Christian background—except for Taiwan, which came in fourth in the "marriage and children" category. Among the lowest listings, none of the countries had a Christian heritage (apart from the complex case of Mozambique, which has a mixed religious population and came in seventh from the last in health, but fourth from the top in employment).

Jesus Is a Teacher

Learn a child her ABCs, and she'll be free for life.

Most religious leaders, from Moses to Mao, emphasized education, at least so people would read their books. But the gospel has done spectacular things with chalk.

Christianity invented the university. Believers established almost all pre-Civil War American colleges and schools in Africa, Latin America, China, and India. Great European universities remain medieval towns shadowed by church towers. At Oxford, Christ Church bells ring you to bed, even if you wake up at three in the morning to drunken songs from undergraduates.

Missionaries also taught young children and started schools for women, outcastes, and hill tribes.

If the education of continents weren't enough, missionaries helped to reduce hundreds of languages to writing. Among Martin Luther's many achievements is that he helped create modern German. In India, southern China, Africa, Southeast Asia, and America, other written scripts created for ministry continue to serve as the basis for all writing.

Before schooling them, Christians often had to rescue children from something worse. The prophetic call that ended human sacrifice in Israel, Rome, and Europe was caught up by Islam, then spread (through missions) to New Guinea, the Burmese hills, and India. In Oxford I got to know believers who rescue children in Peru and old women in Nigeria, both abused as witches. Of course today secularists help as well, and Richard Dawkins would, I am sure, be welcome to join them. But to blame Christianity for "abusing" children without mentioning the billions it has liberated is grossly ignorant or dishonest. The river of life that flows for the healing of the world's children flows from the throne of God, through his prophets and his Son.

Revolution Begins at Home

Liberation often advances at glacial speed. One of the greatest, slowest-moving trends towards freedom has been the rise of monogamy. Polygamy makes most everyone less free and happy. If one man marries four girls, three men are left out in the cold. (Or they can go to war to steal women from "out-groups," which helps explain the success of early Muslim conquests!)

Women in polytheistic societies are often tightly controlled. It's hard to herd camels and watch four women at the same time (let alone several hundred, as an emperor might have). One needs to hobble the ladies somehow: bind feet, lock doors, put veils over faces—or keep women illiterate and tell them they need to worship their husband (along with trees, rats, and ghosts) to escape the bad karma that made them female. Another "good trick" that Sumerian, Byzantine, Turkish, and Chinese rulers discovered was to castrate poor or disgraced men and have them keep an eye on the ladies.

Joseph's brothers became jealous of his coat of many colors and sold him into slavery in Egypt (Genesis 37). Actually they were half-brothers, sons of different mothers. Children suffer from polygamy as well, from a distant father, and from sibling rivalry that is intensified by competition between women. V.S. Naipaul writes,

> These multiple Muslim marriages, though often comic to people outside, caused untold pain to many of the people involved, and the pain could travel like disease from generation to generation, with people seemingly driven to pass on the abuse—the jealousy, the torment, the neglect—from which they had suffered.[40]

Monogamy followed Christian missions. The rise of the nuclear family liberated billions of people from loneliness, castration, and gang warfare at home.

Christ Mellows Caesar

The relationship between Christianity and pluralism is complex. Dawkins thinks the founding fathers of the American republic had little use for Christianity. Some Christian apologists say, "America was founded as a Christian nation." Almost all the Christians I polled agreed that "America was founded on Christian principles."

The founding fathers were of two minds about Christianity, as fair-minded historians admit. On the one hand, they often recognized the contribution the Bible had made to Western civilization and retained a great deal of faith themselves, in the understated style of the time.

Modern democracy came at the tail end of a long process of growing plu-ralism in Europe, with Christian thinkers from Ambrose to John of Paris to John Locke playing key roles.[41]

Influenced by Enlightenment ideas as well as Puritan idealism, the American founders also keenly recognized that an unhealthy relation-ship had grown up between church and state in Europe. The corrup-tion followed a familiar pattern. Humble believers do good work—copy books, clear land, wipe the brow of the sick, feed the hungry. Good works lead to influence, then power, then wealth. The institutional tail begins to wag the ecclesiastical dog. Lovers of money and power find the preacher's platform and the prestige created by good works useful. ("As soon as the coin in the coffer rings, the soul from purgatory springs!") Then a new generation of reformers arises to clean house and create new institutions. This is the ancient pattern of Christian history: death, resurrection, new life.

Pluralism grew slowly in Western culture, like a sheltering tree from a small seed. The tree began to bear fruit long before the Enlightenment. Consider the names of some zealous believers and their influence on politics: Alfred the Great, Ambrose (who rebuked an emperor), Augus-tine (who separated "city of God" and "city of men"), Bartelome de Las Casas (who stood up for Native Americans), Bede the historian, Bene-dict (who taught the aristocracy to work!), Bonhoeffer, Burke, Carey, Don John (who sunk the Muslim fleet at Lepanto), Erasmus, Gregory the Great, John of Paris, John Paul II, Locke, Luther, Roy, Solzhenitsyn, Sun Yat-Sen, Walensa, Wesley, Wilberforce, Wycliffe. Look at what ani-mated them, and what they accomplished—not by themselves, but with millions of others—and it is evident that the relationship between plu-ralist democracy and Christian faith has been intimate and fruitful.

Nor has the need for that influence ended. To paraphrase Stalin, how many divisions did the pope have in 1989? Why did Poland, the most Christian country in Europe, throw off communism first? Why did people power in the Philippines begin with the conversion of Benigno Aquino in prison and end with people on their knees? Why was the first sane modern reformer in China (Hong Rengan, cousin to the first insane reformer, Hong Xiuquan) also one of the first Protestants? Why was the

"Arsenal of Democracy" that pulled Europe back from the brink three times in the twentieth century also the most pious Western nation?

In *Jesus and the Religions of Man*, I summarized the unique stance Christian theology takes towards politics:

> Christianity, then, differs from some religions on the question of church and state in four regards. First, while Jesus had bigger fish to fry, he did not counsel us to withdraw from society or politics, like Buddha. Second, he never promised a utopian end to con-flict, as did Marx. In fact, he promised wars and persecutions of all kinds—not because Christianity hates humanity, but because people are ambivalent towards truth. Third, unlike Islam and other revolutionary religions, Christianity prescribes separation of church and state. And fourth, it provided the theoretical prin-ciples which served as a basis for modern freedoms: the doctrine of sin, legal equality, a special duty to the poor, and a special warning for the rich.[42]

Sam Harris describes the history of Christianity as "principally a story of mankind's misery and ignorance."[43] The New Atheists do what they can to make it look that way. I don't want to be glib in response and portray Christian history as one glorious flying carpet ride up to heaven. Jesus was not a wizard, and the gospel is not a magic wand that we wave over the planet to turn men and women into angels. If the New Testa-ment promises a rose garden, it plays up thorns more than petals.

But when we follow the movements that have liberated humanity most profoundly, we find that the gospel played a profound role in almost all of them.

Like proteins in a cell, followers of Christ read this code to build up not just the church (in-group), but also society (out-group). I've only scratched the surface. For example, I've met hundreds of people who have been freed from drug addictions through Jesus.

These historical effects don't seem far-fetched or convoluted. One can chart a clear and often direct causative course from the Gospels to the work of reformers, missionaries, doctors, and teachers. Jesus taught. He healed. He was kind to women. He welcomed children. He said, "Give to Caesar what is Caesar's, and to God what is God's" (Matthew 22:21). He staged no coup and started no cult beyond the Jordan. Jesus taught us explicitly to love others, including Samaritans, and he taught us even more powerfully by the implicit example of his life.

But what about the crimes of Christianity? Harris was not just blowing smoke, after all: Christian history does involve a lot of misery and ignorance, too.

No honest person who has been involved in churches for long can deny the existence of backbiting, pettiness, intrigue, or of course (everyone's favorite) scandal. The conservative church I grew up in didn't tell us whom to vote for, but one of our pastors had affairs with teen girls in the youth group. Our church lost its building in a lawsuit when it left the larger denomination. How often have I heard a bitter atheist begin their "testimony" to unbelief, "I was raised in a pious Catholic/Baptist/evangelical home"?

Stretch that out in red letters across history, and you get some idea of the other side of what the church has done wrong.

There are two questions to ask. First, have Christians done a lot of evil? Every reasonable person will say yes in a heartbeat.

The deeper question, however, is this: What is the source of that evil? What effect have the teachings of the New Testament themselves had on this planet? To answer that question, we must look more closely at motives—and also, at times, separate legend from fact.

Or a Curse?

"Whatever the confused, muddle-headed, mingy-minded
intellectuals of today may think, Christian Europe was a
noble cause—however abominably it behaved towards the
Jews—particularly when compared to that of its enemies."

—PAUL FERGOSI[1]

The old adage "Do no harm!" surely applies to religion as well as medicine. Even if belief in God has done a lot of good, what about the evil perpetrated in his name?

Whenever the effect of Christianity is discussed, five episodes are almost always mentioned: the Crusades, the Inquisition, the persecution of accused witches, the slave trade, and pogroms against Jews. Typically, Daniel Dennett gives three positive examples of what religion accomplishes (civil rights, science in early Islam, the self-respect members of the Nation of Islam gain) of which one is Christian, while all his negative examples (the Inquisition, pogroms, and Catholic opposition to condoms in Africa) involve Christians.[2] Sam Harris writes of the Inquisition,

> There is no instance in which so many ordinary men and women
> have been so deranged by their beliefs about God; nowhere else
> has the subversion of reason been so complete or its consequences
> so terrible.[3]

Harris and Dawkins aren't satisfied with blaming Christianity for obvious crimes. Following a spate of recent books about "Hitler's pope,"

155

they also implicate "Christian theology" in the Holocaust. "Knowingly or not, the Nazis were agents of religion," Harris claims.[4] Dawkins suggests that most of the soldiers who carried out Hitler's crimes against Jews "were surely Christians."[5]

Most skeptics admit few of their Christian neighbors are fire-breathing dragons, and even Dawkins concedes that the bishop of Oxford is an amiable fellow. Many suppose this is because the religion has been watered down. Ignoring 1500 years of Christian history, Hitchens even supposes that "charity and relief work" are "the inheritors of modernism and the Enlightenment"![6] The bigger problem now, some "concede," is Islam, which is stuck in the Middle Ages, from which the West has emerged like a coal miner from a cave-in. Christianity once "regarded apostasy as a capital offense," Dennett tells us. "Of the Abrahamic faiths, Islam stands alone in its inability to renounce this barbaric doctrine convincingly."[7]

Jesus said you will know a tree by its fruit (Matthew 7:18-20). The legitimacy of a teaching can therefore be judged by its effects. Harris writes, "It really matters what billions of human beings believe and why they believe it."[8]

"Saints are sinners, too," some Christians respond glibly, then drop the subject as quickly as possible. That won't do. The claim isn't only that there are bad apples in the gospel barrel, or even that some criminals co-opt Christianity to do evil. The claim is that there's something in this faith, when taken seriously, that leads to the murder of the innocent. The charge demands honest consideration.

What If Urban II Had Nukes?

Let's begin by dropping one of the charges. By 1095, Europe had been under Muslim assault for four centuries. Muslim armies had conquered much of Byzantium, north Africa, and Spain, pushing into southern France, Switzerland, and to the gates of Rome. Pope Urban called on Europeans to liberate Jerusalem from its Turkish occupiers and go to the aid of the "Greeks" against Islamic imperialism. He complained that the "accursed race" of the Persians had "invaded the lands of those Christians and depopulated them by the sword, pillage, and fire," enslaved, raped, and tortured the inhabitants, turned churches into mosques, and "dismembered" the Byzantine empire.[9]

He was right. I see nothing vile about defending a friend against a bully at the risk of one's own neck. True, recruits were not always of high caliber. After the conquest of the city of Ma'arra, the French gave French cuisine a vile name in the Middle East by boiling and grilling the defenders.[10]

The obsession with the Crusades, a momentary response to attacks on Europe that lasted more than a millennia, are, in my opinion, unfair and unhealthy. Had the West remained on the defensive, we might be speaking Arabic today—or lining our sons up outside thatch huts for Turkish lords to induct as janissaries into slave armies. It seems hypocritical to attack our ancestors for defending themselves against aggression when NATO checked socialist jihad by threatening to nuke a thousand Ma'arras. Would Urban II have agreed to MAD?

Less ambiguous horrors are, unfortunately, not hard to find. It's impossible to deny that self-described Christians played a role in many of these crimes, or that they often found a way to justify them from the Bible.

The New Atheists unconsciously offer a "debating point" by which to escape blame for much of this should we adopt it. If the evil Christians do is a problem for believers, Dawkins and Harris see the good done by the followers of Jesus as a problem for skeptics. Early scientists such as Isaac Newton did "claim" to be religious, Dawkins admits. But that was before Darwin, when atheism wasn't really an option.[11] Harris draws out the logic of the argument:

> It is a truism to say that people of faith have created almost everything of value in our world, because nearly every person who has ever swung a hammer or trimmed a sail has been a devout member of one or another religious culture.[12]

In fact, medievals were less "devout" than we often assume.[13] But if we grant that medieval Europeans were "Christian" in some sense, why should Harris's argument only work *against* religion? If Christianity deserves no credit for plotting the course of planets or writing the Magna Carta because "everyone was religious" when these things were accomplished, why blame it for the Inquisition? The elite were educated in monasteries and religious universities. Just as everyone gives lip service to democracy and science today no matter how big a tyrant or fool he may be, in the Middle Ages Christianity was the "myth" to which propagandists of the day had to appeal, whether to burn a witch or set her free.

Ideas are like Harry Potter's "any flavored candy," or Forrest Gump's chocolates: There is a certain quantum variability to what comes out of the historical selection process at any moment.

Influence is hard to pin down. How can we trace the flow of an idea from its intellectual origins through such a complex, ingenious, and devious organ as the mind and out into human actions?

Look first at the original idea—the seed, the scriptural DNA. When it comes to Christian theology and the New Testament, unlike amino acids in a cell, theological and Scriptural "coding" is written in plain English (or Greek), visible for all to see. We can also plainly see how nature acts "on its own." We've seen nonreligious societies, and can also look at animals and get an idea of how people might act without religious teaching.

Some ideas are *explicit*. The apostles John and Paul wrote about the divinity of Jesus, which is why Christians have always believed him divine. Jesus taught and healed, setting an example for his followers. Other doctrines are *implicit*, and their logic mixes slowly, like juices in a crockpot. The New Testament has little to say about slavery—it's taken for granted, but undermined by pervasive calls to love one another, talk about freedom, and the assumption that Christians form a unified spiritual family. Still other doctrines or practices grow up in the face of commands against them, which we *subvert* for our own purposes. Buddha rebuked a disciple for making love to his wife, but later Buddhists (acted on by common impulses) made peace with sex. Karl Marx prophesied the end of Das Kapital. Deng Xiaoping said "to get rich is glorious," creating "socialism with Chinese characteristics," which turned out to be a form of capitalism.

Most of the reforms I talked about in the last chapter show strong implicit or explicit New Testament warrant. Jesus taught, healed, and told his disciples to do the same. Jesus' followers overstepped class boundaries because their Master systematically erased them. One young Indian leper began crying when Dr. Paul Brand put his hand on the man's shoulder. "Have a I done something wrong?" he asked his assistant. "No, doctor," she responded. "Until he came here no one had touched him for many years."[14] Dr. Brand consciously followed the direct example of Jesus, who healed by touching untouchables.

Jesus and the Inquisition

It's harder to find warrant in the New Testament for torturing heretics. Jesus told no story of a "bad Samaritan" who put a backslider on the rack. Paul was beaten by the state, accused by Jewish enemies, and betrayed by Christian brethren, but never raised a hand in reprisal.

The Inquisition seemed to have three sources: political expedience, Roman precedent, and theological rationalization.

In a sense, torture doesn't need to be "explained." Making someone feel pain until he does what you want is what Daniel Dennett calls a "good trick," and can be witnessed on any playground. Few, if any, civilizations have failed to make use of this trick. Roman law admitted the testimony of slaves only if they were first tortured. Chinese police were, and are, famous for their ingenuity in the art, as were the Soviets. Indian gurus even tortured themselves.

In A.D. 385, the Emperor Maximus had Pricillian and six followers beheaded as heretics, over the protests of Ambrose. St. Augustine took a fateful step down this path when he allowed himself to be talked into the idea that state force could be used against sectarians. Apart from Charlemagne's ruthless campaigns against the Saxons, though, laws that sanctioned the killing of heretics remained mostly "on the books" until the thirteenth century. Then, in response to threats from without (Islam) and heresies within, the church rationalized a series of methods collectively known as the Inquisition. St. Aquinas defined heresy as "a sin which merits not only excommunication but also death."[15] In 1252, Pope Innocent IV allowed inquisitors to use torture so long as it didn't involve bloodshed, mutilation, or death. Over the next few centuries, thousands of heretics—Jews, Muslims, Protestants, and Catholics—were killed for thought-crimes. Many others were tortured.

The model for Dostoevsky's Grand Inquisitor may have been Tomas Torquemada, the "hammer of heretics." A pious and learned man,

Torquemada burnt Talmuds and Islamic literature and helped engineer the expulsion of the Jews from Spain in 1492. Relying on secret denunciations, he had people tortured and delivered to the state for burning. Some 2000 are said to have been killed by the Spanish Inquisition over several centuries.

Hopefully we have learned from history. Ma Bell's unofficial slogan "We don't care because we don't have to" sums up much that is wrong with monopolies, including religious ones. Torture is (at least) a radical form of poor customer service: Buy our product, or else! The government shouldn't be in the business of telling people where to go on Sunday. The church is better off getting knocked around by the media, or even the state, than enduring too much official love. Churches are at their best when they compete for market share through good works.

No one blames Buddha or Confucius for the Japanese Inquisition, which killed as many Catholics as the Spanish killed non-Catholics. Why blame Jesus when people do the opposite of what he taught?

In 1859, a young man from Geneva attempted to meet Napoleon III in the town of Solferino in northern Italy, where he'd just fought a battle. Henri Dunant grew up in a family of devout Calvinists and was mentored in caring for orphans, the sick, the poor, and parolees. Dunant found thousands of wounded men lying about the battlefield, with no one to give them water or tend to injuries. He rallied local townspeople to help. Afterward, he devoted his life to bringing care to the wounded. This work was the origin of the Red Cross and the Geneva Conventions, which have done much to ameliorate human cruelty.

Would Jesus Burn Witches?

Persecution of "witches" is another crime commonly and reasonably laid at the door of the church. Surely this evil wouldn't have occurred apart from religious dogma! Atheists, after all, don't believe in witches.

Bertrand Russell claimed the church murdered "millions of unfortunate women."[16] Dan Brown put the figure at five million. Research has caused historians to radically revise such figures. It now appears some 40,000 were killed, of whom three quarters were women. Most murders occurred in border towns where church and state were both weak. Ironically, the Inquisition actually protected accused witches in Spain.

What role did Christianity play in the persecution of witches? A more complex one than is usually assumed.

The Old Testament does seem to give explicit warrant for what would come: "Do not allow a sorceress to live" (Exodus 22:18). Some modern witches argue, however, that the Hebrew term referred not to Wiccan herbalists, but "black magic."[17]

A maniac rushed up to Jesus, claiming that a "legion" of demons possessed him. While the disciples hid in the bushes, Jesus set the man free, apparently without raising his voice (Mark 5). When a possessed slave girl dogged Paul's footsteps, yelling and disrupting his sermons, he healed her at the cost of getting flogged and thrown into prison himself (Acts 16). With examples such as these, the early church repealed pagan laws against witchcraft. Charlemagne pronounced the death penalty against the "pagan superstition" of burning supposed witches. Canon law described anyone who thought people could fly on beasts in the dead of night as "beyond doubt an infidel," and instructed priests to clear up such nonsense at the grassroots.[18]

There was a lot to clear up. Like everyone else, Europeans had always practiced, and feared, witchcraft. "I curse Tretia Maria and her life and mind and memory and liver and lungs mixed up together," one Greco-Roman tablet read.[19] During the Renaissance, stories with no biblical warrant cropped up—people turning into animals, magical sticks that you merely told, "Go, devil, go!" and would fly you off to a synagogue where (it was assumed) terrible things were going on. The case of Johannes Kepler's mother seems to have been the norm: a sharp-tongued woman in a small town who prescribed herbal remedies was persecuted, for spite and profit, by a former hooker with powerful friends, "people who had wanted some petty vengeance, people who had seen their chance to get their hands on his mother's small estate."[20]

Why did the hunting of witches and widespread belief in the phenomenal powers of the devil become popular just then? Even atheists and skeptics such as Thomas Hobbes and Jean Bodin advocated the killing of witches, the latter of whom wanted it done in the slowest possible fire. Rodney Stark argues it was one of several "collateral results" of conflict between Europe and Arabia. James Connor adds that "like an earthquake," the Reformation "had cracked Western Christianity, stable since the fifth century."[21]

When two tectonic plates meet, volcanoes often erupt at weak points near the subterranean line of contact. Here in the Pacific Northwest, snowy volcanic peaks mark that line about a hundred miles from the sea. So too in Europe, two great civilizations collided. Muslim armies conquered most of the known world, putting Europe on the defensive. Then the Reformation opened up a new "fault line" within Europe. At weak points, Rhone Valley towns where authority was in doubt, violence broke out.

Of course that doesn't excuse Christians who persecuted witches. Stark argues that medieval theologians found witchcraft useful. They needed it to explain why folk herbalists often healed as well as or better than doctors.

But Christians have also protected many "witches." In the Middle Ages, sometimes it was devout Christians who came to their senses first. Puritan pastors in New England condemned the use of "spectral evidence." Two Dai minority villages in southern China were founded by "pipa devils" who had been cast out of their own villages, then befriended and helped by missionaries. The Scottish missionary Mary Slessor once defied a mob commissioned by a Nigerian chief to murder a dozen people he accused of using witchcraft to cause a tree to fall on his son and die. I know Christians called by God to continue to protect people falsely accused of witchcraft in Africa and South America.

The Christian record on witches, then, is mixed.

Witchcraft is only one form of the more general phenomena, however. When a village is threatened by plague, invasion, or cultural unraveling, people often take their anxieties out on those who stand out from the crowd—a poor person, a minority or cripple, perhaps even an especially handsome or rich person, such as Marie Antoinette. This tendency to pick on vulnerable members of a community has deep roots in the psyche and can even be seen among animals. While atheists are not supposed to believe in witches, unbelief by itself doesn't automatically check such impulses.

Rene Girard, the world's leading theorist of scapegoating, sees the Gospels as the historical force that exposed this trick as evil. One example he gives is the story of Peter warming his hands by the fire while Jesus was on trial. Edging up to the fire, Peter joined a little community. The cost of joining it was ritual denunciation of the scapegoat. By denying Jesus, Peter effectively took the side of the oppressors against the innocent. The Bible relentlessly exposes that act as sinful:

> The Gospel is not gentle with persecutors...It unearths even in our most ordinary behavior today, around the fire, the ancient gesture of the Aztec sacrificers and witch-hunters as they forced their victims into the flames.[22]

Scapegoating operates with or without religion. Religious conservatives scapegoat gays, secularists scapegoat believers, and Europe and Arab nations sometimes seem to want to make peace by throwing that little postage-stamp of a state, Israel, to the wolves.

Jesus' words are, therefore, doubly prescient. "Whatever you did for one of the least of these brothers of mine, you did for me" (Matthew 25:40).

Is Christianity Anti-Semitic?

Sam Harris, who is himself Jewish, calls anti-Semitism "intrinsic to both Christianity and Islam," as "integral to church doctrine as the flying buttress is to a Gothic cathedral."[23] Only "the mad work of the Christian church" could have demonized the Jews. In one instance, he notes, 3000 Jews were murdered for desecrating communion bread! By 1933, only a few generations had passed "since the church left off disemboweling innocent men before the eyes of their family, burning old women alive in public squares, and torturing scholars."[24] Harris admits the Nazis didn't care for Christianity either. But hatred of Jews was "a direct inheritance from medieval Christianity."[25] Some Christians, however, did help Jews. Others aided the Nazis, including (Harris claims) Pope Pius XII. Christopher Hitchens also calls Pius XII "pro-Nazi."[26]

Dawkins agrees.[27]

Did Jesus only care about Jews, as Dawkins claimed? Or is Harris right that the gospel teaches us to hate Jews? Perhaps we should leave Dawkins and Harris to hash it out between themselves and come up with a single, coherent accusation. (Or read the New Testament honestly, and admit the patently obvious fact that the Gospels consistently tell us to love everyone!)

But I don't want to be glib. Too many innocent people died. It's understandable if some of their descendants suspect the roots of the problem may lie in the New Testament. But let them read it honestly.

The New Testament is almost entirely a Hebrew composition. Two writers do speak harshly of "the Jews," however. John tells us that the Jews tried to stone Jesus (John 10), and later shouted for his execution (John 18). According to Luke, Paul rebuked the Jews of Rome for "calloused" hearts and ears that "scarcely hear," and promised to preach to the Gentiles instead (Acts 28:27 NASB)—a promise many Jews wish Christians would keep!

An outsider shouldn't talk as freely as members of a family. Rebuking Jews is a very Jewish thing to do. But later abuse of the Hebrew Scriptures to justify anti-Semitism is not only obscene, it is absurd. "Christ-killer"? The whole point of Christianity is that Christ laid his life down for the salvation of all peoples, "first for the Jew, then for the Gentile" (Romans 1:16).

Even in the book of John, Jesus is presented as Jewish. His mother is Jewish, the people he heals are Jewish, and he livens up a Jewish wedding with Israeli wine. He prays to the Jewish God and is raised to life to meet Jewish friends by the Sea of Galilee and catch kosher fish. The Nazis would hardly quote the teaching, also in John, that "salvation is from the Jews" (John 4:22). Nor did they echo Paul when he explained his feelings about his people: "For I could wish that I myself were accursed...for the sake of my brothers" (Romans 9:3).

If you can read anti-Semitism into the New Testament, you can read it into anything.

Not that reading was the strong suit of the medieval pogromists. Laymen were forbidden, by the Council of Narbonne in 1229, to read any part of the Bible. Most people couldn't read anyway! As for priests, in 1222, the Council of Oxford described parish clergy as dumb dogs. In 1551, fewer than half of the priests in Gloucester could name the Ten Commandments.[28] Most popes, of course, did know their Bible, and protected Jews. "Of all the dynasties in Europe," wrote Jewish historian Cecil

Roth, "the papacy not only refused to persecute the Jews...but through the ages popes were protectors of the Jews."[29]

If persecuting Jews isn't taught, explicitly or implicitly, in the New Testament, why did anti-Semitism only appear among Christians and Muslims?

The answer, of course, is that it didn't. Jews were enslaved in Egypt. Queen Esther rescued her people from genocide in Babylonia. Clement of Alexandria, a second-century Christian, defended Jews against the bigotry of his pagan opponent, Celsus. Jews were the focus of Stalin's "doctors' plot" (though fortunately he died before this proscription for disaster was administered). In Japan, millions of copies of anti-Semitic books have been published. The Buddhist sect Aum Shinrikyo put out a tract called *Manual of Fear: The Jewish Ambition—Total World Conquest,* blaming the children of Abraham for the slaughters in Cambodia and Rwanda!

By contrast, over a span of 350 years, America has never seen a pogrom. Jews also seemed to live relatively peacefully in Europe until "eruptions" of violence during the medieval conflict with Islam.

Anti-Semitism, like witch hunting, is part of a larger phenomena. Where haven't minorities come to grief? Koreans in Japan, Chinese in Malaysia, blacks in America, Tutsi in Rwanda—the list is endless.

Most Christians in America agree with Harris that the world owes the Jewish people deeply. In answer to a survey I took, the vast majority of respondents agreed that America should support Israel. Many said they saw the Israeli cause as just, and they didn't care for the tactics of Hamas and the PLO, aside from offering theological or historical justification. I agree that the world—Arabs as well as Europeans—owed the Jewish people a state after World War II, and owe them a chance to live in peace, within protectable borders, today.

What About the Holocaust?

Of course it's a terrible shame that anyone cooperated with the Nazis. That's easy to say, sitting in a leafy twenty-first-century American or English neighborhood! But what is surprising about murder and cowardice from an evolutionary point of view? It's just as Dawkins and Hauser predict: one looks out for one's own, not for the "out-group."

What's surprising is when people risk their lives to save people of another race.

A few years ago, the Israeli embassy set up an exhibit at Nanjing University—a city sensitive to mass murder because of the terrible slaughter the Japanese carried out there during World War II. Along the main road leading into the school, photos and brief biographies told the stories of about 20 people who saved Jews from the Holocaust. Among the four or so Asians, two ascribed their actions to faith in God.

Bulgaria was the only Axis nation that ended the war with more Jews than it began (about 50,000). They would likely have died were it not for the work of three men: Metropolitan Stefan, head of the Orthodox Church in Sofia, Metropolitan Kyril, and Dmitur Peshev, vice president of Parliament and an orthodox Christian. The plan was to ship the Jews to Poland. Kyril threatened to lie across the tracks in front of the first train. He pulled off his robes and climbed the fence into the compound where the Jews were kept, saying, "Wherever you go, I'll go." The prime minister threatened to arrest Metropolitan Stefan for his equally outspoken actions to save Jews, and shut down churches to prevent mass (fake) christenings.[30]

Such examples could be multiplied: Martin Niemöller, who told Hitler to his face, "We too have a responsibility for the German people, laid upon us by God"; Corrie ten Boom and her pious family, who hid Jews in a false room and went to Buchenwald for it; Pastor Andre Trocme, who persuaded the village of Le Chambon to give refuge to 2500 Jews in France. The confessing church was the "sole coherent opposition to Hitler's religious (and therefore racial) policies within Germany."[31]

But since Dawkins and Harris attack Pius in particular, as a Protestant, let me speak in praise of him and the Catholic Church.

The Pius Wars

The role of Pope Pius XII in the Holocaust has been so thoroughly debated that Joseph Bottum wrote an overview optimistically entitled, "The End of the Pius Wars." The debate had become "like a giant game of Whack the Mole: Up pops some new accusation against Pius, splat goes the hammer of critical response, and undeterred up pops the mole somewhere else."[32]

Hitchens writes, "Many Christians gave their lives to protect their fellow creatures in this midnight of the century, but the chance that they did so on orders from any priesthood is statistically almost negligible."[33] (Of course, according to a fisherman named Peter, every Christian is a priest—2 Peter 2:9.) Dawkins claims the Catholic Church supported Hitler. This "support" manifested itself in Pius XII's "persistent refusal" to speak out publicly against the Nazis. Dawkins adds, "Either Hitler's professions of Christianity were sincere, or he faked his Christianity in order to win—successfully—co-operation from German Christians and the Catholic Church."[34]

Jewish leaders often disagree. Israeli historian Pinchas Lapide claimed, on the contrary, that Pius "was instrumental in saving at least 700,000, but probably as many as 860,000 Jews from certain death at Nazi hands."[35] Sir Martin Gilbert, Winston Churchill's official biographer, credited the Catholic Church "under the leadership and with the support of Pope Pius XII," with saving "hundreds of thousands" of Jews.[36] While the extent of his involvement is disputed, if anything close to this is true, these are hardly "negligible" numbers. Golda Meir said, "When fearful martyrdom came to our people, in the decade of the Nazi terror, the voice of the Pope was raised for the victims."[37]

Pius was a cautious and diplomatic man, and operated in Mussolini's shadow in Rome. But among contemporaries, friend and foe, there was little doubt where he stood. In 1937, he helped draft an encyclopedic for his predecessor, Pius XI, which said the Catholic Church was "for all peoples and nations." Therefore, "Whoever exalts race, or the people, or the State, about their standard value and divinizes them to an idolatrous level, distorts and perverts an order of the world planned and created by God." The Nazis caught the drift: "[Pius XI] is virtually accusing the German people of injustice towards the Jews, and making himself the mouthpiece of the Jewish war criminals."[38]

Germany refused to send a representative when Pope Pius XII was installed in 1938. Hitler would later even consider kidnapping the pope, whom the SS called "the chief Rabbi of the Christian world."[39]

True, Pius declined to condemn Hitler publicly, as Roosevelt's State Department asked him to do. This was not because he was "Hitler's pope," but for at least four good reasons that University of Washington historian James Felak suggested to me. First, it was unlikely such a condemnation would have been heeded. Often even Catholics simply ignore inconvenient papal messages, a fact which any survey of American opinion on abortion confirms. Second, public denunciations would probably have backfired. "If you were a Jew hidden in a monastery," Felak asked, "Would you want the pope to speak out publicly?" Quite likely Hitler would have cracked down on Catholic organizations, leading to the arrest of even more Jews. Third, of course, that would have fatally damaged the Catholic Church as well. And fourth, the pope was hoping to play a broker deal between the warring powers, as the papacy had in times past. The State Department did not want him to condemn both Hitler and Stalin together, since America was allied with Stalin.

But the new pope did more than talk. While documents have not been found, many church officials say he instructed them to aid Jews to escape the Holocaust. Castel Gandolfo, the papal estate in the hills 20 miles from Rome, became a refuge not for nine travelers (like Rivendell), but for 500 persecuted Jews. This Gandolfo held no magic wand to protect his friends—just moral authority. The chief rabbi of Rome subsequently converted to Catholicism—so much for "Hitler's Pope."[40]

What about Dawkins's idea that the Nazis were "surely Christian"? One wonders what Dawkins would say to a "Hail Mary" argument like that in a student paper!

In fact, the percent of SS troops who belonged to the Catholic Church plummeted during the war. While six percent of university students studied theology in 1933, when the Nazis took power, that figure fell to only two percent by 1939. If the Nazis were so pro-Christian, why did young people stop studying Dawkins's least-favorite subject? More importantly, why did the Nazis kill thousands of Polish priests? Why did Dachau become "the largest religious community in the world," as William O'Malley put it, with some 2,750 clergymen interned?[41] How did a "solidly Catholic region like Bavaria…end up having no Catholic schools by 1939"?[42] Why, in newly annexed territories, were children and schoolteachers forbidden from belonging to a church?[43]

Hitler hated Christianity and planned to destroy it when the time came, as he explained in private. If the New Atheists want to do the same, let them take a number.

How Does Morality Evolve?

Dawkins supposes that morality marches ever upward. While there are "local and temporary setbacks," such as the Bush administration, "most of us in the twenty-first century are bunched together and way ahead of our counterparts in the Middle Ages, or in the time of Abraham, or even as recently as the 1920s."[44]

The self-congratulatory tone of this effusion is matched only by the naivete on which it is based. Progress in some areas can reasonably be claimed. The police seldom torture suspects in Western countries, and a public display like the killing of William Wallace as depicted in the movie *Braveheart*, or the actual martyrdom of the three Anglican bishops whose memorials stand in the center of Oxford, or the 26 martyrs above the train station in Nagasaki, is now unimaginable in most countries. But the bloody pillaging of South America by the Spanish, and even the Atlantic slave trade, saw their matches and more (in absolute numbers) during the twentieth century.

John Wesley described Africans as capable craftsmen, courteous, moderate, and students of the stars. A century later, Social Darwinians compared the same people to apes, and justified not just slavery, but annihilation. With no sense of irony, Alfred Kirchhoff's *Darwinism Applied to Peoples and States* suggested the "extermination of the crude, immoral hordes."[45] Clearly he agreed with Dawkins that morality evolves, with "bright" Europeans standing at the apex.

Moral values don't rise in a straight line, like a balloon (shall I say it?) full of hot air. They rise and descend in a wavelike trajectory, caught by the magnetic pull of ideas.

Robert Coles tells the story of a six-year-old black girl he met in New Orleans, the first to attend a formerly all-white school. Every day adults waited at the gate to scream obscenities and threats as she passed. After getting to know the little girl, he found to his shock that she looked back just before entering school to pray for the people yelling at her. Why? "Because they needed praying for," she explained, and because Jesus forgave his enemies from the cross.[46]

That's what I call progress.

Some 2000 years ago, the apostle Paul wrote,

> Love is patient, love is kind. It does not envy, it does not boast, it is not proud. It is not rude, it is not self-seeking, it is not easily angered, it keeps no record of wrongs. Love does not delight in evil but rejoices with the truth. It always protects, always trusts, always hopes, always perseveres (1 Corinthians 13:4-7).

That stops me in my tracks every time I read it. How many of those boxes can Dawkins, Harris, and Hitchens check? Was Paul 2000 years ahead of the moral curve, or are we two millennia behind it? Or can right and wrong be measured by the clock? How do we know the New Testament isn't driving any improvements that are being made?

Consider two Nobel Peace Prize laureates: Mother Teresa (1979) and Yasser Arafat (1994). Sam Harris describes Teresa as a "good person" whose moral intuitions have been "deranged by religious faith." This derangement was exhibited in her Nobel Peace Prize acceptance speech, when she decried abortion as "the greatest destroyer of peace."[47] Dawkins calls her "sanctimoniously hypocritical," proving that a professor who lives on a quiet street in Oxford has the guts to take on a five-foot-tall Albanian nun who washed pus from the face of Calcutta street people (at least after she's dead). Hitchens went so far as to write a book with an obscene title debunking Mother Teresa.

But both Arafat and Teresa were moral innovators, and therefore test Dawkins's theory of progress. Arafat helped invent the hijacking. This involves seizing an airplane full of strangers and threatening to blow them to pieces thousands of feet in the air unless your demands are met. Arafat also explored ways of blowing up land-based civilians, including schoolchildren. His coup de théâtre came in 1972, when Palestinian terrorists murdered 11 Israeli athletes at the Munich Olympics. In other spheres, Arafat broke less ground. He amassed about a billion dollars through drugs, shakedowns, gunrunning, and siphoning off money meant for his people. Then he died, whether of poisoning or AIDS (he was a man of many appetites) is debated.[48] "Bright" Norwegians awarded Arafat the Nobel Peace Prize during a lull in the storm.

Mother Teresa, by contrast, founded the Missionaries of Charity. She took the dying off the streets, fed them, washed their wounds, and prayed for them. Her followers continue to care for "the hungry, the naked, the homeless, the crippled, the blind, the lepers, all those people who feel unwanted, unloved, uncared for throughout society."[49] Some accuse them of telling their patients that God loves them. There are even dark hints that they baptize the dying.

In Bombay I met one of Teresa's victims. He was born a Brahmin, then cast out of his family for converting to communism. When he developed asthma, his comrades abandoned him as well. The opportunistic Sisters of Charity swooped down on this prize human skeleton and gave him food and shelter.

Teresa wasn't a physician or talented administrator. She may have been politically naïve. But most people feel that the Nobel Peace Prize committee honored itself with the prize. A true step of moral progress came when a short Albanian nun copied Jesus by stopping, as he did, for a blind beggar or street person.

Is it a moral advance to vilify a little old lady who spent her life wiping tears from the faces of the dying because one dislikes her religion? Or to accuse a pope who likely saved hundreds of thousands of lives in order to get at the Catholic Church? Is that an improvement on Jesus' archaic "Love your enemies," or Paul's primitive "Love hopes all things"? For that matter, does it improve on Lao Zi ("What heaven succors it protects with the gift of compassion"), Confucius ("When you meet someone better than yourself, turn your thoughts to becoming his equal") or the Buddha ("Foolish people who scoff at the teachings of the wise, the noble, and the good, following false doctrines, bring about their own downfall like the khattaka tree, which dies after bearing fruit")?[48]

The Way is the Way, and cannot be changed. Two kinds of moral innovation are possible, however. You can isolate one precept from the rest—purity, justice, love of one's people—and turn it into madness. Or you can build higher on these old and sure foundations.

Putting It All in Perspective

What should we conclude? Not that any belief system is harmless. Every group of believers or unbelievers who gain power, especially a monopoly of power, oppresses: polytheists, atheists, Christians, Muslims, Hindus and yes, Buddhists. (How do these naive Westerners think the first Dalai Lama came to power?) No successful ideology is free from the shedding of innocent blood.

So what's the problem—ideology or human nature? Should believers stay out of politics? And instead, meditate in the hills, or starve themselves and breathe through cloth to avoid harming paramecium?

"Accepting Jesus" does not, I admit, magically transform the beast within. Jesus didn't say it would. He once rebuked his followers for wanting to call fire from heaven on a disinterested village (Luke 9:54-55). If the Christian share of crimes may seem large, I think that's for four reasons. First, the "Christian" West gained the power to rule most of the world. Second, we know our own history better, and therefore, so does everyone else. Third, there is a lot of dishonest propaganda going around. And finally, I think the world expects more from followers of Jesus. Whatever they say, even skeptics know in their hearts that Jesus is good. The whipping of slaves, burning of heretics, pogroms against minorities, and the scandalous personal lives of "televangelists" become obscene not because of evolution, but in the light of the gospel. In the greater scheme of things, Torquemada is the evolutionary norm, a symptom of the Fall. Mother Teresa is harder to explain, which may be why New Atheists try so hard to explain her away.

Teachers and parents have a special responsibility for how we focus and strengthen the intense moral awareness of the young. They may act like savages, but they expect to be taught better. Morality doesn't progress automatically. It relapses when we forget what we've learned, or suppress what we "can't help knowing." A lot of that happened in the twentieth century.

What About the "American Taliban"?

"She was truly devout, poor herself and charitable
not only to the poor but also to the rich."

—Victor Hugo[1]

R ichard Dawkins introduces us to Keenan Roberts, a pastor in
Colorado who runs "hell houses." In these institutions, actors depict
abortionists and homosexuals screaming under torture under the gloating
supervision of the devil. Children (optimum age: 12) are brought to
these delightful theme parks to see what to expect if they die in their
sins. This, a shocked Richard Dawkins informs us, is what "mainstream"
religion has become in America today.[2]

Dawkins may not believe in hell, but he believes in the tactic. With
Sam Harris riding shotgun (or, one might say, pitchfork), he guides us
through that Hell House of religious fanaticism called America. Among
others, he interviews a Lutheran terrorist who shot an abortion doctor
and his bodyguard. He tells about a boy who wore Christian "hate
speech" on a T-shirt to school. He drops in on political figures who
blame a lesbian for the destruction of New Orleans, or run on a platform
of "intolerance," "hatred," and "theocracy." Dawkins notes, ominously,
that while the person who made these campaign promises, an activist
named Randall Terry, is "not yet" in power, "no observer of the American
political scene at the time of writing can afford to be sanguine."[3]

A number of recent and popular American books confirm the general outlines of this story. Michele Goldberg writes darkly in *Kingdom*

173

174 ⚖ The Truth Behind the New Atheism

Coming (New York: W.W. Norton, 2007) of a gathering theocratic storm. Kevin Phillips warns of *American Theocracy* (New York: Viking, 2006)— a book Dawkins cites. Chris Hedges paints a particularly dark picture in *American Fascists: The Christian Right and the War on America* (New York: Simon & Schuster, 2006). Sam Harris points to an article by sociologist Gregory Paul that suggests Christianity in America correlates to a higher rate of murder, unwed pregnancy, and, yes, abortion.[4] Even Jimmy Carter suggests that right-wing Christians support Israeli attacks on the Arabs in order to bring about World War III and the return of Christ.[5]

America has become a polarized society, and those who dislike religion often acquire atheism in the context of hard-fought political battles over abortion or gay rights. Non-American readers may find these images of a superpower run by religious fanatics titillating, as apocalyptic myths often are.

But while the United States no doubt has its share of fanatics and odious preachers, the general truth is radically different. Look closely at the facts, and it becomes clear that the critics not only are wrong, but generally don't even know what they're talking about. I will argue not only that Christianity has done America good in the past, but that serious followers of Jesus, far from being a threat to democracy or their neighbors, act as what Jesus called the "salt of the earth" (Matthew 5:13), preserving the best qualities of American society.

A Few Easy Targets, To Warm Up

Richard Dawkins's case against Christianity in America is essentially anecdotal, while Sam Harris makes use of more systematic data. Visit Madame Tussaud's wax museum, and you'll want to see Jack the Ripper. In many tours of the American Hell House, Pat Robertson plays a similar function. (Hedges calls James Dobson and Pat Robertson the "ruling elite" of American fascism.[6]) Dawkins offers two stories:

> In 2005, the fine city of New Orleans was catastrophically flooded in the aftermath of a hurricane, Katrina. The Reverend Pat Robertson, one of America's best-known televangelists and a former presidential candidate, was reported as blaming the hurricane on a lesbian comedian who happened to live in New Orleans. You'd

think an omnipotent God would adopt a slightly more targeted approach to zapping sinners...[7]

In a footnote Dawkins admits he's not sure if the story, which he found on the Web, is true. But "whether true or not," it's relevant because "it is entirely typical of utterances by evangelical clergy...on disasters such as Katrina."

One is numbed at first by the fatuity of the reasoning. Then, like drops of dew gathering around flakes of dust in the stratosphere, unease precipitates fast and furiously into questions.

First, how many readers trouble to read footnotes? Given that some don't, wouldn't it be better to admit uncertainty about something so basic as the accuracy of a damning quote in the body of the text?

Second, if the quote is so typical (and Robertson does say some very foolish things), why not offer one known to be accurate? It turns out this one was invented by the spoof Web site Dateline Hollywood, which explains on the site's "About" page:

> Dateline Hollywood was founded in 360 B.C. as "Gladiators Weekly" to cover the booming entertainment industry in the coliseums of ancient Rome. Its pioneering analysis of the statistics of lion mauls and emperor thumbs up/down made it the original publication to take the business of entertainment seriously.[8]

Third, isn't it a bit undignified for a respected Oxford professor to mine Internet "gotcha" quotes that he isn't sure are accurate to attack the faith that created his civilization? (And even his university?)

Dawkins wants us to think Robertson's failed candidacy in 1988 renders crude comments he made (maybe) some 20 years later "mainstream." But anyone who is of age, not a convicted felon, and a native citizen has the right to run for president of the United States. It helps if, like Robertson, you're rich.

Dawkins then quotes Robertson (citing a BBC Web page this time) saying that God won't protect the people of Dover, Pennsylvania, because they voted proponents of Intelligent Design out of office. Dawkins concludes, "Pat Robertson would be harmless comedy, were he less typical of those who today hold power and influence in the United States."[9]

It is surprising how much of Dawkins' case against American Christianity is of this nature. Dawkins points to a quote from Ann Coulter, which he also found on the Internet, as Exhibit A: "We should invade their countries, kill their leaders and convert them to Christianity."[10] He takes this quite seriously, having no idea who Coulter is, and not knowing that (like Michael Moore or Gore Vidal) she is a star of political soaps. "Come on, Bill" she'll explain to an interviewer with a wink, "you have to take it in context!" Dawkins implies that Randall Terry, who promised "theocracy" and "hatred," is about to be elected to high office. In fact, Terry ran for the state legislature in a conservative district in Florida and lost badly.

By contrast to Robertson or Terry, George Galloway, a Scottish politician who publicly rhapsodizes over the thought of Tony Blair being killed and the charms of Saddam Hussein, is an elected member of the British Parliament. Galloway's extravagant foolishness is the subject of similar urban legends. One might cite him (in some cases accurately) calling the collapse of the Soviet Union the great catastrophe of his life, or fawning over Saddam Hussein, and conclude, "George Galloway would be harmless comedy, were he less typical of those who today hold power and influence in Britain." If a failed local politician in Florida or a blowhard televangelist portend theocracy and fascism in America, what sort of omen should we take Galloway's more successful career to be? Does this mean Old Trafford (where the Manchester United soccer team plays) will soon be used to behead English children who fly kites? If every nation were defined by its nuts, we would need to cage the planet to keep the squirrels out.

Of course, Dawkins's sloppiness doesn't prove his concerns about "Christian terrorism" and the "American Taliban" are entirely imaginary. But they show why we need to be wary of political pig-piles and generalizations from a distance based on a few suspect sources. Let's look more closely at Dawkins's more serious concerns and at what American Christians really think about politics.

Christian Terrorism?

Dawkins spends three pages on Paul Hill, a Lutheran minister who was executed in Florida for killing an abortion doctor. Interviewing his confederate, Michael Bray, Dawkins found a serious and even likeable young man. Hill was not a psychopath, he concluded—"just very religious...dangerously religious."[11]

But there's a twist: Hill was executed under Florida governor Jeb Bush, the president's brother. If a company of like-minded extremists is about to take over the United States, with George Bush "typical" of that movement,[12] why is his brother (also a Republican) executing the vanguard? America is supposedly on the verge of a Taliban takeover because George Bush, a right-wing Christian who executes killers and dislikes abortion, is in office. A Lutheran pastor shoots an abortion doctor, and is executed by the president's own brother! It seems the American Taliban has begun eating its own.

And why does Dawkins spend so much time on Hill in a country where more than 200 million people see themselves as Christians? Are there no other ideological terrorists in America to worry over?

There are. Jim Jones, a New Age Marxist (he reportedly claimed to have been Lenin in a past life!), encouraged 900 followers to kill themselves in a dramatic act of assisted suicide. The Unabomber, whom we will meet later, was a "bright" if ever there was one. He taught math at UC Berkeley and blew up two dozen or so innocent people in a seriously misguided attempt to slow the dehumanizing spread of technology. An agnostic named Timothy McVeigh blew up 168 people in Oklahoma City. Buford Furrow, a member of a group called Christian Identity, shot three people to death at a Jewish community center in Los Angeles. (Dawkins probably realizes that "Christian Identity" is hard to recognize as orthodox Christian, even when it isn't killing folk.) And America had already endured the first World Trade Center bombing, sarin gas through the mail, Muslim gunmen, the second World Trade Center bombing, and a successful attack on the Pentagon.

In a predominately Christian country in grave threat of conquest by the "American Taliban," Dawkins finds one Christian terrorist who killed two people. No reasonable Christian would blame our skeptical or Muslim neighbors for the hundreds or thousands who have died at the hands of fanatics who place themselves in those camps. That Dawkins focuses on such an exceptional case to represent the danger of Christianity in America involves no small act of stacking the deck and a de facto admission of how hard it is to find American Christians who are also terrorists.

Does Faith Up the Murder Rate?

At this point, Harris rides to the rescue with a broader set of data. Perhaps it can be shown that American Christians are a generally violent lot, Harris suggests, citing sociologist Gregory Paul. Conservative Christians, as is well known, tend to support the Republican party. It turns out that 62 percent of cities with a lower crime rate are in Democratic states. 76 percent of the most violent are in red (Republican) states. Dawkins injects a note of caution: "correlative evidence is never conclusive."[13] But obviously all three men think they are on to something.

"Correlative evidence"? In fact, while Paul's study was widely cited in the media, there is no real evidence at all here. What is the claim? That murders increase during Mardi Gras (New Orleans has the highest murder rate in America) because people are out of sorts from fasting? That crack sellers whose turf battles up the murder rate in Washington, DC (where homocide is second in the nation) crowd into church on Wednesday night to study the book of Colossians?

Every serious observer of American society knows why the murder rate is higher in some cities than in others. It isn't Republican politics: Every large American city is overwhelmingly Democratic, New Orleans and Washington, DC in particular. (Colorado Springs, however, home of Focus on the Family and where Dawkins interviewed Bray, has one-tenth the murder rate of Washington, DC—and voted for Bush over Kerry two to one.) It isn't a matter of a denser concentration of Sunday school teachers. The difference is cultural: a difference between the breakdown of extroverted cultures and the slower breakdown of more introverted cultures. Half of all murders in America are committed by blacks, mostly young and male. Northern Europeans are more inclined to self-murder. (The suicide rate in Europe, especially Scandinavia, is thus the mirror image of the murder rate in America.)

I don't deny, however, that there can be a relationship between Christian faith and crime. I've met many former criminals who became Christians because of the desperation engendered by drug addiction. I've known ex-gangsters who started large churches in neighborhoods where Christians were rare.

A study by David Larson of the National Institute for Healthcare Research found that church-going cut crime and other risks among young black males in poor inner-city neighborhoods by 50 percent. Felons who attend Prison Fellowship Bible studies (founded by Chuck Colson) are two-thirds less likely to reoffend. John DiIulio, a political scientist at Princeton, argues that the church, applying "tough love" and other biblical principles, is the one institution that has given real help to the people who live in the poorest American neighborhoods:

> I know that most volunteers in this country are people of faith. Most charitable dollars are church dollars...But...the biggest asset of the Christian community is Christianity.[14]

What's the difference between these two perspectives? Paul is looking at American society from 10,000 feet in the air. (One can play all sorts of games with statistics from that distance—in "Does God up the Murder Rate?" I describe many of the games Paul plays, which render his study essentially worthless, despite all the media attention it gained.[15]) DiIulio, by contrast, talks with real people in the slums and observes what really affects their lives.

Do Christians Want Theocracy?

All right—so Christians are not going to establish theocracy through violence, nor does Christianity engender violence. But isn't it true that a major Christian movement, called Reconstructionism, aims to establish the biblical analogue of sharia law in American?

"If secularists are not vigilant," Dawkins warns, Christians will establish "a true American theocracy."[16] But what evidence is there that American Christians want such a thing?

I grew up in conservative American churches (including the Presbyterian Church in America, which Hedges describes as a particularly dangerous "schismatic sect"[17]). I don't remember anyone telling us to vote Republican. Since then, I've visited over 300 fellowships around the world, almost all evangelical, of many affiliations. I know these people better, I think, than Jewish journalists from the Bronx such as

Goldberg, or *New York Times* writers from Harvard Divinity School, such as Hedges. (As for Dawkins, I'd be happy to give him a tour of churches in Oxford if he'll give me a tour of pubs!)

In four-and-a-half decades, I don't think I've ever heard a Christian pastor advocate theocracy. Nor have I heard any tell us to assault unbelievers. I have heard pastors talk about loving our enemies. I even heard one sermon (from David Aikman) about taking secular journalists out for lunch!

What do Christians think about faith and politics?

I surveyed two groups of conservative Christians. The first was at Westside Presbyterian Church, which belongs to the evangelical wing of the largest Presbyterian denomination in the country. (My parents met there more than 50 years ago.) The second was at Cedar Park Assembly, one of the most politically active and conservative large congregations in the Northwest. Almost everyone who responded to my survey was conservative politically and had been a Christian for more than three decades.

Given all that has been written about the "American Taliban," how do you expect such members of the "indoctrinated elite" to respond to the statement, "America does not need a Constitution. The Bible provides the best specific rules for a legal system in a Christian country?" Of the 58 people who answered my survey, not one agreed. Over 90 percent thought, on the contrary, that the Constitution should be interpreted more strictly.

How should the Bible apply to public policy? I asked, "How does the Old Testament legal system apply today?" Most agreed with the statement, "The Old Testament legal system was for a particular period in history, and should not be applied wholesale to modern America." Some were dissatisfied with the choices I offered and wrote in alternatives such as, "The Old Testament law was fulfilled in Christ, and its principles, though not necessarily its specific, historically limited consequences, are still very applicable."

True, a large minority at Cedar Park (42 percent) agreed that "the government should favor Christian belief." (Only two at the Presbyterian church thought so.) But that would be the status quo in England. Cedar Park is at the forefront of opposing same-sex marriage in Washington state. Yet only 20 percent of these highly committed believers agreed that homosexual acts should be prosecuted. (Far fewer of the evangelical Presbyterians did.) Although Dawkins interviewed an American Christian who thought adulterers should be executed, no one in my survey even agreed that "witches should be put to death, as in the Old Testament."

The claim that American democracy hangs by a thread—and is kept together by secular termites holding hands—appears greatly exaggerated. Out of 42 statements on the survey, the most popular was the claim that "America was founded on Christian principles." While this can mean many things, it certainly doesn't mean American Christians think democratic and Constitutional government is a bad thing!

What Taliban?

The phrase "American Taliban," which Dawkins uses often, sums up the apocalyptic visions of the New Atheists and their allies well. "The Afghan Taliban and the American Taliban," he warns, "provide a horrifying modern enactment of what life might have been like under the theocracy of the Old Testament."[18]

The Taliban was a movement of Pashtun tribesmen from southern Afghanistan whose armies conquered most of that country and imposed a rigid form of Islam upon the population. Under their rule, women weren't allowed to work or study. Music was forbidden. Taliban leaflets warned, "If any music cassette [is] found in a shop, the shopkeeper should be imprisoned and the shop locked."[19] Kite shops were abolished, and pigeons (popular for racing) were killed. A soccer field built with Western aid was inaugurated with an execution between the goalposts. Ancient Buddhas carved on a mountainside were blown up. Those who flew airplanes into skyscrapers were vouchsafed a "right of refuge."

Do the New Atheists expect the armies of the "American Taliban" to march on Washington? Are Christians planning to ban music? Rock, classical and—of course—Gospel emerged from church music to begin with. Bernard Lewis marks polyphony—harmony or counterpoint in a choir, ensemble, or orchestra—as a defining quality of Western civilization.[20] Do the Southern Baptists plan to keep their women indoors? (That would empty their churches!) Are believers set to blow up Mount

Rushmore now that Dawkins has outed the founding fathers as near-atheists?

But of course the purpose of Hell House is not to offer a realistic description of subterranean geological structures. Dawkins wants us to see devils and feel appropriately scared.

Aside from the wax villains Dawkins points to, the "radical agenda" for the real "American Taliban" appears to consist of three main planks: (1) Marriage is best carried out between people of opposite sexes; (2) the birth of children is preferable to their deaths (this from the same religion that outlawed infanticide and lions shredding people in the arena); and (3) students might usefully be informed that there are books that express skepticism toward the purely material explanations of origins.

Leaving the rights and wrongs of these issues aside, it seems to me these are legitimate public policy issues for people in a democracy to discuss.

Harris mocks Christians for protecting the life of a blastocyst, a three-day-old human of 100 or so cells, "souls in a Petri dish."[21] For a person who shakes his fist at God for allowing children to be abused, is this the most cautious position? Just a generation or two ago, neo-pagans and Enlightenment atheists killed millions of "subhuman" Jews and "cow devils and snake spirits." The influential philosopher Peter Singer tells us now that subpar children are worth less than a pig or dog. Some old folks in "progressive" Holland now die involuntarily at the hands of their own doctors. Female infanticide is reappearing in China and India.[22] (among all religious communities in India, but most rarely among Christians, the Indian census shows).

Wherever you draw the line between human and nonhuman, isn't it obvious that the gospel of Jesus stands on the right side of it? In fact, it was usually the gospel that drew the line.

If the alleged parallels between the Christian right and the Taliban don't lie in policy, perhaps they lie in how Christians intend to achieve them? But the Taliban achieves their goals with bullets. American Christians have tried to achieve theirs by voting for politicians who agree and lobbying elected representatives.

Are the two "Talibans" allied, then? But it was a candidate of the religious right in America and the most pious British prime minister in decades who worked together to overthrow the Afghan Taliban and restore music, kites, and schools to the children of Afghanistan.

Peculiar media figures and oddball fanatics aside, I suspect the myth of the "American Taliban" is driven less by empirical fact than by theory. The "American Taliban" is a kind of "missing link" deduced from a Dawkinsian view of religion.

One of the unspoken laws of post-9/11 discourse seems to be that if one must speak ill of Islam publicly, one must show how the same criticism applies to Christianity. For every evil non-Christian religious act or movement that occurs or exists, there must be an equal or greater Christian act or movement that corresponds. A similar theory of symphonic skullduggery was popular before the threat was Islam. In 1993, Presbyterian pastor Robert McNeilly wrote in *The New York Times* that American Christians were "even more" dangerous than communists, though the latter had killed 100 million innocent people.[23] (During the Cold War itself, many pastors of that sort actually seemed to see Communism as a pretty good idea.)

How Bad Was Hebrew Theocracy?

American Christians, we have seen, do not want to return to the theocracy of the Old Testament. We don't think it applies to us, at least not as a detailed legal code. Jesus said, "Give to Caesar the things that are Caesar's," and for thousands of years, Christians have taken that as a warrant for developing space between church and state.

But was Hebrew theocracy really so regressive? Not compared to modern Oxford or Palo Alto, of course, but to other ancient Middle Eastern states, or even to the Afghanistan of A.D. 2000?

Unlike the Taliban, ancient Jews loved music: Psalm 150 mentioned eight instruments with which to praise God, along with dancing. Women could and did do business. Barley and fruit was left in fields for the poor to harvest. Holidays were set aside for community camping and feasting. Having lived among Taiwanese shopkeepers who work 16 hours a day seven days a week, I agree with Thomas Cahill, who called the Sabbath "one of the simplest and sanest recommendations any god has ever made."[24]

Historian Donald Treadgold points out that Israel was the only state in the ancient near Middle East with much freedom. "Hebrew society was unique in the ancient near East in managing to avoid the techniques, devices, and institutions of despotism."[25]

We don't want to go back to stoning idol-worshippers, or burning heretics, as in Renaissance Europe. But for the time, in important ways ancient Israel represented great progress.

But Dawkins's most virulent and ominous argument against contemporary Christianity has to do with children.

The Case Against Letting Christians Raise Kids

Dawkins tells how a boy in Ohio won, in court, the right to wear a T-shirt that says, "Homosexuality is a sin, Islam is a lie, abortion is murder. Some issues are just black and white!" Dawkins comments that the parents "couldn't" have defended their son's right to wear such a shirt, "because free speech is deemed not to include 'hate speech.'"[26]

Apparently the judge in the case disagreed.

Such a T-shirt may not violate either school rules or the Constitution, but does, I think, violate the teachings of the apostle Paul, who said Christians should speak the truth in love (Ephesians 4:15). But is this really "hate speech"? The shirt calls certain behaviors (abortion and homosexuality) wrong, and a certain belief (Islam) false. Why define the expression of such views as "hatred"? If the Constitution doesn't let us say something is wrong or false, what good is it?

On the very next page, Dawkins accuses a group of Muslims of a "tendentious lie." Indeed that's about the kindest comment he gives on theistic religions (recall Dawkins's 23-adjective assault on Yahweh: "misogenist, homophobic, racist, infanticidal, genocidal..."). So why is a 12-year-old American boy guilty of a "hate crime" for a frankness that earns a British professor fame and fortune?

Similar hypocrisy is more ominously on display later in the book. Dawkins represents James Dobson ("founder of today's infamous 'Focus on the Family' movement") as the "sinister" modern-day equivalent of the Jesuit who said, "Give me the child for his first seven years, and I'll give you the man." Driving through Colorado, Dawkins spots a bumper sticker that reads, "Focus on your own damn family," laughing in agreement. But mulling it over, he ponders, "Maybe some children need to be protected from indoctrination by their own parents"[27] (see chapter 9).

Having read some of Dobson's books and listened to him on the radio over the years, I doubt he has ever advocated taking children away from their (nonabusive) parents. On the contrary, his listeners (among whom Dawkins is obviously not one) often hear him encourage parents to be intimately involved in the lives of their children. Dobson is precisely about focusing on our own families.

By contrast, in the final sentence of the line quoted, Dawkins admits his own intention to "focus on," or intrude in, other peoples' families. He develops this idea (as promised) in chapter 9. In that chapter, he begins with the story of a Jewish child in Italy who was taken from his parents by the Catholic Church to be raised as a Christian. After telling us he "dislikes unfairness even more" than religion, Dawkins says that being brought up Catholic is "undoubtedly" worse than child abuse![28] Relating a few horror stories to justify the absurdity, he quotes, with (lightly qualified) approval, the following comments by psychologist Nicholas Humphreys:

> Children have a right not to have their minds addled by nonsense, and we as a society have a duty to protect them from it. So we should no more allow parents to teach their children to believe, for example, in the literal truth of the Bible...than we should allow parents to knock their children's teeth out or lock them in a dungeon.[29]

What happened to "focus on your own family"?

Dawkins began the chapter by horrifying us with the case of a child being taken from a family that taught him the wrong religion. Before many pages have passed, he wants us to feel horror for exactly the opposite reason: parents are allowed to teach kids any religion. The Catholics were narrow for saying only one religion was true. Dawkins is more broad-minded: he thinks children have a right to be indoctrinated into thinking they're all evil, no matter what their parents say. Harris also complains about the "failure of our schools to announce the death of God in a way that each generation can understand."[30]

But, you might remind me, the case of the Jewish child is true, while Dawkins has not kidnapped any religious children. (Nor do I expect him to—he lets his mouth and the zeal of his young friend Harris run away with him at times...or perhaps it is the other way around.) But the question is more than theoretical. Religious children in Communist countries were often taken away from their parents for precisely the reasons Dawkins gives. Sergei Kourdakov grew up in an orphanage in Siberia. He tells a horrifying story of how a boy called the Deacon was beaten and abused for his faith:

> It was later that I learned his mother and father were believers in God and lived in Orgutsovo, only seventeen miles away. Because they were believers and had taught the Deacon about God, they had been brought before a judge, declared unfit parents, and stripped of their parental rights for life. He would never see his mother and father again, even though they were only seventeen miles away...The little Deacon was my first contact with anybody who believed in God, and I will never forget him.[31]

Pardon me if I find Dawkins's thinking on this subject a bit ominous.

Harvard psychologist Robert Coles, Pulitzer Prize-winning author of *Children of Crisis* (the product of decades of research), doesn't share Dawkins's (or the Soviet state's) gloomy view of the role of faith in the upbringing of children. Like DiIulio, rather than culling horror stories from the Internet or *The New York Times,* Coles tells down-to-earth stories of how Christian faith helps children he has come to know personally. He summarizes, "In 20 years of work among poor people here and abroad, I have found Christ's life a constant source of inspiration to this century's poor."[32]

Nor is all the inspiration just emotional. As DiIulio suggested, there is solid empirical evidence that religious faith not only makes people feel better, but also makes them act a whole lot better, on average.

Who Really Cares?

In his recent book *Who Really Cares,* Arthur Brooks, professor of public administration at Syracuse University, summarizes years of research on giving and other forms of charity and generosity in the United States and, to a lesser extent, Europe. He found that people with strong religious beliefs are far more generous than unbelievers. People who go to a worship service once or more a week give $2,210 to charity a year, while people who seldom or never attend average $642.[33] They also volunteer twice as much. They even give more to secular causes than people without religious faith!

No European country is in the same league as Americans when it comes to private giving: "The closest nation, Spain, has average giving that is less than half that of the United States."[34] Americans give three and a half times as much as the French, seven times as much as the Germans, and 14 times as much as the Italians. Americans are far more likely to volunteer, help a stranger, even give money back when given too much at the store. Brooks shows that religious people in Europe are also more generous. All the studies seem to agree: "Religious people are, inarguably, more charitable *in every measurable way*."[35]

People involved in a healthy church know what Brooks is talking about. We see people volunteer in prisons, stop on street corners to help beggars, go overseas as doctors to poor countries, and go around (as my parents do) to visit shut-ins, take food to the sick, fix roofs and toilets and sinks. One can find such people in the streets and prisons of Oxford, even offering a slice of cheese in the name of the Lord to foreign students. Dawkins ignores all these people just as he ignores the institutional evidence all around him—the great university, once a monastery, at which he works—that the Christian faith created much of what he loves.

Even some atheists have expressed embarrassment at the tone Dawkins in particular adopts. He chooses as dialogue partners the stupidest Christians he can find, portraying the loopy as normal. He compliments himself for "honesty," but accuses a child of "hate crimes" for saying the same thing! He compares American Christianity to the Taliban, and says the Nazis were Christian. He even hints at measures against Christian parents.

My argument is not just that some skeptics go overboard in their criticism of Christianity. We have seen that there is objective evidence that whatever its problems, in some ways the American church still does

188 ❦ The Truth Behind the New Atheism

act as "the salt of the earth," as Jesus said, preserving the good in society, or "the light of the world," illuminating our path in the right direction.

Most of the problems of the church (sexual immorality, cultists, self-righteousness, inordinate fear of science) come when we ignore the gospel, or the best (and worst) of Christian history. The real problem with American Christianity is that we are not yet nearly Christian enough.

Can Atheism Make the World Better?

"It is obvious that a high level of education in a general sense has often failed to protect twentieth-century minds from homicidal, or suicidal, aberrations. As we have seen, these have often been generated by men of high educational standing. And it has often been in colleges and universities that the bad seeds first bore fruit."

—Robert Conquest[1]

"I may, it is true, twist orthodoxy so as partly to justify a tyrant. But I can easily make up a German philosophy to justify him entirely."

—G.K. Chesterton[2]

"Human culture is predisposed to the permanent concealment of its origins in collective violence."

—Rene Girard[3]

Sam Harris is brutally candid. What kind of God would let a man "rape, torture, and kill" a little girl?[4] What was God up to when a tsunami struck Asia and 100,000 children were "simultaneously torn from their mother's arms and casually drowned"?[5] Hearing such stories, I'm almost ready to shake my fist at the sky, too. I have no idea why God allows such things. I often ask, but have been given no reply. This ancient argument against God is renewed every day in the news, in prayer requests, and in accounts of, say, how smallpox devastated the Native Americans.

But if one hates suffering, shouldn't one applaud the religion whose followers invented science, the modern hospital, and the Red Cross, and helped end slavery, the caste system, foot-binding, and widow burning? Yet Harris is equally passionate in his dislike for Christianity.

As critics add to the list of Christian crimes—inquisitions, theocracies, Nazism, terror, child-molesting priests, pigheadedness, bad test scores, bad poetry (compared, at least, to Shakespeare)—even the sleepiest reader is bound to raise an eyebrow. "What about old Joe Stalin? He was an atheist, wasn't he? And didn't he kill a lot of people?"

He was, and he did. On an *average* wintry day of Stalin's 25-year reign, he and his comrades processed more souls across the River Styx than were killed in *three centuries* of the Spanish Inquisition, from Argentina to Andalucia. Yet skeptics bring up the Inquisition relentlessly (it's mentioned on 21 pages of *The End of Faith* and *The God Delusion*). The New Atheists are like the rabbit in C.S. Lewis's Chronicles of Narnia who sits by the Great Waterfall and hears a pin drop in a castle at the far end of the country.

Dawkins and Harris have heard this objection. Stalin is therefore mentioned on nine pages of their books, usually as a problem to be solved, or "debating point," as Dawkins puts it.

This isn't just a "debating point" to me. I researched faith and communism under Donald Treadgold, a leading historian of Marxism-Leninism. I've eaten meals with people who lost loved ones or spent decades in prison for their faith. So I'm prepared to take up the question of what atheism had to do with the Gulag, and will do so shortly.

But Stalin wasn't the only atheist of modern times. Nor did he emerge from a vacuum. What have atheism and Darwinian ethics done for the human race in general? Are there signs that, once freed from the "delusions" our ancestors suffered under, the human race will breath a big sigh of relief and finally make progress? Or does the "death of God" mean, as Dostoevsky warned, that "everything [including Gulags] is lawful"?[6] Let's begin our inquiry in America.

Did the Unabomber Work Alone?

Ted Kaczynski was among the brightest of the brights: a Harvard grad who earned a Ph.D. degree with a dissertation at Michigan State that won a prize for the best in math. He taught at the University of California Berkeley, then retired to the woods of Montana, from where he mailed incendiary devices to people working in technology. Over the years, his homemade explosives killed three people and maimed 23.

Harris mourns "the failure of our schools to announce the death of God in a way that each generation can understand."[7] Harvard did not fail Kaczynski that way. In *Harvard and the Unabomber*, Alston Chase, who took some of the same courses as Kaczynski, noted, "The Gen Ed courses in social science quickly introduced us to the relativity of morals and the irrationality of religion."[8] Readings included Marx, cultural relativist Margaret Mead, existentialist Jean-Paul Sartre, positivist A.J. Ayer, Sigmund Freud's antireligious (and naive) venture into anthropology, *The Future of an Illusion*, and "countless other writers who had absorbed the messages of these doctrines." The future Unabomber took German, where Nietzsche, who announced the "death of God" as clearly as anyone, was on the menu. He read and reread a novel by atheist Joseph Conrad about a professor who retired to the woods.

Kaczynskis wrote in what became known as *The Unabomber Manifesto*, "There is no morality or objective set of values." Chase notes that this statement shows he "learned his Harvard lessons well. He was merely expressing the positivist view of ethics—omnipresent in the curriculum—that philosophers call the 'emotive theory.'"[9]

But it was an experiment in mind control by psychologist Henry Murray that may have pushed Kaczynski over the edge.

Murray should interest Harris, as a student of mind. Murray was an influential psychologist. He was also an atheist who identified with Captain Ahab, seeing his target, the whale, as a stand-in for God.

After World War II, the United States was locked in competition with the Soviet Union across a broad front: ICBMs, satellites, wheat production, Olympic hockey, even mind control. Some guinea pigs were given LSD. A few subjects died or went insane. Professors at Harvard, Cornell, and Stanford were involved. Professors Timothy Leary and Richard Alpert followed their own advice to "turn on, tune in, drop out," and helped invent the hippie. Dawkins argues that the Templeton Foundation "corrupts science" by rewarding scientists who write positively about religion. What about this?

Kaczynski participated in what Murray described as a "stressful disputation." A student would write an essay on his personal ideals, which was then brutally "deconstructed" in a face-to-face confrontation with a lawyer.

> He was frustrated, and finally brought to expressions of real anger, by the withering assault of his older, more sophisticated opponent...while fluctuations in the subject's pulse and respiration were measured on a cardiotachometer.[10]

A young man of genius with a broken family and few friends, Kaczynski seems to have been deeply affected by these assaults.

Kaczynski read works by Lewis Mumford and Jacques Ellul decrying the mechanization of society. Kaczynski saw the danger clearly (Chase quotes Chesterton's felicitous epigram: "the madman is the man who has lost everything except his reason"). An unhappy home life, and a head full of hopeless philosophy, left Kaczynski with few spiritual resources and no "chest" (as C.S. Lewis called it) to mediate between his swollen head and atrophied spirit. He corresponded with Ellul, who had written of hope in Jesus Christ. But the young man rejected that path.

In some ways, Reverend Paul Hill and Dr. Ted Kaczynski were a lot alike. Idealistic and thoughtful young men, both saw credible dangers—different ways in which modern society dehumanizes us—and sought radical solutions.

Dawkins tells us Hill was "dangerously religious."[11] Would it be fair to call Kaczynski "dangerously secular"? At least, probably only mathematicians would have heard of him if he had listened to Ellul and trusted in Christ.

The role academia played in the creation of the Unabomber is in some ways even more troubling than sexual abuse scandals involving priests or teachers. Lust has always been with us. But the urge to experiment on the innocent out of a passion for scientific truth reminds one of how some wealthy medievals reportedly dragged people off the street to test homemade torture devices. As Chase notes, "The same narrow focus on value-free science that led Nazi concentration camp doctors to commit atrocities encouraged many of these well-meaning scholars to cross ethical lines."[12]

Academic psychology has been largely liberated from theology. A survey in 1969 of 60,000 academics showed that only a fifth of psychology professors attend religious services regularly (compared to 42 percent even in the life sciences). Atheistic psychology professors at Harvard who work for democracy would seem just the sort on whom one could pin hopes for a "bright" future.

Of course, every barrel has its bad apples. It would be just as unjust to judge all atheists by a few unscrupulous or lunatic professors as to describe Hell House as a typical religious institution. Still, ideas do have consequences. Dostoevsky noticed worrying signs among the Russian intelligentsia of his day. Soon after, post-Christian thinkers made entire countries their laboratories, or torture chambers. Was atheism irrelevant?

Family and friends hold us back from our worst, even if only wearing mismatched socks. But with the twentieth century a few short years to port—a century of engines, flying machines, atoms that split, and emptying churches—the New Atheists demand that we look seriously at the relationship between ideas and tyranny, and rightfully so. Darwin gave the cognoscentea a chance to become "intellectually fulfilled atheists." What difference did post-Christian ideas about race, class, and sex make?

Can Thoughts Kill?

"You will know them by their fruits" (Matthew 7:16 NASB). Often the logic of an idea bears fruit quickly. The Gnostics believed the world was "filthy mud" created by a malevolent deity. Many eschewed marriage, and their tribe died out. Hitler's *Mein Kampf* was published in 1925. Dachau opened in March 1933, two months after Hitler was sworn in as chancellor of Germany. Jim Jones preached Armageddon, and apocalypse soon visited his village in Guyana.

Dawkins writes a lot about the "magic of big numbers." Time plus variation plus natural selection give rise to a variety of animals. Whether or not that works in genetics, seeded with time and ideas, the mind can be infinitely fertile.

Buddha, Confucius, and the apostle Paul all taught compassion. Over time, their followers justified torture. The seventeenth-century ruler of Japan, Tokugawa Ieyasu, was a supporter of Pure Land Buddhism. Ieyasu seemed to see the idea of God as dangerous and imported a secularist form of Confucianism from China, and an inquisition was on in Japan. Clearly, it is impossible to invent an abuse-proof ideology.

Still, the seeds matter, too. Seed a commune or nation—a "culture"—with an idea, and what develops over the first generations directly expresses what went in. If there's an internal logic to *The Origin of Species*, or the modern turn away from God, we should notice it most among people who develop "evolutionary ethics" in the test tubes of post-Christian societies.

Darwin to Hitler?

Dawkins once wisely wrote, "We should not derive our ethics from Darwinism, unless it is with a negative sign."[13]

What caused the Holocaust? Simple. Having rejected Christian morality, some of Darwin's followers derived their ethics from evolution with a positive sign.

Richard Weikart tells the story in *From Darwin to Hitler*.

Ernst Haeckel, the leading popularizer of evolution in Germany, argued that evolution held five implications for ethics: (1) Evolution proves mind is a part of body; (2) it implies determinism, since the soul can be explained by the laws of nature (as Dennett tries to do); (3) it implies moral relativism, since standards change over time (we "move on," as Dawkins put it); (4) moral character must be at least partly hereditary; and (5) natural selection must somehow produce morality. Haeckel was the Dawkins of his day—his books on evolution were among the most popular nonfiction in Germany.[14] He was also the first prominent advocate in Germany of killing weak and sickly babies, holding up the Spartans and "redskins" as examples.[15]

I hope we still find this shocking.

Ludwig Woltmann suggested that blond, blue-eyed Teutonics were at the apex of the evolutionary ladder. Some called for gradual and peaceful extermination of backward races. The French Social Darwinist Georges Lapouge thought Darwinian mechanisms could work more quickly, writing coldly:

> In the next century people will be slaughtered by the millions for the sake of one or two degrees on the cephalic index (i.e., measuring

brain size)...the last sentimentalists will witness the copious extermination of entire peoples.[16]

In the first years of the twentieth century, Darwinian racism wormed
its way into colonial propaganda. Kaiser Wilhelm II foresaw a battle for
life and death between whites and Asians. Some officials denied that
natives had a right to live. A German missionary complained that "the
average German" in Africa called the natives "baboons" and treated
them as such. In 1904, General Lothar von Trotha, citing "the struggle
of the fittest," ordered the annihilation of the Hereror tribe in what he
called a "racial war." With liberals applauding, and Social Democrats and
the Catholic Centrists demurring, an estimated 65,000 men, women,
and children were butchered, forced into the desert to die of thirst and
starvation, or worked to death as slaves.[17]

Hitler was not, then, a bolt out of the blue. In a society that had
been seduced by Arthur Schopenhauer's "will" and Friedrich Wilhelm
Nietzsche's "will to power" and contempt for Christian kindness, many
Germans still went to church, but the fashionable ideas that moved society derived from evolution and the death of God.

When Hitler said "The gulf between the lowest creature which can
still be styled man and our highest races is greater than that between
the lowest type of man and the highest ape," he was echoing decades
of social evolutionary thought.[18] Nazi propaganda derided philanthropy
as a positive evil: "In the past few decades, mankind has sinned terri-
bly against the law of natural selection." This may not have been good
science, but such ideas had become "reputable and mainstream" among
scholars, "especially among the medical and scientific elites."[19]

G.K. Chesterton foresaw the direction evolutionary logic would take
decades before Hitler came to power:

> The kinship and competition of all living creatures can be used as
> a reason for being insanely cruel or insanely sentimental...It is one
> way to train the tiger to imitate you, it is a shorter way to imitate
> the tiger.[20]

Daniel Dennett writes of the "universal acid" of Darwinism. Weikart argues that the Holocaust was the result of eight decades of corro-
sive action. Some saw World War I as a Darwinian struggle among *volks*,

others as a Christian duty. But by 1933, German voters had a choice between two post-Christian and self-consciously "scientific" creeds. My high school Russian teacher, who was from Berlin, explained, "We knew what the communists were like, so what could we do? We voted for Hitler."

"Each of us shares a common humanity with members of other races and with the other sex," Dawkins writes, "both deeply unbiblical ideas that come from biological science, especially evolution."[21] But National Socialism and Marxism-Leninism murdered the innocent—not because party members didn't know about evolution, but because they knew and approved the "shorter way" of imitating the tiger, the deeper evolutionary law of kill or be killed. Racism was "progressive." Feckless sentimentalists such as Chesterton and his popes protested in vain.

I'm not, of course, suggesting that Dawkins, Harris, or the vast majority of modern Darwinists do other than despise Naziism. But rather than blame Pius XII for saving only half a million Jews, or Mother Teresa for only giving comfort to the dying, Dawkins should come to grips with the history of the ideas Weikart relates.

Instead, Darwin and Harris putter around evolutionary theory as if they'd lost their glasses. "Is there a moral basis here? That's not it. Oh, over there! No?" They grope for a postreligious basis for morality. If not God, who? If not evolution, what? But their answers are strangely muddled.

Dawkins suggests that what makes abortion immoral is the suffering of the fetus. "At what age does any developing embryo, of any species, become capable of suffering?"[22] Does that mean killing is okay if it doesn't hurt? All right, asks Harris, how about if we use intelligence, language use, or moral sentiments as criteria? "If people are more important to us than orangutans because they can articulate their interests, why aren't more articulate people more important still?"[23] But that lands us back in Social Darwinism and "one or two degrees on the cephalic index."

Dawkins tries again. "The granting of uniquely special rights to cells of the species Homo sapiens is hard to reconcile with the fact of evolution."[24] "Progressive" thinkers thus chip away at the value of humanity on old frontiers: abortion, euthanasia, infanticide. But I thought we couldn't derive morality from evolution, "except with a negative sign"? After the horrors of the twentieth century, for God's sake (and for our own as well!), let's paint a dark red negative sign beside all such innovations, ranging from the banal to the ominous, and return to the eternal Tao.

Did Atheism Build the Gulag?

Most of us were born in the twentieth century. Why does the thirteenth seem fresher in the minds of some skeptics?

"I do not believe there is an atheist in the world who would bulldoze Mecca," Dawkins writes, "or Chartres, York Minster or Notre Dame, the Shwe Dagon, the temples of Kyoto or, of course, the Buddhas of Bamiyan."[25] I've stood in Buddhist temples in China and watched artists at work, cleaning up after Chairman Mao, an atheist who singlemindedly (but not singlehandedly) defaced three millennia of China's spiritual treasures. My screensaver cycles a photo I took of Mao's name scrawled on a rock at the summit of Mount Tai, where emperors came for thousands of years to worship the Supreme God. It's not much to look at, as calligraphy goes.

The New Atheists understandably want to think atheism had nothing to do with all this. "There is no evidence that his atheism motivated his brutality," Dawkins says confidently of Stalin:[26]

> Individual atheists may do evil things but they don't do evil things in the name of religion. Stalin and Hitler did extremely evil things, in the name of, respectively, dogmatic and doctrinaire Marxism, and an insane and unscientific eugenics theory tinged with sub-Wagnerian ranting.[27]

With due respect to Dr. Dawkins, but more to the living and the dead, he should find another debating point.

First, why is it "insane," from an evolutionary point of view, to kill people outside your genetic or community line? Male tigers do it all the time, and Dawkins tells us Jesus wanted us to do it, too. He's confused about that, but he knows it follows from his own premises.

Second, has Dawkins never heard the term "dialectical *materialism*"?

Stalin didn't kill alone. Lenin, Mao, Pol Pot, both Kims, Ho, Castro, Ceaușescu, and Honecker were also atheists. In one-third of the world, Communist parties announced the death of God on billboards, chalkboards, radio waves, and blank walls. Secret worship services in homes, forests, and caves were forcibly broken up, along with the faces of many who attended. Millions were *Tortured for Christ*, as the title of a book by Baptist ex-con philosopher Richard Wurmbrand succinctly put it. They had rats driven into their cells, were made to drink urine for communion, or were put into the "carcer" (a cupboard with sides studded by steel spikes) for writing the name *Jesus* on a cell wall.[28] Children of religious parents were kidnapped by the state and taught atheism in truly "Darwinian" state orphanages. None of that counts against the atheist record, according to Dawkins, because in some undefined sense these crimes were not "for the sake of atheism."

Harris attempts to nail that sense down. Communism was "cultic and irrational." While Stalin and Mao "paid lip service to rationality, communism was little more than a political religion."[29] "I know of no society in human history that ever suffered because its people became too desirous of evidence in support of their core beliefs."[30]

So the problem, apparently, is not belief in God, but "unjustified belief" in anything! Well of course! And we have seen that the view that Christianity asks for "unjustified belief" is itself unjustified! But Harris is playing a shell game. The point was supposed to be that religion is harmful, and that things will be better if we get rid of it. Now he is admitting that the real problem is failing to live up to a particular moral virtue—honesty. Yes, and it would also be hard to find a society that suffered from obeying Paul's injunction to charity too fervently! Bad things happen when we turn our backs on the commands of God. But that hardly lets the philosophy that encouraged us to "abolish all religion and all morality" (that's the order Karl Marx and Friedrich Engels put them) off the hook.

David Aikman, former Beijing correspondent for *Time* magazine, wrote his doctoral dissertation on atheism in the Marxist tradition. Aikman examined the spiritual lives of Karl Marx, Friedrich Engels, and Vladimir Lenin, the founders of communism. He showed that the "systematic assault upon religious belief in Communist countries" had deep roots in the anti-God culture in which these men developed their ideas.[31]

Marx was the prototype of all young men who go away to college and lose their faith under the influence of godless professors. The young Marx was sunny and pious. In college, he read Shelley and the romantics. Then he transferred to the University of Berlin and lost his faith in God. He was particularly enchanted by two popular romantic stories. The first was the tale of Prometheus, who stole fire from the gods for the benefit of man and was punished for his impiety. (In his doctoral thesis, he quoted Prometheus: "In a word, I detest all gods."[32]) The other was the story of Faust, who sold his soul to the devil. References to these deeply anti-Christian myths are scattered throughout Marx's writings, but are most vividly reflected in his early poems. The motifs that occupied Marx, Aikman relates, were "doom, revenge, damnation, reaching for heaven, vying with God."[33] Like many great madmen, Marx expressed himself in verse:

> So a god has snatched from me my all
> in the curse and wrack of Destiny.
> All his worlds are gone beyond recall!
> Nothing but revenge is left to me!...
>
> I shall build my throne high overhead
> Cold, tremendous shall its summit be.
> For its bulwark—superstitious dread,
> For its marshal—blackest agony.[34]

Marx then fell in with a group of anti-God philosophers known as the Young Hegelians. Bruno Bauer, who taught theology at University of Berlin and for whom the line between debunking and mocking the Gospels was thin, was one of the most violently anti-Christian writers alive and deeply influenced the young man. Ludwig Feuerbach introduced the idea that God was a substitute for mankind. Moses Hess linked atheism and communism.

The implication of these ideas was clear to many contemporaries. Another of the Young Hegelians, Arnold Ruge, broke with Marx, telling his mother that communism "would lead to a police state and slavery."[35] Ruge, of course, had never heard of Stalin, and therefore could not blame him for soiling Marx's good name, as later apologists still do.

Engels was even more pious when young, and lost his faith reading David Strauss's *The Life of Jesus*. "Why does not someone write a devastating refutation?" he wrote his friend Fritz Graeber.[36]

Marx and his followers entered the tunnel with eyes wide open, intensely aware that their new society would be built on repudiation of God, and warned that terrible things might happen. Much of the program was implicit in the atheism of the day: the Enlightenment myth, the end of religion, Science with a capital "S," society as an arena for struggle. The philosophy of the Gulag was reached quickly because it was obvious. Marxists agreed with Ernst Haeckel that man has no soul and can be explained by nature, and that moral standards are malleable.

Alexander Solzhenitsyn spent eight years in Stalin's camps. He researched the question long and deeply, and wrote thousands of pages on the "Red Knot," as he called the Russian revolution. He offered a succinct explanation for the Gulag: "men have forgotten God." Of course atheists can and usually do choose to embrace moral rules of one sort or another. But murder also came fast and hard upon the death of God.

Do Atheists Fight?

In a phrase he might have written while humming John Lennon's *Imagine*, Dawkins says he cannot think of any war fought in the name of atheism. Why would anyone fight "for the sake of absence of belief"?[37]

A more scientific question would be, "Do people who disbelieve in God fight any less?"

In a remote region in China, I was told I was the first American to visit since they had shot a pilot down during the Vietnam War. I walked across the clean new concrete bridge at the border, reading a pledge to "friendship" between the two countries etched into it. Why was the bridge new? The last one had been blown up when China invaded Vietnam in 1979.

In fact, atheism played a central part in the ideology of one or both sides of most of the great wars of the century: the October Revolution, the Russian Civil War, invasion and suppression of the states that went into the Soviet Union, the Soviet-German war, the Chinese Civil War, the Korean War, the Vietnamese invasion of Cambodia, the Sino-Indian war, the Chinese invasion of Tibet, and so on. And mass atheism is still young; who knows what more flowers may grow from this root?

Why would anyone fight for the sake of an absence of belief? Ask the combatants! It may be that nations, like drunks in bars, enjoy a good brawl once in a while. Need one explain aggression to a zoologist?

Would You Rescue a Drowning Child?

Marc Hauser and Peter Singer asked subjects to choose whether a hypothetical action, such as wading into a pond to save a drowning child, was morally "obligatory," "permissible," or "forbidden." Finding no difference in how atheists and believers answered, Hauser noted that "atheists and agnostics are perfectly capable of distinguishing between morally permissible and forbidden actions." They confidently inferred, "The system that unconsciously generates moral judgments is immune to religious doctrine."[38] Dawkins concluded, "We do not need God in order to be good—or evil."[39]

I'm glad to know almost everyone said they would risk ruining clothes to save a child (and alarmed, with Dawkins, at the 3 percent who said they wouldn't!). But the gentlemen failed to distinguish between what a person *says* he would do and what he would *actually* do.

If you risk not trousers but life, might there not be a difference between how those who believe in God and those who don't act? Dennett complains that Christians are too willing to die for their faith.[40] Why would that happen only when doctrine is at stake, and not the life of a child? Studies show that believers are far more generous with money and time. Isn't that a better reflection of how people act than a hypothetical Internet survey? In the Gulag, Solzhenitsyn found, millions of believers cast "a light, like a candle." They were practically the only ones, he said, to whom the dog-eat-dog philosophy of the camps failed to stick (see his portrait of the Baptist, Alyosha, in his novel *One Day in the Life of Ivan Denisovich*). It was the very fearlessness Dawkins complains of (in another context) that put believers at the forefront of revolutions in Manila, Moscow, Romania, and Poland. Of course there were freedom-loving atheists alongside them.

Dawkins and Harris are stuck in a trap of their own devising. They believe faith is a pernicious "meme" that forces believers to do extreme things, such as dying for an abstraction. But they also want us to believe that the logic of evolution will have no negative impact whatsoever on unbelievers. What is this law that makes only the negative consequences of a religious idea effective, and only the positive consequences of atheism play out?

Dawkins even tries to pin Stalin on Christianity. "His earlier religious training probably didn't [motivate him] either, unless it was through teaching him to revere absolutist faith, strong authority and a belief that ends justify means."[41] (In fact, Stalin lost his faith at the age of 13, and entered seminary just for the education.) Dawkins can't bring himself to admit that atheism had anything to do with what an atheist running a party of atheists, spreading anti-God propaganda, and specializing in the murder of believers did. In fact, Stalin *didn't* revere authority. He made a long, successful career of knocking off rival authorities. Just as Prometheus fought the gods to bring fire to man, so Marx and his followers assigned themselves the role of destroying religion and bringing blessings to the proletariat.

A better way to defend the honor of atheism might be to say that any idea can be used to oppress. That's plainly true. But if the road to hell is paved with good intentions, start with bad intentions—"survival of the fittest," nature "red in tooth and claw," "you need to break some eggs," "you only go around once," "eat, drink and be merry, for tomorrow we die"—and you get there more quickly.

A Jewish poet in New York in the 1930s named Joy Davidman was attracted to the communist party for what she saw as its concern for the underdog. When she talked to a friend about joining, Davidman made the mistake of mentioning this concern. Her friend responded caustically, "Wait a minute. You mean you want to join for the sake of other people?" Realizing her faux pas, Joy responded, "To hell with other people! I want to join the Communists for my own sake." Her friend smiled; she was in.[42]

It *does* matters what billions of human beings believe and why they believe it. Marx and Engels wrote that communism "abolishes all eternal truth, all morality." That alone helps explain the pale grey idols, the soulless art and propaganda, the ugly post-God architecture, the slave labor camps.

But Davidman's story illustrates the biblical truth rediscovered by Hauser and Singer: So long as we remain human, we can't really get rid of moral truth. It can be driven underground. It can be rationalized away. It may nag at us until we drown our conscience in alcohol or blood. But we "can't not know."

Does Atheism Liberate?

The best argument against religion in theory has always been religion in practice. Dawkins correctly notes:

> From Kosovo to Palestine, from Iraq to Sudan, from Ulster to the Indian subcontinent, look carefully at any region of the world where you find intractable enmity and violence between rival groups. I cannot guarantee that you'll find religions as the dominant labels for in-groups and out-groups. But it's a very good bet.[43]

It's an excellent bet. Jesus warned, "I send you out as sheep in the midst of wolves" (Matthew 10:16).

But correlation does not prove causation. Groups often choose religions to "flag" themselves against enemies. If they have no religion, they pick secular labels. Three hundred people were reportedly killed in fights between Red Guard factions on the campus in southern China where I later studied. My teacher's husband also died. Communist cells splinter faster than Presbyterian churches in Seoul, and much more lethally: Trotskyites, Right Revisionists, the Gang of Four. Nor are radical feminists, socialists, Freudians, or objectivists famous for mutual amity.

When people fight over power, they justify themselves (often sincerely) by whatever dogma are lying around (what Jacque Ellul called "myths"). In the mid-twentieth century, most myths were secular: communism, nationalism, fascism, socialism, democracy. These were the flags under which people rallied. Now secular gods have died, and people are picking up new flags. To think getting rid of religion will give us "nothing to kill or die for" (as John Lennon put it) is not merely naive, it's a mark of gross historical amnesia.

Sexual Liberation: Are We Having Fun Yet?

The final revolution of the twentieth century is one over which we need not dispute responsibility. Harris readily concedes—no, complains—

that Christianity restrains our libido. He mocks the idea that "the Creator of the universe will take offense at something people do while naked," adding, "This prudery of yours contributes daily to the surplus of human misery."[44] Indeed, unbelievers have been at the forefront of sexual liberation. "We all jumped at" evolutionary thought, said Aldous Huxley, "because the idea of God interfered with our sexual mores."[45]

Alfred Kinsey, another believer who lost his faith under the tutelage of a godless professor, cast off the inhibitions of his pious youth under the intellectual influence of William Wheeler (a Harvard etymologist who, like Edmund Wilson, followed Solomon's advice to "study the ant"). Kinsey's studies of human sexuality were published in what are called the Kinsey Reports, best-selling scientific books that helped launch the sexual revolution. Kinsey was a dedicated researcher, filming his wife in bed with students, among other innovations. His research methods have been panned for poor sampling (too many prison inmates and pedophiles) and gross ethical lapses. His results—he claimed ten percent of males were homosexual—inflated margins at the expense of the center.

Margaret Sanger, the founder of what became Planned Parenthood, published a magazine called *The Woman Rebel*, whose slogan "No Gods! No Masters!" succinctly summarized her philosophy. She believed that "ethical dogmas of the past" blocked evolution and "the way to true civilization." This would come through sex, by which "mankind may attain the great spiritual illumination which will transform the world." The rebel woman had "the Right to destroy" and "the Right to be an Unmarried Mother."[46] If Kinsey was the father of sexology, Sanger can be seen as the mother of the single-parent household—though she spent her own spare time chasing lovers across oceans.

Sexual freedom has been preached, and practiced, by leading skeptics with enthusiasm for 200 years.

What "great spiritual illumination" has been achieved? Harris blames America's high rates of abortion, teen pregnancy, and sexually transmitted disease on Christianity.[47] This is like blaming him for the fact that most Americans still believe in God! If the Bible says, "Do not commit adultery," it is absurd to blame it for what happens when people do just the opposite!

Popular culture supports La Revolución. The "Material Girl" got rich by teaching girls they could tomcat, too. Madonna merely popularized what post-Christian thinkers had been saying for decades. Sanger advised her 16-year-old granddaughter to have sex three times a day. Planned Parenthood removed the most obvious consequences, though its founder died lonely. Margaret Mead wrote about "love under the palms" in Samoa, in one of the most successful acts of scientific frauds (after Kinsey's) of the twentieth century. Aldous Huxley, whose grandfather debated Samuel Wilberforce, wrote about a brave new world in which all the girls were easy. These fantasies were all the rage when the sixties generation grew up (as was B.F. Skinners' *Walden Two*, about a prototypical commune). Sixties kids did as they were told; some professors even chipped in the acid. The violent crime rate in every state in America as much as tripled over the next two decades.

Public schools seldom stand in the dike. Schools speak out clearly against intolerance, racism, and drug use, but rarely against promiscuous sexuality. In the rural high school I sometimes substitute at, a sign posted on the library window for the gay and lesbian club lets students know the administration is not about to spoil the fun.

Who should we blame for promiscuity but the church, the one institution that speaks out against it? (Though less often than it should.)

Glenn Stanton, in *Why Marriage Matters*, studied the most extensive surveys of sexuality in America and concluded, "The public image of sex in America bears virtually no relationship to the truth":[48]

> First-time, lifelong monogamous marriage is the relationship that best provides for the most favorable exercise of human sexuality, the overall well-being of adults, and the proper socialization of children. Marriage has no close rival. It stands independently above any other option: singleness, cohabitation, divorce, and remarriage.[49]

Harris points out that some kinds of social dysfunction have not reached the same level in Europe yet. That's because they've put away their Bibles, he wants us to think. Yet while living in Oxford, I often woke up to lovers' quarrels at about 3:30 in the morning. One might have been loud enough for Dawkins to hear on the other side of town:

206 @ The Truth Behind the New Atheism

"Of course I've got other women! If you want to be a * nun, go ahead" (faint sound of lady crying).

Never mind abortions and sexually transmitted diseases. I'll tell you what bothers me most. Sometimes, when my boys say, "Quiz, Daddy!" at dinnertime, or we take the dog down to the river, I wonder: How many children can't use the word *Daddy* or *Mommy* because their parents are too "liberated" to bother making house? How many single mothers try to work and raise children by themselves? How many young men are in the criminal justice system because they didn't have two parents to discipline and love them? (Lack of a father figure is a common thread among criminals.)

If the Creator cares about human beings at all, he certainly must care what "people do while naked." And what perverse reductionism this phrase unconsciously reveals! As Mother Teresa told Harvard students,

> Nakedness is not only for a piece of cloth. Nakedness is the loss of human dignity, the loss of respect, the loss of that purity which was so beautiful, the loss of that virginity which is the most beautiful thing that a young man or a young woman can give each other because of their love.[50]

I wonder how many students had heard that before?

The fact that God's book damns human sexuality (without damning it), channeling this powerful force in productive directions, gives us reason to think he really does care.

A Better Place Without God?

In conclusion, I see no evidence that the world will be better without God. We can try to persuade ourselves Communism was a fluke, that it was "lack of reason," not faith, that sent a third of the world into a murderous tailspin. We do share "deep conscience." But the logic of ideas— you only go around once, moral relativity, we're all material girls and boys, man as a "survival machine" for genes, survival of the fittest, the relativity of morality, the tendency to exalt government to the throne of God—can and do subvert what we know is right.

Consilience

"Do not think at all that I have come into this world
because I wanted to destroy the old law, to chop it
down amongst this people."

—Heliade[1]

Richard Dawkins's most famous maxim may be, "Evolution makes it possible to be an intellectually fulfilled atheist." That worked for Edward Wilson. He began as an amateur naturalist chasing snakes through the ponds and reeds of rural Alabama. Reading Ernst Mayr's *Systematics and the Origin of Species*, Wilson arrived at what he described, in his book *Consilience*, as an "Ionian Enchantment." "Suddenly," he wrote, "I saw the world in a whole new way." The sciences were unified, and the world was orderly, and could be "explained by a small number of laws." He traced this conviction of unity to Thales of Ionia in the sixth century B.C., who believed that all matter was ultimately made of water. For Wilson, evolution was what bound all forms of life (at least) together. Evolution allowed him to see nature not as a grab bag of unrelated specimens, but a subtle web of cause and effect, an ordered chain of being linked by a story. "The animals and plants I loved so dearly reentered the stage as lead players in a grand drama."[2] Everything was connected, from the flat-tailed water snake to the gods of the Parthenon.

Wilson also found continuity between science and the religious feelings of his childhood. We all look for something bigger than ourselves:

We are obliged by the deepest drives of the human spirit to make ourselves more than animated dust, and we must have a story to tell about where we came from, and why we are here. Could Holy Writ be just the first literate attempt to explain the universe and make ourselves significant within it? Perhaps science is a continuation on new and better-tested ground to attain the same end.[3]

Wilson's program sounds to some rather as Roman propaganda sounded to Calgacus: "They make it a desert and call it peace." The New Atheism expands the boundaries of science, critics feel, with the same reckless disregard for the true good of future subjects as the Roman legions conquering Britain.

But unity of knowledge is something Christians have always affirmed, too. "All truth is God's truth," said Clement of Alexandria. That's why Robert Boyle not only studied chemistry, but paid to have the Bible translated into distant languages. That's why the collection of monastic institutions that surrounded his home had come to be called a *university*.

Which unity makes better sense of life? Which brings a peace to the soul more like a fruitful garden than a barren desert? Jesus claimed to be "the way, and the truth, and the life" (John 14:6 NASB). Can he reconcile different levels of our nature, as he claimed?

The Music of Life

One of the triumphs of Baroque music is that it most brilliantly developed an audible way to express the polyphonic character of life. It did this by weaving rhythms and melodies into a whole by what is called *counterpoint*:

> It is hard to write a beautiful song. It is harder to write several individually beautiful songs that, when sung simultaneously, sound as a more beautiful polyphonic whole. The internal structures that create each of the voices separately must contribute to the emergent structure of the polyphony, which in turn must reinforce and comment on the structures of the individual voices. The way that is accomplished in detail is..."counterpoint."[4]

Music and astronomy (the "music of the spheres") have always seemed to go together. Johannes Kepler wrote of the *harmonice mundi*. Searching for the most basic laws of physics, Brian Greene catches notes of what he calls a "cosmic symphony."[5] In a book that gently chided Dawkins for overreaching, Oxford physiologist Denis Noble wrote of the "music of life," offering polyphony as a metaphor for advanced organisms:

> The great advantage of these keys is that, provided that each musical part is written in the same key, and certain rules concerning intervals are followed, the results are very harmonious. The medieval modes, however, didn't disappear. They became assimilated, just as unicellular organisms did not disappear when multicellular forms evolved.[6]

Here, too, the goal is unity within diversity. But a consilience that leaves some of the melodies of life out is too simple—"mono-tonous" in the literal sense. That, it seems to me, is the problem with atheism. It's not that it doesn't explain anything. Rather, it can't explain everything. Skepticism fits some moods. But a more polyphonic worldview is needed to bring all life into unity.

The New Atheism reveals its simplistic grasp on reality in many ways. First, the most cocky atheists often fail to recognize the limits of science. Second, their theories leave too many facts out. Third, they refuse to ask certain obviously important questions. Fourth, to obscure the failure of their theory, some are driven to play a game of "let's pretend."

The Limits of Science

While few people today deny the glory of science, like the Roman Empire, it has limits. Science is limited in three ways: in knowledge, origin, and explanatory power.

As we've seen, all knowledge—without exception—is built on a solid foundation of faith. We can't know anything without reasoned trust. Not only is it impossible to do science without faith, materialism drives us to such follies as positivism, determinism, and (a contribution of the New Atheists) meme theory, according to which thought itself is just a bug in the brain. But just as visible light is only a small part of the electromagnetic spectrum, so there are ways of knowing that lie both north and south of science in the spectrum of cognition. Logic, moral intuition, memory, and mathematics are all grasped more directly. On the other hand, most of what each of us knows comes less directly by trust in other people. The "fear of the Lord" is the beginning and end of wisdom, touching both ends of the spectrum, the foundation and goal of reasoning.

Not only is science limited in what it can tell us, it is derivative. Modern science was born as but one part of a "Galilean Enchantment" that is still sweeping the world. Like Wilson, the first modern scientists saw animals and plants as players in a single epic drama. The world could be explained by a set number of laws because it was created by a Law-giver. Paul Davies noted, "Science did not spring ready-made into the minds of Newton and his colleagues." Rather, it arose from the Greek and also the "Judaic worldview, according to which the universe was cre-ated by God at some definite moment in the past and ordered according to a fixed set of laws."[7]

Even the intuition that laws should be simplified is Christian. The Bible consolidated the functions of Ares, Hermes, Zeus, Aphrodite, Apollo, Poseidon, and their kin. Theism reduced lawgivers to One. Jesus reduced moral laws to two on which all the law and prophets depended, and then offered *agape* as an ethical Unified Theory. "Love the Lord your God with all your heart and with all your soul and with all your mind. And…love your neighbor as yourself. All the Law and the Prophets hang on these two commandments" (Matthew 22:37,39-40).

If I say, "There are many things science can't explain," you may reply, "Just wait! It will!" Of course one can't refute a prediction about the future. Like the Roman Empire by the time of Agricola, science has been expanding at a rate that would lead to complete dominance were it to continue. But boundaries around the empire have sharpened, and in some cases—quantum irregularities, the big bang, anthropic coincidences, the Sky God, the "resurrection of the Son of God"—a God-shaped vacuum grows, just about where Christian theology has generally marked it.

Reading the New Atheism, I am sometimes reminded of the mechanics in the movie *Doc Hollywood*. A doctor crashes his car in a small Southern town on the way to an important interview in California. After weeks of work, the mechanics finally show him the repaired hot rod, good as new—with a few extra parts lying next to it on the ground. We always have parts left over, they explain with a shrug.

Wilson's intuitions are healthy. Truth is one. But when you simplify theories, you must not leave too many facts lying around unreconciled. Many of the most natural questions not only show that scientific explanations leave "gaps" in our knowledge, but often that they become more profound the more we learn. They beg a deeper reconciliation.

Random Acts of Inquiry

A man named Job was once given a pop science exam. How do eagles know where to build nests? Where do mountain goats deliver lambs? What laws guide galaxies? How does human instinct work? It's taken the human race a long time to answer some of these questions. Some we're still working on, along with Adam's duty of naming all the animals.

But with every answer deeper questions open up—like distant valleys from the peak of a "conquered" ridge.

Why is there something rather than nothing? If the rate of expansion of the early universe were smaller by one part in one hundred million billion, or greater by one part in a million, some say the universe would have collapsed, or stars and planets would not have formed.[8] Why do the size, shape, and laws of nature turn out so precisely correct? Why did we "luck out" in the production of hydrogen, carbon, and heavier metals, produced only in large suns and in the supernovas that spewed into space the heavy elements that form the cobblestones of High Street?

Who thought of making things out of strings? (If they are?) Why are multiple dimensions bound up in every atom? (If they can be found there?) Why are the facts of physics so strange, revealing layer under layer of surprises, yet so elegant and harmonious that beauty often serves as a mark of truth in physics?

Why is our planet just where it needs to be, in a "Goldilocks Zone," neither too hot nor cold, in deadly space? Why does the Earth's crust float? (On Venus it sinks apocalyptically into the mantle every so often.) Why is our atmosphere clear and light, while one neighbor planet suffocates in a mantle of carbon dioxide and the other is a barren wasteland that loses much of its tiny allotment of CO_2 to "snow" at the poles every winter? Why do our companions in space stabilize rather than disorder our motion, with Jupiter and Saturn taking hits from comets and asteroids aimed at us? The possible causes that led to these conditions—for example, an ancient Mars-sized planet that struck Earth at just the right angle long ago, forming the moon and stripping our original atmosphere—can be deduced. But that doesn't strip this elegant universe of its wonder.

How did life begin? Did it need to be such a baroque long shot at every turn? How did the human form and mind change so much so quickly, as if the Spirit breathed new life into man in the blink of a geological eye?

Why is life so beautiful and terrible at the very same instant? Who told tribes in Australia, Africa, China, America, and the South Sea islands about the same God who also haunts the dreams of physicists and astronomers? How did Paul and Augustine predict a widespread theism that Hume, Dennett, and Dawkins overlook? (And that people like Karen Armstrong and Emile Durkheim write about when they are describing the facts, then forget about when they formulate theories to explain them?)

How did one tribe of wandering nomads know their "seed" would bring a blessing to all peoples? Why have some 23 percent of all Nobel Peace Prize winners belonged to that little tribe, which makes up one four-hundredth of the world's population? How did Jewish shepherds know the universe had a beginning 3000 years before Nobel Peace Prize winning descendants admitted the fact? Why did Iron Age bedouins affirm the unity and universal responsibility of humanity, doctrines denied by city mouse sages and scientists? (But now definitively affirmed by genetics?)

Why was so much of the world awaiting a savior? Why did the Jewish prophets say the "Messiah" would be the "light of the nations so that My salvation may reach to the end of the earth" (Isaiah 49:6 NASB). Did Isaiah, Micah, and Hosea forget about in-group morality? Why did Daniel, Mencius, Virgil, and the Diamond Sutra all predict saviors who would be born at about the same time? And why, at about that time, were wise men in the East said to have spotted a star announcing one born "King of the Jews"? Just when, as it turns out, Jupiter, the "king's planet," met Saturn in the night sky three times within a few months in 6 B.C.? ("Jupiter encountering Saturn in the Sign of the Fishes would have meant that a cosmic ruler or king was to appear in Palestine at a culmination of history."[9])

Jesus lived and taught well before 1859. Why do his teachings go to my heart, while an Oxford scientist's "amended Ten Commandments" ("Enjoy your own sex life [so long as it damages nobody else] and leave others to enjoy theirs in private whatever their inclinations"[10]) strike me as vacuous? Will such inane platitudes cause the AIDS epidemic to ground to a halt, cement families together, and challenge the hearts of future generations to self-sacrificial love?

Among eminent Jesus scholars, wrote philosopher Raymond Martin, N.T. Wright's approach to history is "far and away the most sophisticated and articulate."[11] After sifting carefully through thousands of pages of early Christian evidences, Wright argued that many lines of evidence affirm the resurrection of Christ. "The proposal that Jesus was bodily raised from the dead possesses unrivaled power to explain the historical data at the heart of early Christianity."[12] How do atheists know God can't do that?

Two friends told how, when they were about to commit suicide, strangers came up to them (one in Singapore, the other in Taiwan) and said, "Don't kill yourself! God loves you." A young man I met in central China told me his friends laughed at him for believing. "But I'll always believe in God," he replied fiercely, telling me how his wife was healed of brain damage. I have met dozens of intelligent and honest people whose stories, if true, would alone spell the doom of the materialistic paradigm. When atheists hear such tales, why do they feel obliged to dismiss them as delusional or untrue? Why are they so confident they have the universe, and everything behind it, in a box?

"Where are the Hittites?" Walker Percy asked. "Why does no one find it remarkable that in most world cities today there are Jews but not one single Hittite, even though the Hittites had a great flourishing civilization while the Jews nearby were a weak and obscure people...?"[13] How did the prophets, who couldn't have named half the continents, know Israel would be scattered among them, survive, then return (even after an almost 2000-year exile)? Why are there Jews today in Rio de Janeiro, Sydney, and Tel Aviv—but no Hittites, Isaurians, Phrygians, Phoenicians, Idaeans, Carthaginians, or Philistines? Why is my name David and not Goliath?

Some of these questions involve what might be called "gaps" in scientific or historical knowledge. Some may, in time, be closed, I suppose. But others have to do with the nature of things, or how facets of reality—melodies—come together to produce a richer harmony.

Can evolution make one an intellectually fulfilled atheist? Maybe, if man really does live by bread alone, and you don't mind the bread a little stale ("Pro-'crust'-ean bread," baked to fill a person with a sociobiological soul).

Will further research narrow the "gaps"? Or will it deepen them, etching the boundaries of another kingdom on the fringes of science (and beneath it as well), a "God-shaped vacuum" in human understanding?

Two Ways to Be Childish

Given not just anthropic coincidences and other scientific clues to divine activity, but also a variety of human experience that also helps foster the "God delusion," faith seems not only reasonable, but reconciling. The Christian story makes sense of a much larger field of data than evolution on its own.

In response, New Atheists sometimes play a game of "let's pretend." Let's pretend Jesus only taught in-group morality (because evolutionary theory doesn't explain what he did teach). Let's pretend Mother Teresa was the problem with India. Let's pretend the Bible cannot be read as a single book with a coherent divine message. Let's pretend Bible-thumpers didn't end slavery, invent the university, write the Hallelujah Chorus, paint the Sistine Chapel, challenge crazy gurus (religious and secular), heal and teach millions of the poor, and show the world why the caste system, foot-binding, infanticide, and human sacrifice are wrong. Let's pretend morality improves on its own. Let's pretend American Christians (of whom Pat Robertson and Paul Hill are typical examples) plot to tear the U.S. Constitution to shreds. Let's pretend the Gulag was a fluke. Let's pretend Stalin was the only unpleasant Marxist. Let's pretend the universe explains itself. Let's pretend the origin of life has been solved. Let's pretend Solomon, Plato, Lao Zi, Augustine, Pascal, and Burke have nothing to teach us now that we have Marc Hauser and Peter Singer. Let's pretend prayers are never answered.

Christopher Hitchens admits his main critiques of religion were developed by his early to mid teens. Indeed, as "bright" as some prominent New Atheists are, adolescence is evident not only in their tone, but also in their bibliographies. Why did Richard Swinburne have to tell Dawkins he had written books giving evidence for God? Shouldn't Dawkins read eminent opponents before he rebukes them savagely in public? Why didn't Dawkins realize that the cosmological argument for God's existence is still a going concern in serious philosophical circles? How come only friendly Jesus scholars appear in his footnotes? Why hasn't he even read C.S. Lewis, his "neighbor" and the most popular Christian thinker of the twentieth century? Why does Dennett appear ignorant of the Sky God hypothesis? Where does one find reference in this wilderness to contrarian thinkers such as Rene Girard, Rodney Stark, Arthur Brooks, or even Alexander Solzhenitsyn?

The kingdom of God, said Jesus, is for children. All of us are children, in one way or another. But we choose how to be childish. Just as science artificially concentrates on narrow domains of thought, so children close their eyes and pretend, or hide in a box or under a chair, to artificially limit their world. On the other hand, like great thinkers, children learn by asking unexpected questions. The first narrows our field of vision, the second broadens it.

Dawkins tells us we must not ask questions about "purpose" and "meaning." He refers to the asking of such questions as "childish teleology."[14]

Children do indeed ask such questions.

A week ago as of this writing, our beautiful yellow Lab suddenly became sick, probably from foraging a tainted piece of meat. I took him to the vet. The next night, when we visited him, he labored to breath, foam forming at his mouth. As we spoke to the vet in another room, he stopped breathing. Stroking his fur, our boys cried, "Why? Why did Elwood have to die?" They asked about the cause of death—and that's what I concentrated on at first, concerned for safety. But more urgently, they asked about meaning. What purpose did it serve for their best friend, a healthy and happy young animal, obedient and playful, who swam in the river a block from our home, skied and played baseball (he was a wonderful fielder), to suddenly lose control of his hind legs, then lungs, and die?

Faced with greater tragedies, "Why?" is the most-asked human question. If we often have to answer (as I did), "I don't know," that hardly renders the question irrational. Perhaps discounting questions of meaning is one way to fence ourselves off from the pain of childhood. But as Blaise Pascal understood, life forces us back to such questions—from Dawkins's neat intellectual empire into the realm of meaning and purpose.

Sometimes we may be given positive intimations of purpose.

When the Jewish people were threatened with an early genocidal episode, a man named Mordecai asked younger cousin Queen Esther, "Who knows but that you have come to the kingdom for such a time as this?" Throughout history people have received a similar "calling" that set their lives within a larger "drama": Augustine, Patrick, Queen Bathilda, Francis of Assisi, Martin Luther, Bartolomé de las Casas, John Wesley, William Wilberforce, Alexander Solzhenitsyn, Benigno Aquino.

For me, a calling, which I have been pursuing ever since, came one Sunday evening in Hong Kong at the age of 23. But in a deeper way, God speaks to us all. The moral law is among the means by which God reveals purpose and meaning to the just and the unjust, like rain that comes to moisten parched soil.

What a burden the New Atheists carry! To be "brights" in a world of dims. To learn nothing about human nature from anyone who wrote before 1859. To despise saints.

Wilson is right: Consilience is also about what "tribe" we choose to join. One reason I am a Christian is that following Jesus doesn't force me to leave the rest of the human race (and its full experience) behind. Christ allows me to become an intellectually fulfilled humanist.

Tutors to Christ

Justin Martyr called Greek philosophers "tutors" to bring the world to Christ. Clement of Alexandria reminded his readers of the myth of Pentheus, who was torn into pieces by the Bacchants. He argued that Christ joins the truths of different schools into one coherent whole. Each sect "vaunts as the whole truth the portion which has fallen to its lot. But all, in my opinion, are illuminated by the dawn of Light."[15]

Atheists make two accusations against Christianity. The first is that Christianity sees no beauty or truth or value in other religions. The second is that Christianity itself evolved from other faiths, which some-how discredits it. The two accusations conflict, and are both untrue.

Skeptics tell us that Christmas is just the birthday of Mithras. Easter is the goddess of the dawn. Halloween is just a druid ghost festival.

The word *just* here is unjust. The Christian tradition preserves pagan holidays because (as Clement explained) the Gospels conciliate truth wherever it lies.

The gospel thus breaks down barriers between people. East and West "never shall meet," wrote Rudyard Kipling, until they lie at "God's Great Judgment Seat."[16] Judgment occurs (Christians believe) at the cross. In Christ, there is neither slave nor free, rich nor poor, male nor female, Greek nor Jew (Galatians 3:28). Distinctives are not lost, but woven together in a pattern, like melodies in a Bach fugue.

Christians have long said Jesus joins us not only to the Hebrew tradition but to other great spiritual traditions. The gospel finds a "middle path" between saying all religions are equally true and despising them all as equally false. Jesus fulfills the deepest truths in each tradition, while challenging abuse and untruth that every religious tradition (including our own) invariably kicks up.

Christians pray to the Father God with our nomadic ancestors. We climb Mount Tai with Confucius, echoing his words, "Tian xia wei xiao"—"Under heaven, everything is small." (The relative minuteness of earthly affairs is even clearer through the Hubble telescope or look-ing back from space at the "plae blue dot" that is Earth.) We worship at the Temple of Heaven with a long line of Chinese emperors. We call Socrates and Plato "tutors" to truth. We identify with Odysseus (Clem-ent suggested) as he was tied to the mast of his ship, as if to the cross, so he could safely sail past the sirens to his true home. With Chinese philosopher Yuan Zhiming we may call Lao Zi a "prophet of God" who foresaw how weakness would overcome strength in the life of Jesus. With reformer Krishna Banarjea some Indian Christians see Prajapati, the cre-ator in Hindu mythology who sacrificed himself for all before the cre-ation of the world, as a shadow of the truth: "Sacrifice the instrument by which Sin and Death are annulled and abolished."[17] We can renounce the world with Buddha, then fight at Lepanto (or in the Sudan, or with

218 ⊛ The Truth Behind the New Atheism

the International Justice Mission in brothels outside Phnom Penh) to free slaves:

> Breaking of the hatches up and bursting of the holds,
> Thronging of the thousands up that labour under sea
> White for bliss and blind for sun and stunned for liberty.[18]

Dawkins owns a T-shirt that reads, "Atheists for Jesus." There's something touching about this gesture. But more important is the fact Jesus is for Richard Dawkins, the scientist, atheist, and man. It was a Galilean Enchantment that Galileo, Kepler, Boyle, and Pascal fell under, and that nurtured the intellectual culture that produced them—like the three good fairies who protected Sleeping Beauty until she came of age.

No one denies false gods more ringingly than the Hebrew prophets. While Daniel Dennett thinks himself bold to question God, the Bible foreshadows the most honest cries of atheism as well. "Does it please you [God] to oppress me, to spurn the work of your hands, while you smile on the schemes of the wicked?" (Job 10:3). "My God, my God, why have you forsaken me?" (Matthew 27:46).

Life is a wager, said Pascal. Hell is too heavy a club for me to lift over readers' heads. (Nor do I know anything about it.) I would rather ask, which story will you bet on? Who will you work beside? What role in consilience has Christ called you to play? Which enchantment will you fall under?

Some spells, after all, liberate rather than enslave.

Mirror, Mirror on the Wall

Wilhelm Grimm, a leading authority on fairies and their ways, was also an astute student of the New Testament. He read it in Greek, underlining passages that reflected themes he and his brother developed in their stories.[19] With Christian imagery and Wilhelm Grimm's Bible in view, the most popular of the Grimm fairy tales, *Snow White and the Seven Dwarves*, can be read as a sort of altar call to modern atheists.

Snow White is a picture of the human soul. Threatened by her jealous stepmother, she fled and found refuge with seven dwarves who carried candles. (In the book of Revelation, seven candles represent the churches, whose duty it is to protect endangered souls. "Love your neighbor as yourself"—Mark 12:31. Murphy compares them to medieval Benedictine monks, whose motto was "pray and work."[20]) The stepmother tracked down Snow White and tempted her three times. (As Jesus was tempted in the wilderness.) Seduced by vanity, the girl succumbed to the first two temptations, putting a beautiful poison comb in her hair and allowing a bodice to be tied too tightly, choking her. She fell down as if dead. (Christianity affirms the material world as real and good, created by a good God, but warns against inordinate attachment to pleasure: "You cannot serve both God and Money" [Luke 16:15]). The dwarves came home and revived Snow White by applying the sacraments. ("John baptized with water"—Acts 11:16.) The stepmother then brought a poisoned apple, as in the Garden of Eden. Snow White ate it and fell down "dead, and she remained dead." The dwarves anointed her with oil and water, but couldn't bring her back to life. They placed her in a glass coffin and laid it to rest on a hillside. Three birds came and nestled in a tree nearby: an owl, a raven, and a dove. (These birds represented the benevolent influence of German, Greek, and Jewish traditions, "all illumined by the Dawn of light" as Clement put it.) But while all cultures contain truth, none can save. Finally the king's son arrived and revived her ("I am the resurrection and the life"—John 11:25), and took her into his kingdom.

Science has played many roles in this story. It has played the role of dwarves, protecting and extending human life, providing us with food and safety—all that Francis Bacon hoped for and more. It has played the role of the owl, bringing wisdom and literally giving us "wings to fly."

Science has also played the role of the witch.

"Brights" cheerfully midwifed the birth of every modern form of barbarism. Hardly any travesty of justice, any "boot stamping on a human face forever," has not been instituted in the name of science: Social Darwinism, eugenics, abortion, the new infanticide, free love, LSD, gas chambers, the Gulag. Slave ships were a technological advance. A leading psychologist helped drive Ted Kaczynski mad. Scientists were the heroes of every Marxist state. Abimael Guzman, founder of the vicious Shining Path revolutionary movement in Peru, was a college philosophy professor. Pol Pot taught French literature. Stalin, Mao, and Hitler were poets with an almost magical faith in "Mr. Science," as he was called in China.

Now we face new challenges. All involve science, either incidentally or in essence: a resurgent and increasingly well-armed Islam (whose most fanatical leaders are usually well-educated), the rise of China and India, global warming, virtual realities that divorce us from virtue and reality, technologies that threaten our very humanity.

Stanley Jaki called Jesus the "savior of science." Anyone who can't see it needs a savior (and we may soon need a savior from it again) has not been paying attention.

Like the seven dwarves, the church has protected, fed, and given a home to wanderers and refugees. The Christian record is far from perfect. Often it is abysmal. But it would be foolish to deny that followers of Jesus have done a great deal for the world. Faced with such challenges, however, we need more than a proscription from Doc Kepler. We need more than Elder Happy greeting us at the church door with a liturgical program. We need more than a sermon from Reverend Grumpy or Bishop Dopey. We need more than multiculturalists settling near our coffin to "kah" and "coo" and ask, "Whoooo?" in a thousand languages.

Rumor has it the king's son may show up again. Even so, come.

Notes

Introduction

1. Tomoko Masuzawa, *The Invention of World Religions* (Chicago: University of Chicago Press, 2005), 75.

2. Richard Dawkins, *The God Delusion* (London: Bantam Press, 2006), 31.

3. Richard Dawkins, *The Selfish Gene,*(Oxford: Oxford University Press, 2006), 198.

4. Dawkins, *The God Delusion*, 20.

5. Sam Harris, *Letter to a Christian Nation* (New York: Alfred A. Knopf, 2006), 74.

6. Dawkins, *The God Delusion*, 158.

7. Alan Orr, *The New York Book of Reviews*, January 11, 2007.

Chapter 1—Have Christians Lost Their Minds?

1. James Boswell, *Life of Johnson* (New York: Charles Scribner's Sons, 1917), 382.

2. Daniel Dennett, *Breaking the Spell: Religion as a Natural Phenomena* (New York: Penguin, 2006), 230-31.

3. Sam Harris, *Letter to a Christian Nation*.

4. Sam Harris, *The End of Faith: Religion, Terror, and the Future of Reason* (New York: W.W. Norton, 2004), 15.

5. Ibid., 19.

6. Richard Dawkins, *The Selfish Gene* (Oxford: Oxford University Press, 1976), 330.

7. Ibid., 198.

8. Alister McGrath, *Dawkins' God: Genes, Memes, and the Meaning of Life* (Oxford: Blackwell, 2005), 86.

9. Hubert Yockey, *Information Theory, Evolution, and the Origin of Life* (Cambridge: Cambridge University Press, 2005).

10. Dawkins, *The Selfish Gene*, 198.

11. Dawkins, *The God Delusion*, (London: Bantam Press, 2006), 65.

12. Ibid., 64.

13. As cited at http://users.ox.ac.uk/~orie0087/framesetpdfs.shtml.

14. Ibid., 23.

15. Alister McGrath, *Dawkins' God: Genes, Memes, and the Meaning of Life* (Oxford: Blackwell Publishing, 2005).
16. Ibid., 86.
17. Dawkins, *The God Delusion*, 54.
18. J.P. Moreland, *Love Your God with All Your Mind: The Role of Reason in the Life of the Soul* (Colorado Springs: NavPress, 1997), 41.
19. Ibid., 199.
20. Nicholas Wolterstorff, *Divine Discourse: Reflections on the Claim that God Speaks* (Cambridge: Cambridge University Press, 1995).
21. Michael Shermer, *Why Darwin Matters: The Case Against Intelligent Design* (New York: Harry Holt & Co, 2006), 37.
22. W.F. Trotter, public domain.
23. Dawkins, *The God Delusion*, 104-05.
24. Ibid., 199.
25. Blaise Pascal, accessed at http://www.brainquote.com/quotes/quotes/b/blaisepasc105085.html.
26. Dawkins, *The God Delusion*, 222.
27. Lisa Jardine, *Ingenious Pursuits* (New York: Nan Talese, 1999), 8.
28. Dawkins, *The God Delusion*, 282.
29. Francis Bacon: *A Selection of His Works*, Sidney Warhaft, ed. (Indianapolis: Odyssey Press, 1965), 205.
30. Dawkins, *The God Delusion*, 51.
31. Dawkins, *The God Delusion*, 283.
32. Carl Sagan, *The Demon-Haunted World: Science as a Candle in the Dark* (New York: Ballantine, 1996), 13.
33. Dawkins, *The God Delusion*, 200.
34. Ibid., 286.
35. *Francis Bacon: A Selection of His Works* (Indianapolis: The Odyssey Press, 1965), 205.
36. Dawkins, *The God Delusion*, 282.
37. For choice examples, see *Philosophers Who Believe: The Spiritual Journeys of Eleven Leading Thinkers*, (Downers Grove, IL: InterVaristy Press, 1997).
38. Dawkins, *The God Delusion*, 284.

Chapter 2—Are Scientists Too "Bright" to Believe in God?

1. Daniel Dennett, *Breaking the Spell: Religion As a Natural Phenomena* (New York: Penguin, 2006), 21.
2. Daniel Dennett, *New York Times*, July 12, 2003.
3. Carl Sagan, *The Demon-Haunted World: Science as a Candle in the Dark* (New York: Ballantine Books, 1996), 13.
4. Dawkins, *The God Delusion* (London: Bantam Press, 2006), 34.

5. Ibid., 99-100.

6. Ibid., 1-3.

7. Joseph Needham, *The Shorter Science and Civilization in China: An Abridgement of Joseph Needham's Original Text* (Cambridge: Cambridge University Press, 1978), 84.

8. Rodney Stark, *For the Glory of God: How Monotheism Led to Science, Witch-hunts, and the End of Slavery* (Princeton: Princeton University Press, 2003), 162.

9. Stark, "Secularization, RIP," *Sociology of Religion*, Fall 1999.

10. Bertrand Russell, *Religion and Science* (London: Oxford University Press, 1935), introduction.

11. *Francis Bacon: A Selection of His Works*, Sidney Warhaft, ed. (Indianapolis: Odyssey Press, 1965), 307.

12. Edward Wilson, *Consilience: The Unity of Knowledge* (New York, Alfred A. Knopf, 1998), 22.

13. G.K. Chesterton, *St. Francis of Assisi* (New York: Doubleday, 1989), 135.

14. Dawkins, *The God Delusion*, 150.

15. Huston Smith, *Why Religion Matters: The Fate of the Human Spirit in an Age of Disbelief* (New York: HarperCollins, 2001), 96-98.

16. Sam Harris, *The End of Faith* (New York: W.W. Norton, 2004), 52-53.

17. Edward Wilson, *Naturalist* (Washington, DC: Island Press, 1993), 43-45.

18. As cited at nobelprize.org/nobel_prizes/medicine/laureates/2001/nurse-autobio.html.

19. Dawkins, *The God Delusion*, 15-16.

20. Dawkins, *The God Delusion*, 34.

21. Huston Smith, *Why Religion Matters*, 96.

22. Stephen Hawking, *Brief History of Time* (New York: Bantam, 1988), 8.

Chapter 3—Does Evolution Make God Redundant?

1. Jonathan Wells, *Icons of Evolution* (Washington: Regnery Publishing, 2000), 235.

2. Alan Grafen and Mark Ridley, eds., *Richard Dawkins: How a Scientist Changed the Way We Think* (Oxford: Oxford University Press, 2006), 28.

3. Charles Darwin, *Origin of Species* (Edison, NJ: Castle Books, 1859, 2004), 209.

4. Donald De Marco and Benjamin Wiker, *Architects of the Culture of Death* (San Francisco: Ignatius Press, 2004), 96.

5. C.S. Lewis, *Reflections on the Psalms* (New York: Harcourt, Brace & Co, 1958), 111.

6. Francis Collins, *The Language of God: A Scientist Presents Evidence for Belief* (New York: Free Press, 2006), 125-26.

7. Lewis, *Reflections on the Psalms*, 109.

8. Sam Harris, *Letter to a Christian Nation*, (New York: Alfred A. Knopf, 2006), 48.

9. See http://www.christian-thinktank.com/pred2.html.

10. Stephen Jay Gould, *Bully for Brontosaurus: Reflections on Natural History* (New York: W.W. Norton, 1991), 385-401.

11. Michael Shermer, *Why Darwin Matters: The Case Against Intelligent Design* (New York: Henry Holt & Co, 2006), 74.

12. Francis Collins, *The Language of God*, 111.

13. See Fazale Rana and Hugh Ross, *Who Was Adam? A Creation Model Approach to the Origin of Man* (Colorado Springs: NavPress, 2005), 227-43.

14. "A Priest Serving in Nature's Temple: Robert Boyle's Career Blended Faith, Doubt, and the Use of Science to Heal Disease and Fight Atheism," *Christian Century*, November 2002, 28-31.

Chapter 4—Some Riddles of Evolution

1. Edward Wilson, *Consilience* (New York: Alfred A. Knopf, 1998), 6.

2. Dawkins, *The God Delusion* (London: Bantam Press, 2006), 123.

3. Darwin, *The Origin of Species* (Edison, NJ: Castle Books, 2004), 207.

4. Steven Jay Gould, *Bully for Brontosaurus* (New York: W.W. Norton, 1991), 145.

5. Gould, *Bully for Brontosaurus*, 110.

6. Jack Cahill, *WorldNetDaily*, February 15, 2007.

7. *Commentary*, September 1996, letters.

8. *Commentary*, September 1996.

9. Accessed at www.talkorigins.org.

10. Ibid.

11. Dawkins, *The God Delusion*, 128.

12. Dennett, *Breaking the Spell*, 61.

13. Huston Smith, *Why Religion Matters* (New York: HarperCollins, 2001), 188.

14. Dawkins, *The God Delusion*, 137-39.

15. Richard Dawkins, *The Blind Watchmaker: Why the Evidence of Evolution Reveals a Universe Without Design* (London: W. W. Norton & Co, 1986), 144.

16. Francis Collins, *Language of God* (New York: Free Press, 2006), 69.

17. Paul Davies, *God and the New Physics* (New York: Simon & Schuster, 1983), 69.

18. Fazale Rana and Hugh Ross, *Origins of Life: Biblical and Evolutionary Models Face Off* (Colorado Springs: NavPress, 2004), 163.

19. Hubert Yockey, *Information Theory, Evolution, and the Origin of Life* (Cambridge: Cambridge University Press, 2005), 117.

20. Ibid., 119.

21. Ibid., 144.

22. *Commentary*, February 2006.

23. Dawkins, *The God Delusion*, 137.

24. Rana and Ross, *The Origin of Life*, 125.

25. Dennett, *Breaking the Spell*, 120.

26. Giuseppe Sermonti, *Why Is a Fly Not a Horse?* (Seattle: Discovery Institute, 2005), 15.

27. Lee Spetner, *Not by Chance! Shattering the Modern Theory of Evolution* (New York: The Judaica Press, 1998), 141.

28. Ibid., 131.

29. Calvin Bridges, *The Mutants of Drosophila Melangaster*, Carnegie Institution of Washington Publication 552, Washington, D.C., 1944.

30. See Fazale Rana and Hugh Ross, *Who Was Adam?* (Colorado Springs: NavPress), 155-67.

31. David Berlinski, *Commentary*, September 1996, correspondence.

32. Walker Percy, *The Message in the Bottle* (New York: Farrar, Strauss, & Giroux, 1984), 38.

33. Collins, *The Language of God*, 137.

34. Howard Newcombe, "Problems in the Assessment of Genetic Damage from Exposure of Individuals and Populations to Radiation," *Human Populations, Genetic Variation, and Evolution*, Laura Newell Morris, ed. (San Francisco: Chadler Publishing, 1971), 125.

35. Dawkins, *The God Delusion*, 125.

36. Ibid.

37. Ibid., 181.

Chapter 5—Did God Evolve?

1. Lin Yutang, *The Importance of Living* (New York: Capricorn Books, 1974, 1937), 409.

2. Daniel Dennett, *Breaking the Spell* (New York: Penguin, 2007), 20-24.

3. Ibid., 253.

4. Ibid., 70.

5. William James, *Varieties of Religious Experience* (New York: Random House, 1994), 22.

6. Dennett, *Breaking the Spell*, 108.

7. Ibid., 114-15.

8. Ibid., 114.

9. Edward Tylor, *Religion in Primitive Culture* (New York: Harper, 1958), 10-12.

10. Dennett, *Breaking the Spell*, 113.

11. Dawkins, *The Selfish Gene* (Oxford: Oxford University Press, 1976), 1.

12. Dennett, *Breaking the Spell*, 150.

13. Ibid., 295.

14. Ernest Becker, *The Denial of Death* (New York: The Free Press, 1973), 175.

15. Source unknown.

16. Dawkins, *The Selfish Gene*, 20.

17. Denis Noble, *The Music of Life* (Oxford: Oxford University Press, 2006), 11.

18. Ibid., 22.

19. Dawkins, *The Selfish Gene*, 192.

20. Ibid., 192.

21. Dennett, *Breaking the Spell*, 156.

22. Ibid., 186.

23. Ibid., 186-88.

24. Accessed at www.blackwellpublishing.com/lexicon.

25. Accessed at www.reviewevolution.com/viewersGuide/Evolution_Conclusion. php#88214.

26. Dennett, *Breaking the Spell*, 118.

27. Walker Percy, *Love in the Ruins: The Adventures of a Bad Catholic At a Time Near the End of the World* (New York: Farrar, Straus, & Giroux, 1971), 343.

28. "The Natural History of Religion," *Hume on Religion* (Cleveland: Meridian Books, 1964), 33.

29. Dennett, *Breaking the Spell*, 205-06.

30. Dawkins, *The God Delusion*, 32.

31. Emile Durkheim, *Elementary Forms of the Religious Life*, trans. Karen Fields (New York: The Free Press, 1995), 420.

32. Ibid., 289-94.

33. Stark, *A Theory of Religion* (New York: David Lang, 1987), 86.

34. David Marshall, *True Son of Heaven: How Jesus Fulfills the Chinese Culture* (Seattle: Kuai Mu Press, 2002, 1996).

35. James Legge, *The Religions of China: Confucianism and Taoism Described and Compared with Christianity* (London: Hodder & Stoughton, 1880), 11.

36. Don Richardson, *Eternity in Their Hearts* (Ventura, CA: Regal Books, 1981), 97-98.

37. Nicholas Standaart, *The Fascinating God: A Challenge to Modern Chinese Theology Presented by a Text on the Name of God Written by a 17th Century Christian Student of Theology* (Rome: Pontifical Gregorian University, 1995).

38. Harris, *The End of Faith*, 13.

39. Ibid., 14.

40. G.K. Chesterton, accessed at www.cse.dmu.ac.uk/~mward/gkc/books/everlasting-man.html#chap-I-iv.

Chapter 6—Is the Good Book Bad?

1. Richard Dawkins, *The God Delusion* (London: Bantam Press, 2006), 237.

2. Ibid., 31.

3. Ibid., 237.

4. Dawkins, *The God Delusion*, 240.

5. Ibid., 241.

6. Ibid., 243.

7. C.S. Lewis, *The Voyage of the Dawn Treader* (New York: HarperCollins, 2000), 141.

8. Dawkins, *The God Delusion*, 242.

9. Richard Dawkins, *The Selfish Gene* (New York: Oxford University Press, 1976), introduction.

10. *The Independent*, December 4, 2006.

11. Dawkins, *The God Delusion*, 222-26.

12. As cited in Jay Budziszewski, *What We Can't Not Know* (Dallas: Spence Publishing, 2003), 20.

13. Ibid., 79.

14. *Skeptic*, vol. 3, no. 4, 1995.

15. Dawkins, *The God Delusion*, 253-54.

16. Ibid., 254.

17. *Skeptic*, vol. 3, no. 4, 1995.

18. Marcus Borg, *Meeting Jesus Again for the First Time* (New York: HarperCollins, 1994), 56.

19. Robert Funk, *Honest to Jesus* (New York: HarperSanFrancisco, 1996), 196.

20. Ibid., 179.

21. Richard Weikart, *From Darwin to Hitler* (New York: Palgrave Macmillan, 2004), 116.

22. Dawkins, *The God Delusion*, 265.

23. Ibid., 258.

24. Walter Wink, *Engaging the Powers* (Minneapolis: Fortress, 1992), 129.

25. Dawkins, *The God Delusion*, 247.

26. Nicholas Wolterstorff, *The Divine Discourse* (Cambridge: Cambridge University Press, 1995), 186.

27. Wolterstorff, 185.

28. C.S. Lewis, *Reflections on the Psalms* (New York: Harcourt, Brace & Company, 1971), 111.

29. Ibid., 112.

Chapter 7—What Should an Atheist Do About Jesus?

1. Carl Sagan and Ann Druyan, *The Demon-Haunted World: Science as a Candle in the Dark* (New York: Ballantine Books, 1996), 133.

2. M. Scott Peck, *In Search of Stones* (New York: Hyperion, 1995), 194.

3. Tarif Khalidi, *The Muslim Jesus* (Cambridge, MA: Harvard University Press), 138.

4. Ravi Ravindra, *Christ the Yogi: a Hindu Reflection on the Gospel of John* (Rochester, VT: Inner Tradition, 1990).

5. Ed Viswanathan, *Am I a Hindu? The Hinduism Primer* (San Francisco: Halo Books, 1992), 154.

6. Per Beskow, *Strange Tales About Jesus* (Philadelphia: Fortress Press, 1983), 64.

7. Dan Brown, *The Da Vinci Code* (New York: Doubleday, 2003).

8. Marcus Borg, *Meeting Jesus Again for the First Time* (New York: HarperSanFrancisco, 1994), 113.

9. Kenneth Leong, *The Zen Sayings of Jesus* (New York: Crossroad), 1995.

10. Richard Dawkins, *The God Delusion* (London: Bantam Press, 2006), 93-97.

11. Ibid., 206.

12. Ibid., 37.

13. Ibid., 92.

14. Sam Harris, *The End of Faith* (New York: W.W. Norton, 2004), 94.

15. See David Marshall, *Why the Jesus Seminar Can't Find Jesus and Grandma Marshall Could* (Fall City, WA: Kuai Mu Press, 2005), and *The Truth About Jesus and the Lost Gospels* (Eugene, OR: Harvest House Publishers, 2007).

16. Dawkins, *The God Delusion*, 93.

17. Robert Funk, *Honest to Jesus* (New York: HarperSanFrancisco, 1996), 38.

18. Paula Fredriksen, *Jesus of Nazareth, King of the Jews* (New York: Vintage Books, 1999), 20.

19. Christopher Hitchens, *god Is Not Great* (New York: Hachette, 2007), 174.

20. Dawkins, *The God Delusion*, 93.

21. Richard Fletcher,*The Barbarian Conversion: From Paganism to Christianity* (Berkeley: University of California Press, 1997), 4.

22. Peck, *In Search of Stones*, 394.

23. Dawkins, *The God Delusion*, 95.

24. Ibid., 96.

25. Dawkins, *The God Delusion*, 95.

26. Dawkins, *The God Delusion*, 206.

27. David Marshall, *Why the Jesus Seminar Can't Find Jesus*, 181-201.

28. Ibid.

29. Dawkins, *The God Delusion*, 94.

30. Ronald Nash, *The Gospel and the Greeks* (Phillipsburg, NJ: Presbyterian & Reformed, 2003).

31. Accessed at www.christianthinktank.com/copycatwho/html.

32. Nash, Ibid.

33. Dawkins, *The God Delusion*, 92.

34. Ibid., 97.

35. Ibid., 97.

36. Bart Ehrman, *Lost Scriptures: Books That Did Not Make It into the New Testament* (Oxford: Oxford University Press, 2003), 58.

37. Marcus Borg, *Meeting Jesus Again for the First Time*, 51.

38. *Jesus, a Biography* (New York: W.W. Norton, 1992), 89.

39. Sagan and Druyan, *The Demon-Haunted World*, 194.

40. Harris, *The End of Faith*, 94.

41. Dawkins, *The God Delusion*, 92.

42. Justin Phillips, C.S. *Lewis at the BBC: Messages of Hope in the Darkness of War* (London: HarperCollins, 2003), 148.

43. Dawkins, *The God Delusion*, 253.

44. David van Biema, "God vs. Science," *Time*, November 5, 2006.

Chapter 8—Is Christianity a Blessing?

1. Malcolm Muggeridge, as cited by Ian Hunter, *Malcolm Muggeridge, a Life* (Nashville: Thomas Nelson Publishers, 1980), 188.

2. Denis Noble, *The Music of Life* (Oxford: Oxford University Press, 2006).

3. Robert Hooke, *Micrographia: or Some Physiological Descriptions of Minute Bodies Made by Magnifying Glasses: With Observations and Inquires Thereupon* (London: John Martor, printer to the Royal Society), 113.

4. Dawkins, *The God Delusion* (London: Bantam Press, 2006), 265.

5. Ibid., 271.

6. Sam Harris, *The End of Faith* (New York: W.W. Norton, 2006), 148.

7. Sam Harris, *Letter to a Christian Nation* (New York: Knopf, 2006), 22.

8. Ibid., 35.

9. John Farquhar, *Crown of Hinduism* (London: Oxford University Press), 258.

10. Accessed at http://www.firstthings.com/article.php3?id_article=2068&var_recherche=neuhaus+king+gandhi.

11. Sam Harris, *The End of Faith*, 202.

12. Mohandas Gandhi, *Autobiography: The Story of My Experiments with Truth* (New York: Dover, 1983), 60.

13. Ibid., 265.

14. Vishal and Ruth Mangalwadi, *The Legacy of William Carey: A Model for the Transformation of a Culture* (Wheaton, IL: Crossway Books, 1993), 72-73.

15. Vishal Mangalwadi, *Truth and Social Reform* (New Delhi, Good Books, 1985), 29.

16. *Modern Religious Movements in India* (New York: The Macmillan Company, 1915 [Delhi: Low Price Publications, 1999]), 32.

17. Ibid., 61.

18. Tenzin Gyatso (fourteenth Dalai Lama) *Freedom in Exile* (New York: Harper Perennial, 1990), 190.

19. Accessed at http://trinicenter.com/WorldNews/ghandi5.htm.

20. *Modern Religious Movements in India*, 369.

21. Ibid, 371.

22. Dr. Paul Brand and Philip Yancey, *Pain: The Gift Nobody Wants* (New York: Harper-Collins, 1993), 20.

23. Harris, *Letter to a Christian Nation*, 19.

24. Donald de Marco and Benjamin Wiker, *Architects of the Culture of Death* (San Francisco: Ignatius Press, 2004), 96.

25. Ibid., 114.

26. Bernard Lewis, *What Went Wrong? Western Impact and Middle Eastern Response* (Oxford: Oxford University Press, 2002), 83.

27. Farquhar, *Crown of Hinduism*, 169.

28. Hugh Thomas, *The Slave Trade: The Story of the Atlantic Slave Trade, 1440-1870* (New York: Simon & Schuster, 1997), p. 35.

29. Richard Fletcher, *Barbarian Conversion: From Paganism to Christianity* (Berkeley: University of California Press, 1997), 71.

30. Thomas, *The Slave Trade*, 39.

31. Christopher Hitchens, *god Is Not Great: How Religions Poison Everything* (New York: Twelve, 2007), 176.

32. Thomas, *The Slave Trade*, 451.

33. Ibid., 458.

34. Ibid., 459.

35. Rodney Stark, *For the Glory of God* (Princeton, NJ: Princeton University Press, 2004), 342.

36. Dawkins, *The God Delusion*, 265.

37. NRO, *The New Abolitionist Movement: Donna Hughes on Progress Fighting Sex Trafficking*, January 26, 2006.

38. David Marshall, *The Truth About Jesus and the "Lost Gospels"* (Eugene, OR: Harvest House Publishers, 2007), 125-27.

39. "Country Rankings of the Status of Women: Poor, Powerless and Pregnant," 1988.

40. V.S. Naipaul, *Beyond Belief: Islamic Excursions Among the Converted Peoples* (New York: Vintage Books, 1999), 333.

41. See Brian Tierney, *The Crisis of Church and State, 1050-1300, with Selected Documents* (New York: Prentice Hall), 1964.

42. David Marshall, *Jesus and the Religions of Man* (Seattle: Kuai Mu Press, 2000), 130.

43. Harris, *The End of Faith*, 106.

Chapter 9—Or a Curse?

1. Paul Fergosi, *Jihad in the West: Muslim Conquests from the 7th to the 21st Centuries* (Amherst, NY: Prometheus Books, 1998), 236.

2. Daniel Dennett, *Breaking the Spell* (New York: Viking, 2006), 327.

3. Sam Harris, *The End of Faith* (New York: W.W. Norton, 2004), 79.

4. Harris, *The End of Faith*, 79.

5. Dawkins, *The God Delusion* (London: Bantam Press, 2005), 276.

6. Christopher Hitchens, *god Is Not Great* (New York: Twelve, 2007), 192.

7. Dennett, *Breaking the Spell*, 289.

8. Sam Harris, *Letter to a Christian Nation* (New York: Alfred A. Knopf, 2006), 87.

9. "Speech of Urban," as cited in *The First Crusade: The Chronicle of Fulcher of Chartres and Other Source Materials*, ed. Edward Peters (Philadelphia: University of Pennsylvania Press, 1971), 27.

10. Amin Maalouf, *The Crusades Through Arab Eyes*, trans. Jon Rothschild (London: Al Saqi Books, 1983), 39.

11. Dawkins, *The God Delusion*, 98.

12. Harris, *The End of Faith*, 108.

13. Stark, "Secularization, RIP," *Sociology of Religion*, Fall 1999.

14. Paul Brand and Philip Yancey, *Pain: The Gift Nobody Wants* (New York: Harper-Collins, 1993), 106.

15. Edward Burman, *The Inquisition: Hammer of Heresy* (New York: Dorset Press, 1984), 17.

16. Bertrand Russell, *Why I Am Not a Christian* (New York: Simon & Schuster, 1957), 20.

17. Citing, for example, http://paganwiccan.about.com/gi/dynamic/offsite.htm?zi=1/XJ/Ya&sdn=paganwiccan&cdn=religion&tm=38&gps=131_6_843_537&f=10&tt=14&bt=0&bts=0&zu=http%3A//www.draknet.com/proteus/Suffer.htm.

18. Rodney Stark, *For the Glory of God* (Princeton, NJ: Princeton University Press, 2004), 228.

19. Ibid., 225.

20. James Connor, *Kepler's Witch: An Astronomer's Discovery of Cosmic Order Amid Religious War, Political Intrigue, and the Heresy Trial of His Mother* (New York: HarperSanFrancisco, 2004), 15.

21. Ibid., 14.

22. Rene Girard, *The Scapegoat* (Baltimore: John Hopkins University Press, 1986), 156.

23. Harris, *The End of Faith*, 92.

24. Ibid., 105.

25. Ibid., 101.

26. Christopher Hitchens, *god Is Not Great* (New York: Twelve, 2007), 240.

27. Dawkins, *The God Delusion*, 277.

28. Stark, "Secularization, RIP."

29. David G. Dalin, *The Myth of Hitler's Pope: How Pope Pius XII Rescued Jews from the Nazis* (Washington, DC: Regnery, 2005), 18-19.

30. "Separation of Church and Reich" *Christianity Today*, October 4, 1999.

31. Vincent Caroll and David Shiflett, *Christianity on Trial: Arguments Against Anti-Religious Bigotry* (San Francisco: Encounter Books, 2002), 123.

32. Accessed at http://www.firstthings.com/onthesquare/?p=557.

33. Hitchens, *god Is Not Great*, 241.

34. Dawkins, *The God Delusion*, 277.

35. Dalin, *The Myth of Hitler's Pope*, 11.

36. Ibid., 14.

37. Caroll and Shiflett, *Christianity on Trial*, p. 134.

38. Ibid., 129.

39. Michael Burleigh, *Sacred Causes* (New York: HarperCollins, 2007), 280.

40. Ibid.

41. Caroll and Shiflett, *Christianity on Trial*, 127.

42. Burleigh, *Sacred Causes*, 183.

43. Ibid., 228.

44. Dawkins, *The God Delusion*, 271.

45. Richard Weikart, *From Darwin to Hitler* (New York: Palgrave Macmillan, 2004), 184.

46. Robert Coles, "The Inexplicable Prayers of Ruby Bridges" in Kelly Monroe, ed., *Finding God at Harvard: Spiritual Journeys of Thinking Christians* (Grand Rapids: Zondervan, 1996), 37-38.

47. Harris, *Letter to a Christian Nation*, 35-36.

48. Accessed at http://www.nationalreview.com/mccarthy/mccarthy200411120827. asp.

49. Wikipedia, accessed at http://en.wikipedia.org/wiki/Mother_Teresa.

50. *The Dhammapada*, trans. Eknath Easwaran (Berkeley: Nilgiri Press, 1985), 121.

Chapter 10—What About the "American Taliban"?

1. Victor Hugo, *Les Miserables* (New York: Penguin, 1998), 175.

2. Richard Dawkins, *The God Delusion* (New York: Bantam Press, 2006), 319-20.

3. Ibid., 292-93.

4. In 2005, Paul published an article in the journal *Religion and Society* pointing out that compared to Western Europe and Japan, America has much higher rates of murder, sexually transmitted diseases, youth pregnancy, divorce, and mortality. Americans are also far more likely to believe in God, attend church, and make religion a central part of their lives. While he did not say so explicitly, it was clear readers were meant to assume that religion causes social breakdown. In 2006, sociologist Gary Jensen published a follow-up article in the same journal, titled "Religious Cosmologies and Homicide Rates among Nations." While pointing out weaknesses in Paul's methodology and offering a more ambiguous (and sophisticated) reading of the evidence, in the end, Jensen affirmed a correlation between murder rates and "dualistic" faith, by which he meant belief in God and the devil. He admitted, however, that disbelief in God seemed to correlate to high rates of suicide. I respond to these claims in "Murder and Religion" at christthetao.com.

5. Jimmy Carter, *Our Endangered Values* (New York: Simon & Schuster, 2005), 114.

6. Chris Hedges, *American Fascism: The Christian Right and the War on America* (New York: Simon & Schuster, 2006), 92.

7. Dawkins, *The God Delusion*, 239.
8. Accessed at http://datelinehollywood.com/about-us/.
9. Dawkins, *The God Delusion*, 239.
10. Ibid., 288.
11. Dawkins, *The God Delusion*, 296.
12. Ibid., 291.
13. Dawkins, *The God Delusion*, 229.
14. Tim Stafford, *Books and Culture*, June 14, 1999, "The Criminologist Who Discovered Churches."
15. Accessed at http://www.homestead.com/christthetao/articles/MURDERand RELIGION.pdf.
16. Dawkins, *The God Delusion*, 319.
17. Hedges, *American Fascists*, 57.
18. Dawkins, *The God Delusion*, 288.
19. Ahmed Rashid, *Taliban* (New Haven: Yale University Press, 2001), 218.
20. Bernard Lewis, *What Went Wrong: Western Impact and Middle Eastern Response* (Oxford: Oxford University Press, 2001), 128-9.
21. Sam Harris, *Letter to a Christian Nation* (New York: Alfred A. Knopf, 2006), 31.
22. Ezekiel Emanuel, "Who's Right to Die?" *Atlantic Monthly*, March 1997.
23. Robert McNeilly, *The New York Times* op-ed, August 29, 1993, "Government Is Not God's Work."
24. Thomas Cahill, *The Gift of the Jews* (New York: Doubleday, 1999), 144.
25. Donald Treadgold, *Freedom, a History* (New York: New York University Press, 1990), 32.
26. Dawkins, *The God Delusion*, 23.
27. Ibid., 177.
28. Ibid., 316-17.
29. Ibid., 326.
30. Harris, *Letter to a Christian Nation*, 91.
31. Sergei Kourdakov, *The Persecutor* (Old Tappan, NJ: Fleming Ravell, 1973), 74-75.
32. Robert Coles, *Harvard Diary: Reflections of the Sacred and the Secular* (New York: Crossroad, 1988), 17.
33. Arthur Brooks, *Who Really Cares: America's Charity Divide; Who Gives, Who Doesn't, and Why It Matters* (New York: Perseus Books, 2006), 192.
34. Ibid., 1120
35. Ibid., 40.

Chapter 11—Can Atheism Make the World Better?

1. Alston Chase, *Harvard and the Unabomber: The Education of an American Terrorist* (New York: W.W. Norton, 2003).
2. G.K. Chesterton, *Orthodoxy* (New York: Doubleday, 1990), 125.

3. Rene Girard *The Scapegoat* (Baltimore: Johns Hopkins University Press, 1986), 100.

4. Sam Harris, *Letter to a Christian Nation* (New York: Alfred A. Knopf, 2006), 50.

5. Ibid., 48.

6. Fyodor Dostoevsky, *Brothers Karamazov* (New York: New American Library, 1957), 243.

7. Harris, *Letter to a Christian Nation*, 91.

8. Chase, *Harvard and the Unabomber*, 209.

9. Ibid., 290.

10. Ibid., 233.

11. Richard Dawkins, *The God Delusion* (London: Bantam Press, 2006). 296.

12. Chase, *Harvard and the Unabomber*, 278.

13. Dawkins, *The Selfish Gene* (Oxford: Oxford University Press, 2006), Introduction.

14. Richard Weikart, *From Darwin to Hitler* (New York: Palgrave Macmillan, 2006), 25.

15. Ibid., 146.

16. Ibid., 196.

17. Ibid., 205-06.

18. Ibid., 216.

19. Ibid., 232.

20. Chesterton, *Orthodoxy*, 112.

21. Dawkins, *The God Delusion*, 271.

22. Ibid., 298.

23. Sam Harris, *The End of Faith* (New York: W.W. Norton, 2004), 178.

24. Dawkins, *The God Delusion*, 300.

25. Ibid., 249.

26. Ibid., 273.

27. Ibid., 278.

28. Richard Wurmbrand, *In God's Underground* (Greenwich, CT: Fawcett Publications, 1968), 53.

29. Harris, *The End of Faith*, 79.

30. Harris, *Letter to a Christian Nation*, 43.

31. David Aikman, *The Role of Atheism in the Marxist Tradition* (doctoral dissertation, 1979), 3.

32. Ibid., 138.

33. Ibid., 123.

34. Ibid., 117.

35. Ibid., 174.

36. Ibid., 288.

37. Richard Dawkins, *The God Delusion*, 278.

38. Marc Hauser, *Moral Minds: How Nature Designed Our Universal Sense of Right and Wrong* (New York: HarperCollins, 2006), 421.

39. Dawkins, *The God Delusion*, 276.

40. Daniel Dennett, *Breaking the Spell,* (New York: Viking, 2006), 231.

41. Dawkins, *The God Delusion*, 273.

42. Lyle Dorsett, *And God Came In: An Extraordinary Love Story* (New York: Macmillan, 1983), 35.

43. Ibid., 260.

44. Harris, *Letter to a Christian Nation*, 26.

45. D. James Kennedy and Jerry Newcombe, *What If the Bible Had Never Been Written?* (Nashville: Thomas Nelson, 1998), 26.

46. Donald de Marco and Benjamin Wiker, *Architects of the Culture of Death* (San Francisco: Ignatius Press, 2004), 293.

47. Harris, *Letter to a Christian Nation*, 44.

48. Glenn Stanton, *Why Marriage Matters* (Colorado Springs: NavPress, 1997), 41.

49. Ibid., 11.

50. *Finding God at Harvard: Spiritual Journeys of Thinking Christians*, Kelly Monroe, ed. (Grand Rapids: Zondervan, 1996), 316.

Chapter 12—Consilience

1. G. Ronald Murphy, *The Saxon Savior* (Oxford: Oxford University Press, 1995), 93.

2. Edward Wilson, *Consilience: The Unity of Knowledge* (New York: Alfred A. Knopf, 1998), 4.

3. Ibid., 6.

4. Wikipedia, "Counterpoint," from John Rahn, *Music Inside Out: Going Too Far in Musical Essays* (London: Routledge, 2000), 177.

5. Brian Greene, *The Elegant Universe: Superstrings, Hidden Dimensions, and the Quest for the Ultimate Theory* (New York: Vintage Books, 1999), 146.

6. Denis Noble, *The Music of Life* (Oxford: Oxford University Press, 2006), 96-97.

7. Paul Davies, "Physics and the Mind of God: The Templeton Prize Address," *First Things*, August/September 1995.

8. Francis Collins, *The Language of God* (New York: Free Press, 2006), 73.

9. Paul Maier, *In the Fullness of Time: A Historian Looks at Christmas, Easter, and the Early Church* (Grand Rapids: Kregel, 1991), 54.

10. Richard Dawkins, *The God Delusion* (London: Bantam Press, 2006), 264.

11. Raymond Martin, *The Elusive Messiah: A Philosophical Overview of the Quest for the Historical Jesus* (Boulder, CO: Westview Press, 2000), 134.

12. N.T. Wright, *The Resurrection of the Son of God* (Minneapolis: Fortress Press, 2003), 718.

13. Walker Percy, *The Message in the Bottle* (New York: Farrar, Straus & Giroux, 1978), 6.

14. Dawkins, *The God Delusion*, 181.

15. *Stromata* I: XIII.

16. Rudyard Kipling, "The Ballad of East and West," at http://whitewolf.newcastle. edu.au/words/authers/K/KiplingRudyard/verse/volume XI/eastwest.html.

17. Ivan Satyavrata, "God Has Not Left Himself Without Witness: A Critical Examination of the "Fulfillment" Concept in the Christian Understanding of Other Religions in Indian Christian Thought, with Special Reference to the Contribution of Krishna Mohan Banerjea and Sadhu Sundar Singh to Protestant Fulfillment Theology," Open University, 2001, 139.

18. G.K. Chesterton, "Lepanto," written in 1915.

19. Ronald Murphy, *The Owl, the Raven, and the Dove: The Religious Meaning of the Grimm's Magic Fairy Tales* (Oxford: Oxford University Press, 2000).

20. Ibid., 128.

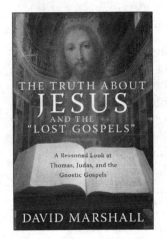

Randall Price

Searching for the Original Bible
Who Wrote It and Why? • Is It Reliable? • Has the Text Changed over Time?

"A fine book for lay and professional readers alike."
PUBLISHERS WEEKLY MAGAZINE

Lost...destroyed...hidden...forgotten.
For many centuries, no one has seen any
of the original biblical documents.
How can you know whether today's Bible is true to them?

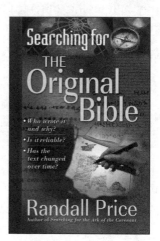

The Bible claims to be a communication from God—a text that is completely reliable. Can you still be confident of this? What about allegations by scholars and in the media that the "Lost Gospels" prove the early church changed the Scripture? Noted researcher and archaeologist Randall Price brings his expert knowledge of the Bible to tackle crucial questions:

- What happened to the original Bible text? If we don't have it, what *do* we have?
- How was the text handed down to our time? Can you trust that process?
- Should other books be included in our Bible—like the "Lost Gospels"?
- How can the text of the original documents be recovered today?
- What about the Bible's claim to be inspired and inerrant?

Current evidence upholds the historic views of orthodox Christianity more strongly than ever. Today's Bible remains the authoritative record of God's revelation for every person—a Book you can build your life and faith on.

"Graphically and accurately traces the...important work that lies behind obtaining the
authentic words that our Lord revealed to his prophets and apostles in the Scriptures."
WALTER C. KAISER JR.
President Emeritus, Gordon-Conwell Theological Seminary

To read a sample chapter, go to www.harvesthousepublishers.com

James K. Walker and Bob Waldrep

The Truth Behind *The Secret*

Is "the Secret" Really
Everything It Claims to Be?

At first glance, the message of *The Secret* is very appealing. It's about using the "Law of Attraction" to make your life better and get everything you've ever wanted. It offers beautiful and powerful promises that, if

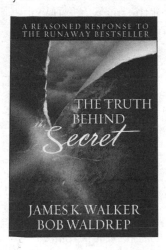

true, could be the ultimate fulfillment of every human yearning. And we're told it's all backed by science.

But there are some very significant secrets behind *The Secret* that aren't being told.

- What are the true origins of the teachings in *The Secret*?
- Who are among the early architects of these teachings?
- What are the dangers of living according to "the Secret"?
- Does science really back the *Secret* teachers?
- And—where is God in all this?

This thoughtful investigative presentation will give you uncensored access to the truth behind the amazing claims made in *The Secret*.

To read a sample chapter, go to www.harvesthousepublishers.com

Richard Abanes

The Truth Behind the Da Vinci Code

What Is Fact? What Is Fiction?

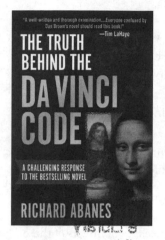

Award-winning investigative journalist Richard Abanes takes you down to the murky underpinnings of this blockbuster novel and movie that has confused so many people. Here's one example of the many questionable points Abanes unearths and scrutinizes:

- *The Code:* Jesus was married to Mary Magdalene, whom he named leader of the church before his death.

- *The Truth:* This fantasy has no support even from the "Gnostic gospels" mentioned in the *Code,* let alone from the historical data.

Probing, factual, concise, and revealing, *The Truth Behind the Da Vinci Code* gives you the straightforward information you need to separate the facts from the fiction.

To read a sample chapter, go to www.harvesthousepublishers.com